iSeries and AS/400®

SQL at Work

Developed by Merrikay Lee, the *at Work* series gives working professionals the tools, techniques, and usable code they need to craft streamlined solutions to everyday challenges.

Merrikay Lee is series editor for the MC Press line of professional books, which comprises more than 75 titles. She has spent more than 20 years as a technical professional in the IBM midrange industry and 15 years in the publishing field. She is the author of four books and has worked with numerous IT technical professionals to develop titles for the IBM midrange community of IT professionals. She is president of Lee Publishing Services Inc. in Dallas, Texas, and can be reached at mlee@leepublishing.com.

iSeries and AS/400®

SQL at Work

Howard F. Arner, Jr.

MIDRANGE COMPUTING
IIR PUBLICATIONS INC.

First Edition
First Printing—March 2001

© 2001 Midrange Computing
ISBN: 1-58347-024-7

Midrange Computing
5650 El Camino Real, Suite 225
Carlsbad, CA 92008–7147 USA
www.midrangecomputing.com

V4R4

In memory of Al Roth. You got me started as a writer by getting me to publish in conference journals. You jump-started my career and put me where I am today, not to mention the whole international travel thing. You are really missed, my friend, and I hope they have Chinese buffets and Indian food in heaven. Though he is gone, the original FBI lives on (in spite of threats from Inland Revenue).

ACKNOWLEDGMENTS

I would like to take this opportunity to thank and acknowledge the following individuals for their contributions to this work. Without your help and encouragement, this would not have come to be.

Kevin Vandever wrote chapter 8, on embedded SQL. As I have absolutely no knowledge of RPG, his work was invaluable to this book. He is also a really cool guy who has immeasurable knowledge of the AS/400 platform. Don Denoncourt wrote the RPG program used in the stored procedures chapter. Merrikay Lee's encouragement and advice was invaluable in the creation of this work. She is a consummate professional who knows how to ride herd over technical writers. My wife, Carla White, gave love and compassion, and kicked my behind when I attempted to play "Age of Empires" or surf the news rather than work on the book. Victoria Mack gave me the job as Microsoft Computing editor for *Midrange Computing* magazine, thereby giving me the confidence to take on this project. Amy Newman got me my first paid article gig and taught me that, amazingly enough, you could get paid for doing something you enjoy. Leah Wilbur taught me how the publishing business works. Christina Conaway continues to incarnate quality writers seemingly from thin air.

Thanks to my dad, Howard F. Arner, Sr. who got me my first job as a tape ape, thus starting my career in the computer business. And of course to my mom, Beverly Arner, for teaching me how to behave in public so I could keep that job (and others). And finally, Albert E. Rust, III Ph.D., who is my best friend, taught me everything I know about both programming and SQL. He also patiently read every word in this book to ensure I didn't say anything stupid.

CONTENTS

INTRODUCTION

SQL, structured query language, is a cross-platform language that allows you to access information on your iSeries or AS/400. In the beginning, SQL was slow, but now it screams. If you are creating client/server and Web-based applications with your AS/400, the best language to use is SQL. If you are venturing into Java, SQL with JDBC is a quick and easy way to guarantee application portability and get data to and from your AS/400. If you are programming in a Microsoft environment like Active Server Pages (ASP) or Visual Basic (VB), or using the Visual Basic for Applications (VBA) macro language, SQL is again your conduit for harnessing the power of the AS/400.

Further, because SQL has support for stored procedures, you can make your business-application logic callable by other programs on other platforms. Industry standards like ODBC, OLE, DB, and Java Database Connectivity (JDBC) are the conduit for this type of activity. Any AS/400 program or command can be called as a stored procedure, and stored procedures can be created in the new AS/400 procedure language, though that option does require you to have the AS/400 C compiler and SQL Development Kit installed on your AS/400.

This book concentrates on teaching you SQL by leading you through examples. As a programmer, I always find that I learn better if I can do something, not just read about it. Therefore, this book takes you through the process of creating an SQL database on your AS/400, populating the database, manipulating records via SQL, and retrieving data. As you move through the book, more and more advanced SQL concepts and queries are featured. As a bonus, the book also covers new features found only in V4R5, techniques for writing stored procedures, and advanced statement-optimization techniques.

Figure I.1 shows how SQL can be used to open your AS/400 to other platforms and applications.

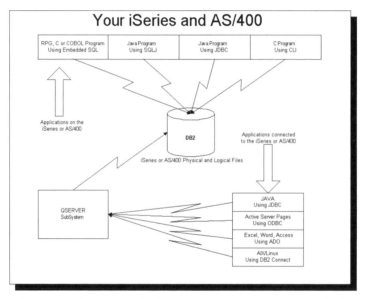

Figure I.1: SQL opens your iSeries or AS/400 to other platforms, application languages, and packages.

I wish that I had had a book like this when I started using SQL on the AS/400. I hope it will help you develop your next-generation 400 applications or open up your legacy applications to the Web.

About This Book

As stated earlier, the goal of this book is to teach you the rudiments and subtleties of SQL. To do this, the concepts of SQL are introduced in what I believe to be a logical order, especially if you have some experience on the AS/400 and are just starting to learn SQL. Read this book from beginning to end; the concepts build from basic to complex. Throughout the book, the SQL examples get increasingly difficult and build on previous chapters. If you have some experience with SQL, you might still get value from the early chapters, as they illuminate differences between AS/400 SQL and DB2 Universal SQL and examine capabilities that only the AS/400 has.

You might notice that I occasionally introduce a concept and then only cursorily explain it. This is because I need to first briefly introduce it, while covering it in complete detail in another section, where it will fit better with your accumulated knowledge. I have made every effort to point out when I am doing this and what section of the book contains the detailed information, but I suggest that you avoid jumping from section to section. This book is organized the same way I teach SQL, progressing from fundamental concepts to advanced techniques. The following is a brief discussion of each chapter.

- Chapter 1 relates information about the DB2 database on the AS/400. It compares terms like "physical file," "logical file," and "library" to their SQL counterparts. Semantics are always difficult when you are learning a new language, so this chapter attempts to bridge the gap between AS/400 terminology and general SQL terminology.

  Along the way, chapter 1 shows you the building blocks of SQL: methods of creating physical and logical files with SQL syntax, ways to add constraints to the physical files on your AS/400, capabilities only accessible on the AS/400 via SQL syntax, differences between DDS logical files and SQL indexes, etc. By the end of the chapter, you should understand key SQL database concepts and how they relate to what you already know about the AS/400.

- Chapter 2 introduces SELECT, the most-used statement in SQL. SELECT is how you ask SQL to retrieve data from your AS/400. This chapter covers all elements of the SELECT statement. It shows you by example how to read data from tables on the AS/400, how to limit the data returned by your queries, how to group data and use aggregate functions to make summary tables, how to filter summary information after it is aggregated, and how to order results.

This chapter starts with simple statements, and then adds more and more features as you progress. My goal, as elsewhere in the book, is to show "real world" examples so that you can see SQL doing things you might be asked to do in your own job.

- Chapter 3 introduces the INSERT, UPDATE, and DELETE statements for putting records into, changing records in, and removing records from your SQL tables. UPDATE and DELETE use some features of the SELECT statements in chapter 2.

- Once you have mastered the basic SELECT, chapter 4 reveals the concepts of joining tables, creating SQL views, and performing advanced manipulation of data using the built-in SQL scalar functions. You will see both forms of SQL join syntax (SQL-92 and the old WHERE clause joins), and become familiar with each type of join that you can perform on the AS/400. The example queries all have some use in the real world: aggregating by timestamps, converting legacy dates to SQL dates, generating Web statistics by day of the week, and ranking Web hits against a Web site.

By the end of chapter 4, you should be an SQL wizard and have a lot of ideas for how you can use the techniques shown within your organization.

- By chapter 5, you will have a thorough grounding in creating SQL databases; inserting, updating, and deleting data with SQL; and selecting records from an SQL database. Now some thought is given to the transactional features of SQL. Transactions are like a big "undo" button that is available to any program, as long as the physical files are journaled. This chapter covers the basic concepts of journaling and commitment control. Because many legacy applications do not use journaling, some discussion of techniques for using SQL against these systems is also presented.

SQL automatically manages the record and table locks placed against database tables for you. This frees you from worrying about throwing and releasing record locks when you program. However, to effectively program in this environment, you must understand how the isolation level of the program affects the automatic locking of records in your SQL tables. Chapter 5 includes information on how you can fine-tune and override these settings within your SQL programs.

- Chapter 6 is probably the most important chapter in this book because it shows you how to interpret information in the AS/400 job log related to how the query optimizer is implementing your queries. The optimizer controls how the AS/400 gets the data you are requesting from the AS/400. Understanding how the optimizer can get to your data, how indexes affect statement performance, and how to "tweak" the optimizer into doing what you want it to do is very important when using SQL in a production environment.

  In addition to debugging and statement-development techniques, this chapter also includes general do's and don'ts of SQL statement writing. Here, I impart my six-plus years of AS/400 SQL performance-tuning to you.

- One of the most useful things on the AS/400 is its support for stored procedures, the topic of chapter 7. Stored procedures allow you to make legacy programs (even OPM programs) available to any platform that can issue SQL statements. The AS/400 also has a built-in stored procedure language that can be used to write business logic procedures in a very high-level dialect. This chapter reviews the stored procedure support: why you would want to use it, how to make stored procedures in CL or RPG, how to call them, and how to write procedures in the AS/400 stored procedure language. In addition, you'll learn a technique for calling any program on the AS/400 as a stored procedure, even if it is not declared.

- Chapter 8 provides several example programs that will be useful starting points for you to learn to exploit SQL at your shop. Programs written to execute natively on the AS/400 can execute SQL in one of two ways, via the Call Level Interface API or via embedded SQL. Embedded SQL is the easiest and most productive interface when executing SQL in native programs. Why would you want to put SQL in a native program? First, OPNQRYF after V4R5 no longer supports opening SQL views that use new features available in SQL. So, if you decide to create an SQL view that uses any of the new database features, you must use SQL to access that information. Second, SQL can make your life easier, as demonstrated in the chapter, by allowing you to add features to your RPG programs that otherwise would be difficult to implement. Finally, you should at least experiment with embedded SQL so that you can learn how to use the SQL language within an application program for the manipulation of data.

- Appendix A details all of the AS/400 scalar functions available for use in your queries. Each scalar is documented, and, if appropriate, example queries are shown that illuminate the scalar's usage. This appendix contains especially valuable information about when scalar functions fail and when they produce erroneous results. The material here is organized by the type of data that the function interacts with: numerical, string, temporal, and other. I find this organization much superior to the AS/400 documentation, as functions are laid out by their intended use, not alphabetically.

- Appendix B details all of the AS/400 system catalog files and how they can be used to get information about your database. Each file and field on your AS/400 is described in the system catalog, so it is a useful repository of metadata. Each catalog file is detailed here, with queries that are helpful in finding out information about your database.

- Appendix C explains how to install the SQLThing program, which is on the book's companion CD. You can use this program to execute all of the examples in this book. In addition, the program allows you to test statements and stored procedures that use parameter markers, and import and export to Microsoft Access databases. You'll also see how to install the HiT Software ODBC driver (trial version) that is on the CD. You should use the HiT ODBC driver if you do not have Client Access installed on your PC. Finally, this appendix walks you through uploading the sample data to your AS/400 using the SQLThing tool.

Conventions Used in This Book

As you go through the book, you will see that SQL statements are formatted so that you can quickly recognize them as code. Here is an example of the formatting that SQL statements take:

```
I AM AN SQL STATEMENT EXAMPLE
```

Sometimes, I need to show you multiple statements with the intention that you will execute the first statement, and then the second. In this case, a semicolon is used as the statement delimiter, like this:

```
I AM THE FIRST STATEMENT;
I AM THE SECOND STATEMENT
```

Note that the second statement does not end in a semicolon. The semicolon just acts as a delimiter of the statements so that you can see the separation between them. Also, remember that in regular SQL statements, the semicolon has no syntactic meaning. It *is* used in the SQL stored procedure language, but if it is included at the end of an SQL statement in an embedded SQL program, it will cause an error.

However, both the Run SQL Statements (RUNSQLSTM) command on the AS/400 and my SQLThing product use the semicolon as a delimiter to mark the end of an SQL statement. Just remember that in the example statements in this book, the semicolon only has meaning in stored procedures; in SQL examples other than stored procedures, it only serves to denote the syntactic ending of an example statement.

Executing the SQL Examples

This book teaches by example, not by lengthy attempts to conceptualize what is happening. I think this is a good approach, but it requires that you be able to run the examples. There are several ways to do this.

Running Statements Using SQLThing: The Preferred Method

The CD accompanying this book contains all of the SQL statements and sample data used in the book. It also contains SQLThing, the graphical SQL tool that can be used from Windows 95, 98, NT, and 2000 to speak SQL with your AS/400. This is how all statements in this book were tested, and all screen captures come from SQLThing. It is the preferred method of running the sample statements, as it requires only an ODBC driver for connectivity with your AS/400 (no AS/400 installed software).

You can obtain the ODBC driver that SQLThing requires by installing Client Access Express, Client Access for Windows 95/NT, or the 60-day free trial of HiT Software's ODBC/400 driver included on the CD. Appendix C details how to set up the SQLThing tool and configure an ODBC data source. It also details how to load the sample data from the CD to your AS/400.

I suggest that you use SQLThing to run the example SQL statements. In fact, SQLThing is the only way that you can run and test parameterized statements that are detailed in chapter 6, and the only way to test stored procedures that require parameters, as described in chapter 7. However, should you choose not to use the product, there are other options available.

Running Statements Using STRSQL

If you choose not to install SQLThing, you may elect to run the sample SQL statements from the Start Structured Query Language (STRSQL) environment provided by IBM. STRSQL is a green-screen interface to DB2/400 that lets you type SQL statements and see the results. If you do not have the AS/400 Query Manager and SQL Development Kit product, you do not have the STRSQL command. In addition, if you don't have the product, you will not be able to execute some of the stored procedure examples shown in chapter 7. These examples require that both the SQL Development Kit and the ILE C compiler products from IBM be installed on your AS/400.

Running Statements Using Operations Navigator

Finally, if you choose not to install SQLThing and do not have STRSQL, you can run the SQL statements from the AS/400 Client Access Express for Windows product's Operations Navigator interface. Operations Navigator has a facility for allowing you to run interactive SQL statements even if you do not have the SQL Development Kit installed on your AS/400. To use SQL from Operations Navigator, open Operations Navigator and select the AS/400 you want to work with from the menu. Then, right-click the Database icon and select Run SQL Scripts. A screen like the one shown in Figure I.2 should appear. From this screen, you can enter and run your SQL interactively.

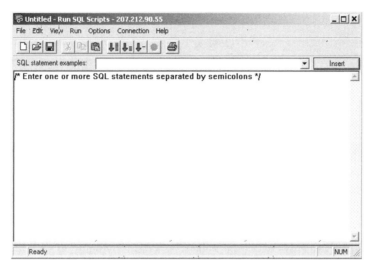

Figure I.2: Operations Navigator has a facility for running SQL scripts.

SQL on iSeries and AS/400

Is SQL on the AS/400 good?

In answer, let me relate a little anecdote. In 1995, I was working for a company that used Gupta's SQLBase product to store data on a Novell file server. SQLBase mimicked DB2 on the big iron, but ran on lowly PCs. We had 40 data-entry operators entering about 40,000 new records a day into our database (which tracked who advertised in newspapers all over the United States). We had a table of over 10 million records that related to a table of over a million advertisers and another table of over 1,000 publications. Our database was more than 2 GB of data.

Because of the rate of growth of the company, I knew that within the year, our database would be over 30 million records. I looked at databases and platforms for about six months and finally decided to move the database to the AS/400, not because of RPG or COBOL, but because of its support of the DB2 database. In my evaluation, the AS/400 is the best database-serving platform around. I chose the AS/400 over DB2 on AIX, SQLServer on NT, or Oracle on Sun because the database on the AS/400 was the only one that had the features I needed to run my business.

I got my first AS/400 in July of 1995, and by September all data was moved to it, and all of our custom PC applications had been ported to talk to the AS/400 as a database server. This was easy because the AS/400 supported ODBC, and all of the in-house applications had been written to the ODBC specification. I had to support not only the in-house data-entry programs, but also online users from around the country. The AS/400 and its implementation of SQL gave me the power to do this. In addition, because of the fantastic processing power of the AS/400, I could do reports on nationwide advertisement occurrences, something I had never been able to do with a PC.

The point? I was one of the original customers actually using the AS/400 as a database server, not as a platform to run RPG and COBOL applications. In fact, I had never written an RPG application until I embarked on this book. However, the AS/400's SQL implementation is so good that a PC programmer (me) would choose this environment over the other popular database server environments. This is the most powerful database platform out there. If it did not support the SQL standards correctly and was not able to run SQL robustly, I would not have been able to use the environment as a server. The platform works, and the platform is powerful. The SQL works, too; don't let anyone tell you different.

Why You Should Learn SQL

I have been using SQL since 1989. Prior to that, and for a few years after, I did most of my database access via a homebuilt database server system or using dBase III compatible files, both of which were very similar to record-level access on the AS/400. I also did a lot of work with proprietary record-level access systems and databases that had their own APIs for manipulation and retrieval of data. The nice thing about SQL compared to record-level and proprietary access is that it totally abstracts you, the programmer, from how you get to or modify the data in your database. All you worry about is informing the computer what data you want to retrieve or modify, not the messy details of how that is going to be done. But what does this really mean?

Think about how you program now. If the boss tells you to go get records X, Y, and Z and then do something to them, you have to look at the file to see what logicals are available so you can design your program to efficiently find the records. If a logical isn't available that meets your requirements, you must create one. This access method requires an intimate knowledge of your database structure and the operating system or APIs available for getting to the data.

The beauty of SQL is that you do not have to know anything about the structure of your database system in order to access and manipulate its data; you are only concerned with asking for the data in a manner that gets the records that you require. This saves a significant amount of time in application development because you spend your time on what you want, not how to get it.

A recent development experience will help explain just how powerful this concept is. I recently created an intranet system for executive financial reporting that gathered all of its data from a legacy AS/400 system. The legacy system had over 1,000 physical and logical files that contained the accounting, inventory, and warehouse information. I spent about two days with the programmers who routinely accessed the accounting information, finding out which physical files contained their general-ledger information and which files contained their inventory and sales data. I did not ask them about logical file formats, just physical files.

I then wrote a series of 20 SQL statements that created summary tables of information based on these physical files. I put the statements into a batch process that could run every night to recreate the summary database. This took about a day.

Next, I designed the drill-down screens that the company wanted. They wanted to be able to see a very high level of data and then be able to successively drill down to more detailed information. The top level showed all financial information for the selected month/year. Clicking on a category drilled to the component summary records that made up that total. Clicking on a component detail showed the general-ledger accounts that made up that component summary. Clicking on a general ledger account showed the general journal entries that made up that account. I spent a total of two days designing all of the SQL statements required to retrieve all of the levels of data and then an additional two days implementing Active Server Pages (ASP) that would serve these drill-downs to users of the intranet.

At no time did I write a "program" to go out and get the data from the legacy system. I did not have to hire an RPG programmer to write a procedure to sum up data and return it to my Web application. I did not have to understand how the legacy application was laid out and which logical files were most appropriate for accessing the data I needed for my pages. I concentrated on writing queries that summed the data the way I wanted it displayed and left the implementation details up to the AS/400. Sure, after the program was complete, I had to add a few logical files to help the AS/400 improve some response times, but I spent the majority of my development time concentrating on implementing the business logic of the intranet application, not writing machine logic to read and summarize the data for views.

More Uses of SQL

Besides freeing you from implementation details and allowing you to focus on business logic, SQL also opens your AS/400 to tools available on other platforms. Most of the Web development that I do for companies uses Internet Information Server (IIS) to deliver data from AS/400 databases to users on the Web. Why do I use IIS instead of developing on the AS/400? The Windows environment has a rich set of graphical report writers, spreadsheet programs, graphing engines, and data analysis tools that are cheap and easy to use. Because almost all tools on Windows expose their interfaces through Component Object Model (COM), it is easy to write a small program in a language like VB that grabs data from the AS/400 via SQL and uses Microsoft Excel to render a graph that is then served to the client browser as a GIF image. Or I use SQL to grab a set of records from the AS/400 and pass them to the Seagate Software's Crystal Reports report writer to produce a PDF report that I then email to a client.

PC reporting and rendering tools are very mature. The AS/400 does not have a lot of tools like this available in its native environment. By using SQL as a conduit for accessing AS/400 data and PC tools for rendering output, you can get the best of both worlds. The AS/400 is the best platform for running your ONLINE TRANSAC-TION PROCESSING (OLTP) systems and, through SQL, you can now have access to sophisticated PC-based tools for transforming and reporting that data.

Finally, SQL makes your AS/400 programs easier to write. Imagine you are asked to summarize your inventory and report the value on hand for each part in each warehouse as a percent of the total dollars on hand in the warehouses and as a percent-to-total dollars on hand in all warehouses. Writing that in RPG, COBOL, or C with record-level access will require several passes through the data or large arrays to accumulate the totals and report them. A single SQL state-ment, in contrast, will not only access all the data, but will produce the per-cent-to-total calculations and order the set based on the percentages. You can then embed that statement into an RPG, C, or COBOL program and not worry about whether a logical file is available to implement the query because the SQL statement implements the query and determines the best way to accomplish the result. This makes your programs easier to read and less susceptible to database changes (such as someone dropping a critical logical file or changing the data precision of a field). SQL abstracts you from the database and makes reporting and analyzing your data much easier.

Go Forth and Conquer

I hope that you enjoy this book and that it helps you use SQL on your AS/400. I tried to put as much information as possible in it while sticking to the premise that it is a book on SQL, not on application programming. I also put in many practical tips and tricks that I have learned over the years so that you can learn them by reading and example, not by the frustrating hunt/peck/poke/call support method. I designed the book so that it will serve beginning SQL users but will also be useful after you learn SQL for information on debugging and perfor-mance techniques.

SQL is important now and, as systems become more and more diverse, it will continue to be important in the future. The trend is toward multitier development, and the best way to implement that is to use SQL for manipulating your data.

Knowing SQL will help your career, but it will also help you do your job better by giving you a whole new way to use data on your AS/400.

Author's Note About "iSeries" and "AS/400"

Throughout this introduction, you may have noticed that, in a few cases, I referred to the IBM midrange box we're so familiar with as either iSeries or AS/400. However, I generally called it AS/400. With the IBM initiative to rebrand the AS/400 by calling it "eserver iSeries 400" comes the challenge of determining how to refer to it when you mean either or both. For simplicity's sake, I refer to the box as the AS/400 throughout this book. But be assured that the topics covered apply to both the AS/400 and IBM's eserver iSeries; both boxes run the same operating system—OS/400.

1

RELATIONAL CONCEPTS AND TERMS

This chapter provides all of the SQL semantics you need to begin learning SQL, and relates them back to what you already know on the AS/400. You'll also learn important differences between AS/400 commands and file specifications and SQL commands and file specifications. There are some things on the AS/400 you can do *only* through SQL. There are also some special capabilities of DDS-based logical files that you need to understand to be a better SQL programmer. Even if you have experience with SQL, you will probably want to read the sections in this chapter on indexes and views to find out about this information.

Some of the concepts and commands introduced in this chapter are explained in detail in subsequent chapters. If, for example, you see information on the SQL SELECT and INSERT statements and wonder what they do, never fear, they will be illustrated in detail later.

Most of the examples in this chapter can be executed using the Start Interactive SQL (STRSQL) command. However, if you do not have the DB/2 SQL development kit installed on your AS/400, you will not be able to use STRSQL. In that case, I suggest you jump to the information in appendix C on installing the SQLThing tool and example database. SQLThing is a graphical tool included on the CD that accompanies this book. It allows you to execute SQL queries and commands from a PC using ODBC to connect to your AS/400. (Even if you have STRSQL, you might find that SQLThing is easier to use.)

SQL on the AS/400

The AS/400 is a somewhat unusual platform, in that almost all data stored on the AS/400 resides in a relational database. Starting with V3R1, IBM called this database *DB2/400* because most customers did not know that the AS/400 had a built-in database. Starting with V4R1, IBM changed the name to *DB2 Universal* to indicate that the AS/400 version of DB2 was compatible with DB2 on all of the other platforms supported by IBM. However, DB2 on the AS/400 has some features and capabilities that DB2 on other platforms does not, and vice versa. These differences are highlighted throughout this book, since they are important when attempting to develop cross-platform applications.

If you are new to SQL, the first hurdle you will need to overcome involves naming conventions. The conventions used in SQL are different from those on the AS/400. So, what better way to start learning SQL than to learn the basic semantics that SQL uses for database elements, and match those names to ones from your AS/400 programming?

The second hurdle is that SQL is actually a two-edged sword. It is both a Data Definition Language and a Data Manipulation Language. (Like the old Saturday Night Live skit: "It's a desert topping! No, it's a floor wax!") A Data Definition Language, referred to as *DDL*, allows you to define SQL data structures, indexes, and views. A Data Manipulation Language allows you to access and modify data stored in the tables, views, and indexes created with DDL.

DDL is important if you are creating an SQL database from scratch. But since you will probably be talking to legacy databases, I am not going to spend a lot of time on DDL language elements, other than introducing you to their concepts and analogs on the AS/400. Yes, you can use DDL elements against physical files already on your AS/400, but you might find that you are more comfortable with DDS (Data Description Specification) for manipulating your legacy data structures.

However, there are some important things that you can do with DDL that you cannot do with DDS, like creating Vector-Encoded Indexes. Conversely, there are things that you can do with DDS that you cannot do with DDL, like creating indexes that can be read with SQL SELECT statements. Throughout this chapter, these differences are highlighted, but for a through grounding in DDL, consult the *AS/400 SQL Reference*. Despite their differences, DDL and DDS both have the same goal: to allow you to create physical files, called *tables* in SQL, in which to store data on your AS/400.

Foundations of a Relational System

As I mentioned earlier, many people do not realize that the AS/400 has SQL built-in. They also do not realize that the AS/400 is built on the concept of a relational database. The 400 is the model of a relational database system. Therefore, this chapter reviews basic relational database concepts by relating them to the AS/400 terms you are familiar with.

You have probably been exposed to relational database concepts, and many other books do a much more complete treatment of the topic than space permits here. Because this book aims to teach you SQL by example, however, a brief review of relational database concepts and topics is necessary. Let's begin with the database.

The Database

The term "database" is actually a misnomer when applied to the AS/400 because the whole AS/400 file system is one database with separate libraries. However, when referring to a database on the AS/400, most people are usually referring to a single library containing physical files, logical files, and journal receivers. Adding to this confusion is an SQL statement that you can execute on the AS/400 called CREATE DATABASE. CREATE DATABASE takes a single argument: a string representing the name of the database you want to create. Here is an example:

```
CREATE DATABASE SQLBOOK
```

This statement creates a library on your AS/400 called SQLBOOK. In addition to creating the library, a journal will be created (called QSQJRN), and a journal receiver (QSQJRN001) will be created and attached to the journal. Also, the system will create the basic DB2 catalog views in the library (more on these later). Any tables created in this library/database will be attached to the journal created in the library, and subsequent changes to the tables will be journaled.

You could perform the same operation with the following SQL syntax:

```
CREATE COLLECTION SQLBOOK
```

The key concept to understand is that all libraries on any single AS/400 are the database, and you can also refer to any single library of files on an AS/400 as a database. Also, the word "collection" is sometimes used to refer to a library. In fact, the CREATE COLLECTION command can be used instead of CREATE DATABASE.

Just because files reside in one library on your AS/400 does not mean they cannot interact with files in another library on the same AS/400 (or using DB2 Multisystem, a different AS/400). Using "database" to refer to either a library or the entire AS/400 is an appropriate use of the term.

The CREATE DATABASE command can also be used to specify the auxiliary stored pool (ASP) where the objects should exist, as in the following statement:

```
CREATE DATABASE SQLBOOK IN ASP 2
```

This would again create the library SQLBOOK, but in this case it would be in ASP pool 2.

Finally, you can also tell the system to create an Interactive Data Dictionary for the database by executing the following command:

4

```
CREATE DATABASE SQLBOOK WITH DATA DICTIONARY
```

This performs all the functions as the other versions of CREATE DATABASE. In addition, it adds the IDDU data dictionary files into the library and ensures that they are automatically updated for any changes/additions to the library.

Libraries and Qualification

As you know, objects on the AS/400 exist in libraries. Library names can be up to 10 characters long. Remember that, when referring to a database, a person might actually be referring to a library on the AS/400. Also, libraries are referred to as "collections" in SQL grammar.

An SQL statement can be *qualified* or *unqualified* when it is executed. A qualified SQL statement has the library name included before the object that the statement is referencing. An unqualified statement does not list the library, so the AS/400 must search the library list for the referenced object.

I have a simple motto in my development of SQL systems: Qualified good, unqualified bad. I believe it is good practice to always qualify your statements unless you are programming against a system that is to be controlled by library list entries. Even if that is the case, you should always qualify DDL statements if you are unsure of the library list your statement may be executed against. Otherwise, very bad things can happen. Because you can change the structure of databases with DDL statements, you might inadvertently change the structure of a file or drop an index in a library you did not intend to modify. You will not be well-liked if this happens. Qualified SQL statements also execute faster, as the system does not have to search the system catalog to find the library location of the table.

This brings up another point about library qualifiers: the SQL naming convention versus the SYS naming convention. Under the SQL naming convention, the AS/400 supports the period character (.) as a separator between qualifiers. Under the SYS naming convention, the slash character (/) is the separator between qualifiers. I personally prefer the period separator, and that is the separator used throughout this book.

You can choose the naming convention when compiling a program, when setting up an ODBC data source, or when using the STRSQL interactive SQL utility. Always know what naming convention you are using. Otherwise, you will have to continually adjust the syntax of your SQL code. I recently had a project half in SQL and half in SYS notation, and found myself having to search and replace through lots of code to change from one to the other. Pick a methodology and stick to it.

Tables and Physical Files

The table is the foundation of the relational database system. On the AS/400, tables are usually referred to as *physical files* and can come into being in several ways. You are probably most used to seeing physical files that were created using DDS language. DDS is a powerful language that is used to describe physical and logical files. However, SQL has a mechanism for creating files in a database called the CREATE TABLE statement.

An SQL table is a collection of *columns*, which you are used to referring to as fields. A table contains *rows* of data, which you are used to calling records. A table can contain one or more columns to hold data and none or more rows of data. I always think of tables as two-dimensional arrays of data, where the y-axis is a pointer to the row I am interested in, and the x-axis is the fields in an individual record. The terms "record" and "row" are interchangeable, as are the terms "column" and "field." The rest of the book uses the SQL terms "row" and "column" when referring the records and fields.

One thing to really try to get a grip on is that a table is not really a physical file. Data in tables are stored in physical files, but in SQL a table is a set of columns. Tables have no inherent order. You can create a physical file and specify the order of the physical file using DDS, and you can create a table and specify its primary key using CREATE TABLE. However, just because a physical file has an inherent order does not mean that the order will be used when SQL returns data to a program. SQL tables, by default, use the arrival sequence of records when storing data, but reading data from a table using SQL might or might not result in that data being returned in arrival sequence.

Members and Aliases

On the AS/400, a physical file can have more than one member. The member concept is foreign to SQL; SQL systems have no concept of it. When accessing a multimember file, by default SQL accesses the first member in the physical file. If you want to read or write data to a specific member of a multimember file, you have two options under SQL. The first is to create an alias to refer to the member, using SQL's CREATE ALIAS. An *alias* is a keyword that you can use to refer to a physical file or the specific member of a physical file. For example, if you have a table in library X called A, but you want to refer to the table as B, you can use the following to create an alias for A:

```
CREATE ALIAS B FOR X.A
```

Table A still exists, and you can read and write to it, but now you also have a virtual object called B that is a reference to A. Conversely, if you have a source physical file called QCLSRC in library X that contains multiple members, and you want to read the member COSTPGM with an SQL statement, you could issue the following CREATE ALIAS statement to access the member:

```
CREATE ALIAS MYALIAS FOR X.QCLSRC(COSTPGM)
```

After the above statement is executed, it appears to the systems as if a new physical file exists called MYALIAS, which contains the rows from the COSTPGM member of the physical file QCLSRC located in library X.

This option has drawbacks because the alias is now permanently in your database as a reference to the member unless you drop the alias later. To get rid of the alias, you would issue the following SQL:

```
DROP ALIAS MYALIAS
```

The second way to access the member is to issue an Override Database File (OVRDBF) command prior to executing the SQL statement. Here is the syntax for selecting the COSTPGM member of the QCLSRC file in the X library.

```
OVRDBF FILE(QCLSRC) TOFILE(X/QCLSRC) MBR(COSTPGM)
```

The bottom line is that there is no way to create multimember files using SQL; these can only be created via DDS. There is no use for multimember files in a traditional SQL relational system, but they are present in legacy systems and you will have to interface with them.

Making a Table with SQL

When a table is declared, you must specify which columns should appear in the table, their names, data type, data length, and possibly numeric precision if appropriate to the data type. Here is CREATE TABLE statement that creates a table called PARTS in a library called SQLBOOK:

```
CREATE      TABLE SQLBOOK.PARTS
            (PARTID CHAR(20) NOT NULL,
            CLASS SMALLINT NOT NULL,
            SUBCLASS SMALLINT NOT NULL,
            UM CHAR(3) NOT NULL,
            PDESC CHAR(40) NOT NULL,
            CURPRICE DECIMAL(8,2) NOT NULL)
```

The DDS in Figure 1.1 would create an identical table.

```
     A          R PARTS
     A            PARTID         20A
     A            CLASS          4B  0
     A            SUBCLASS       4B  0
     A            UM             3A
     A            PDESC          40A
     A            CURPRICE       8P  2
```

Figure 1.1: DDS code can also create a table.

The statement to create a table always begins with the keywords CREATE TABLE, where CREATE specifies the action, and TABLE is the target structure to be created. It is followed by the qualified name of the table. A qualified name takes the form of *Library.Tablename*. The Library qualifier can be left out of the statement, but if it is, the table will be created in the first library in your library list. You should always qualify a statement fully, so you know where your data is going to be stored.

Next, the CREATE TABLE statement takes a list of columns that are to exist in the table. This list is in the form *<Column-Name> <Data-Type>*. Notice the first entry in the example columns list. It instructs SQL to create a column called PARTID of the data type CHAR, with a length of 20 characters. The NOT NULL keyword following the description of the part ID column indicates that the part ID must be a value when a part is added to the table.

Note that all columns created using DDS are always NOT NULL, whereas columns created with the CREATE TABLE statement can contain nulls unless you explicitly specify the NOT NULL keyword. This is a major difference between SQL and DDS. Remember: In SQL, you can create a table that can have null values by leaving out the NOT NULL keyword. Using DDS, a column in a table can never contain a null value.

Removing Tables from SQL Databases

There are two ways to get rid of an SQL table. Because the table is a physical file, you can always use the AS/400 command Delete File (DLTF) to remove it. Another way is to use the SQL DROP TABLE *<table-name>* statement. The DROP TABLE statement takes a single argument, the name of the table to remove, and the name can be qualified or not qualified. The DROP TABLE statement will remove any logical files or SQL views that are dependent on the table from the database, and then physically delete the table. Here is an example that removes the PARTS table from the SQLBOOK library:

```
DROP TABLE SQLBOOK.PARTS
```

Dropping a table cannot be undone; therefore, be very careful with this statement. I recommend that you always qualify these types of statements to ensure that you do not inadvertently remove a table from the wrong library.

9

Advantages of CREATE TABLE over DDS

Because this table was created in the SQLBOOK library that was created with the CREATE DATABASE statement, the table is a physical file journaled against the QSQJRN journal, which was also created (automatically) during the execution of CREATE DATABASE. If you were to create a library with the AS/400 command CRTLIB, on the other hand, you would not get a journal and journal receiver automatically created for you. So, if you had created this table in a library that was not associated with a journal, the creation would proceed, but you would receive a message in your job log that the table was created but not journaled.

You will find out more about journaling a little later. It's important to know that if you create a table in a library that is not associated with a journal, you will not automatically have journaling on that table unless you manually associate the table with a journal using the Start Journal Physical File (STRJRNPF) command. If a table is not journaled, there are restrictions on how you can use it in an SQL environment. Specifically, you will not be able to use transactions against the table (meaning no automatic back-out of your changes should your program fail), and you will not be able to access information from the table unless you are in certain locking modes on your AS/400. (This is explained in more detail in the section on isolation levels in chapter 5.)

You should also realize that if you use the DDS to create the table in the SQLBOOK library, the table will not be associated automatically with the journal even though the SQLBOOK library was created using CREATE DATABASE. You will still have to use the STRJRNPF command to associate the physical file with a journal.

SQL Table and Column Names

SQL allows for names of table and column objects to be up to 128 characters long. The AS/400 only allows 10 characters for file and field names. So, what happens when you use long names? Consider this example:

```
CREATE TABLE SQLBOOK.MYTRANSACTIONS (TRANSNUMBER INTEGER)
```

This statement creates a table, called MYTRANSACTIONS in the library SQLBOOK, which contains one field called TRANSNUMBER. Because these names are too long, the AS/400 will take the first five characters of each one and add the number 00001 to the end. It will then search the system catalog to see if there is already a table named MYTRA00001 in the library you are attempting to create the table in. If there is, the system will increment the number until it finds an unused number. That will be the system table name.

The same thing will happen with the column name TRANSNUMBER. The system will make a name TRANS00001 and search this table definition to ensure that no other column in this table is named TRANS00001. Since there is not, the field will be stored with the system name TRANS00001.

Using SQL, you have the option to retrieve the data from the table by its system name (MYTRA00001) or by its SQL name (MYTRANSACTIONS). Similarly, you have the option of referring to the TRANSNUMBER column by its system name (TRANS00001) within an SQL statement. However, in non-SQL programming environments, you must use the system name to refer to the table or column.

One way to get around the automatic generation of system names is to always specify a name using 10 or fewer characters. However, I like long names, as they can sometimes be more descriptive and act as documentation to the programmer. So, to avoid getting an ugly generated system name, you are given the option of specifying the system name for columns that violate the length convention. Here is a CREATE TABLE statement where I have specified the system names for the column:

```
CREATE TABLE SQLBOOK.MYTRANSACTIONS (TRANSNUMBER FOR COLUMN
    TRANSNUM INTEGER)
```

The FOR COLUMN TRANSNUM indicates that the system name of the column should be TRANSNUM, whereas the SQL name of the column will be TRANSNUMBER. The system table name will still be an ugly derived name. Therefore, I would suggest limiting table names to 10 characters or less, if practical.

Another way to force the AS/400 to generate system names is to use invalid characters or to have spaces embedded in the name. My advice is to avoid this practice altogether. There are plenty of allowable character combinations for table and column names. Why go out of your way to make your life difficult? The permissible characters for table and column names are the letters *A* through *Z*, the digits *0* through *9*, and the *@*, *#*, *$*, and *_* characters. Use no others.

SQL Column Data Types

Tables are collections of columns, and columns have specific data types. Three basic types of data can be stored: *temporal*, *string*, and *numbers*. Temporal data is data about events in time, such as dates, times, and timestamps. String data is based on characters, but also includes mechanisms for storing double-byte character-set data, and also binary data. Numbers are just that, fields for storing numbers in varying precisions and byte lengths. In addition, V4 brings the concept of *user-defined types*, as well as a new type called a *data link*, to the AS/400. User-defined types are data types that you can define to conform to certain rules. Data links are like hyperlinks to files stored outside the DB2 database system. They are useful for enforcing referential integrity between a record in the database and a physical file outside the database. The following is a discussion of each data-type group, and information about how it is stored on the AS/400.

Storing Characters

Character columns can hold letters and numbers. They are denoted by the DDS symbol A for alphanumeric. The AS/400 has several representations of character data types and support for Coded Character Set Identifiers to assist in character translation between the host and client. The biggest differentiation you need to know about character data types is whether the data type is a single-byte character set (SBCS) or double-byte character set (DBCS). Table 1.1 shows the various data types and their attributes.

Table 1.1: AS/400 SQL Data Types	
Single-Byte Character Strings (SBCS)	
CHAR(X) CHARACTER(X)	A character string of length X.
VARCHAR(X) CHAR VARYING(X) CHARACTER VARYING(X)	A varying string of maximum length X.
LONG VARCHAR	A varying character string. The string can be stored from one character up to the limit of space left in the database row (usually less than 32766 bytes).
CLOB(X) CHARACTER LARGE OBJECT(X) CHAR LARGE OBJECT(X)	A character string of maximum length X . It can store strings up to 15 MB in size.
BLOBBINARY LARGE OBJECT	Just like a CLOB with CCSID of 65535. BLOB data will not be translated between character sets, as it is intended for storing binary information.
Double-Byte Character Strings (DBCS)	
GRAPHIC(X)	A DBCS string of length X.
VARGRAPHIC(X) GRAPHIC VARYING(X)	A variable-length DBCS string of maximum length X.
LONG VARGRAPHIC	A DBCS varying character string. The string can be stored from one character up to the limit of space left in the database row (usually less than 16,370 bytes).
DBCLOB	DBCS version of the CLOB with a 7MB maximum size.

Whether a character column is created as SBCS or DBCS can also depend on the CCSID that your system is set to when you create the column. The following data types default to SBCS character fields.

Character or CHAR(X)

The CHAR(X) entry corresponds to the DDS data type A. This is the basic character-string data type, and each character takes a single byte of storage. A character type field can be from one to 32,766 bytes of data. When characters are stored in the table, they are automatically padded with blanks.

Let's look at an example. Consider a column called UM, which represents a unit of measure for a part, and declare the column as CHAR(6). If you write the value A into the column, the database will actually store "A   ". However, DB2/400 is very liberal about matching character columns in expressions. If you asked for parts where the UM field was equal to "A," you would receive the row where it is actually "A   ". This is cool.

When creating a CHAR type column, you can optionally specify if the column should contain SBCS or BIT data. This is accomplished via the FOR SBCS DATA, the FOR MIXED DATA, or the FOR BIT DATA keywords. Alternatively, to ensure that a column conforms to a certain CCSID, you might specify the keyword CCSID <x>, where <x> is the integer representing the CCSID that you want the column stored in. If the CCSID represents DBCS data, each character stored will require two bytes of storage space (which happens to be the same result as if you declared the column GRAPHIC rather than CHAR). If the CCSID represents a SBCS character set, only one byte of storage per character will be required.

Here are a few examples:

```
CREATE    TABLE SQLBOOK.X
          (COL1 CHAR(10) FOR SBCS DATA,
           COL2 CHAR(10) CCSID 367,
           COL3 CHAR(10) FOR MIXED DATA,
           COL4 CHAR(10) FOR BIT DATA)
```

COL1 will be stored as SBCS data. Note that this is the default setting for CHAR and VARCHAR columns if the CCSID of the server is an SBCS character set. If the CCSID on the server is a DBCS, the default is FOR MIXED DATA like the COL3 definition. In the case of COL3, the column would take 20 bytes to store on the server if the CCSID on the server is a DBCS CCSID. COL2 is defined to use CCSID 367 (simplified Chinese), which requires a DBCS character set. Therefore, COL2 will take 20 bytes of storage, even though it is a CHAR(10) column. Finally, COL4 is specified as a FOR BIT DATA CHAR(10) column. This indicates that the CCSID of the COL4 column will be set to 65535, and the column will not be translated when returned to the client application. In addition, the column will only require 10 bytes for storage, as bit data is always SBCS. FOR BIT DATA is a useful dodge if you want to store binary information in the database and guarantee no translation between character sets.

When declaring any type of character column, you may optionally specify the DEFAULT clause, which will cause the system to store a padded string of the length of the character field if a record is inserted into the table and no value is specified for the character column. Here is an example CREATE TABLE statement that creates a CHAR(20) column that cannot be null and has a default value:

```
CREATE    TABLE SQLBOOK.TEST (MYCOL CHAR(20) NOT NULL
          WITH DEFAULT FOR SBCS DATA)
```

The column is also created to ensure that it contains only SBCS data.

VARCHAR(x) or Character Varying

The VARCHAR column type is like CHAR, but the database will store only the value that you hand to it. In DDS, this is represented by the VARLEN keyword. Each character stored takes one byte of storage space. The length can be from one to 32,740. In the CHAR example, if you stored "A," you can find the row using UM="A" or UM="A   ". If UM were a VARCHAR field, only the value "A" would be stored, so trying to find the row with UM="A   " would fail.

VARCHAR fields also impose a 2-byte overhead, as they need 2 bytes in addition to the maximum length of the field for storing the end-of-data marker. Because VARCHAR fields only store the data you give them, they do not use the maximum storage space in each row. For example, storing the value "ABC" in a VARCHAR field results in storage use of 5 bytes: 3 bytes for the data and 2 bytes for the end-of-data flag.

When specifying a VARCHAR field, you can optionally specify an amount of storage to allocate. The ALLOCATE keyword accomplishes this. ALLOCATE causes the database to automatically reserve *x* bytes of storage in a VARCHAR field for possible data. For example, you might wish to create a table of part descriptions.

Most description are 30 characters or less, but you want to allow for descriptions of up to 80 characters. In this case, you should use a VARCHAR field to store the data and allocate 30 characters. In this way, each record will take at least 32 bytes of storage to store any value, whether the value is "ABCDEFG" or just "A." The additional storage, up to 82 bytes total, will only be used if the description field is greater than the allocated 30 characters for that single record. The following example creates a simple table that has a VARCHAR field and allocates 30 bytes to each record for VARCHAR data.

```
CREATE     TABLE SQLBOOK.TEST
           (PID CHAR(10), PDESC VARCHAR(80) ALLOCATE(30))
```

LONG VARCHAR

The LONG VARCHAR column type is a way to store a whole lot of characters. In fact, a LONG VARCHAR can store approximately 32,740 characters. I say "approximately" because LONG VARCHAR columns can use only the space remaining in a record after all other columns are filled. Because the maximum size of a record is 32,766, to find the maximum storage of a LONG VARCHAR column, you would add up the sizes of all other columns in a record and subtract that value from 32,766. However, if you are storing DBCS data in the LONG VARCHAR field, you need to divide the space by two, as each character takes 2 bytes of storage.

CLOB(x)

CLOB stands for Character Large Object. These fields are cool because they can store up to 15,768,640 bytes of data if the fields are storing SBCS data. In future releases of OS/400, the CLOB data type is likely to be unrestricted in size. The value of x can be an integer representing the maximum number of bytes to store in the CLOB field. Also, x can be expressed in kilobytes or megabytes by adding the K or M keyword after the integer expressing maximum size. For example, CLOB(10 M) specifies a character long object field of maximum 10 megabytes of data. CLOB fields can hold SBCS or DBCS data.

GRAPHIC, VAR GRAPHIC, and LONG VARGRAPHIC

A GRAPHIC is just like a character field, except that it stores data in either DBCS or Universal Coded Character Set (UCS2) data. This indicates that the system will store 2 bytes for every character in a GRAPHIC string. When you declare a GRAPHIC column, you should indicate the CCSID of the DBCS character set that you wish to store data in. Otherwise, the CCSID will be set to 65535, and no automatic character translation can occur between host and client. The following example creates a table containing a GRAPHIC field:

```
CREATE  TABLE SQLBOOK.GTEST
        (ID INTEGER,
         DESCRIPTION VARGRAPHIC(80) ALLOCATE (30))
```

BLOB

A Binary Large Object (BLOB) is almost exactly like a CLOB, except it is for storage of binary information. That information could be pictures, audio files, or document images. The maximum size for a BLOB is 15,768,640 bytes.

LOB and VARCHAR Performance Issues

Large Objects (LOB), VARCHAR, and LONG VARCHAR fields are useful, but you should note that these types could bring about negative performance in your database if not used properly. Also, some aspects of LOB fields should be taken into account during the design phase of your applications. For starters, LOB data cannot be accessed by any means other than SQL. If you design a table with a LOB field, that field cannot be read or used within an RPG, C, or COBOL record-level access program. If you want to deal with a LOB field on the AS/400, then you are restricted to programming in embedded SQL or using client/server-programming techniques. In addition, any varying field can impose performance penalties when not used correctly and varying fields are heavily dependent on the ALLOCATE keyword.

The maximum data the AS/400 can store in a single row is 32,768 bytes. After that amount is reached, any additional data is written to an overflow storage area. If data is stored in an overflow area, it requires two IO operations on the AS/400 to access that data. When the data is stored in contiguous table space, only one IO is required to retrieve the record.

The use of the overflow storage area for storing table data also is heavily dependent on the ALLOCATE keyword. Remember that ALLOCATE controls how much data space will be reserved for each record in the table. So, let's look at the following scenario to see how ALLOCATE will help lessen the use of overflow storage:

```
CREATE   TABLE SQLBOOK.ACLOBTEST
              (ID INTEGER NOT NULL PRIMARY KEY,
               B CLOB(4096) allocate (1024) );
```

The preceding statement creates a table that contains two columns: ID and B. Column B is declared as a CLOB, its maximum length is set to 4,096 bytes, and ALLOCATE space is set to 1,024 bytes. This means any record stored in the table will be, at a minimum, 1,028 bytes in length: 1,024 bytes used in CLOB storage, and 4 bytes used in the storage of the integer.

If you insert a record into the table, and that record contains an integer and 90 bytes of character data, then 1,026 bytes are used on the AS/400. If you insert a record that contains 2,048 bytes of character data, the allocated space of the record is filled with the first 1,026 bytes of data and then an overflow area is created to hold the additional 1,024 bytes of data.

When a program asks to read this data, the AS/400 will read the record and see that some of the data is in overflow storage. As a result, it will then read that data from overflow storage. Note that the read requires two distinct IO operations when data is stored in overflow and, therefore, can be quite costly if your system is IO bound.

What does this mean to application design? First, you should always attempt to estimate a reasonable size to "pre-allocate" in table storage using the ALLOCATE keyword. If most LONG VARCHARS are going to be 10 KB, then make sure that you set ALLOCATE to 10,000. In this manner, you will accomplish two things. First, more of your table data will be stored in contiguous space (thereby increasing the effects of AS/400 Expert Cache). Second, because you have reduced the number of overflow records with a preliminary allocation of estimated storage, you will reduce the number of IO operations required to read the table data.

If you are going to use BLOB and CLOB data, I recommend that you use a separate table for the long data. Image that you have to design a system to hold x-ray images in a medical application. The information pertaining to an x-ray image includes attributes such as the date of the image, equipment operator, patient ID, and, of course, a BLOB containing the x-ray image.

Instead of creating a single table to hold all of this attribute information and the image, a better design (taking into account cache usage and other capabilities of the AS/400) would be to create two tables.

The first table would contain the attributes and then an INTEGER field that would represent the image. The second table would contain an INTEGER that identifies the image and then a BLOB field containing the image data. In this manner—if the application is just looking for attribute information about an image—it doesn't have to retrieve the image data. In addition, because the attributes table is small, more of the attributes records will be held in Expert Cache (thereby reducing IO). Also, because the BLOB data is in a separate table, that table could be moved to an auxiliary ASP (which might be slower, cheaper, or differently configured media for mass storage).

Storing Numbers

The AS/400 allows for two basic types of numbers, *exact* and *approximate*. Floating-point numbers are considered approximate numbers and are available in single or double precision. All other numbers offer precise representations of the decimal precision of the number. Table 1.2 shows the AS/400 SQL numeric data types and their attributes.

Table 1.2: AS/400 SQL Numeric Data Types	
Numeric Data Types with Precision	
SMALLINT	A two-byte number between −32,768 and +32,767.
INTEGERINT	A four-byte number between −2,147,483,648 and +2,147,483,647.
BIGINT	A V4R5 and above 8-byte number between −9,223,372,036,854,775,808 and +9,223,372,036,854,775,807.
DECIMAL(X,Y)DEC(X,Y)	A packed decimal, where x is the length and y is the precision. Y is optional; if not specified, it defaults to zero.
NUMERIC(X,Y)	A zoned decimal where x is the length and y is the precision. Y is optional; if not specified, it defaults to zero.
Numeric Data Types without Precision	
FLOATREAL	An 8-byte (32-bit) floating-point number
DOUBLEDOUBLE PRECISION	A 16-byte (64-bit) floating-point number

SMALLINT, INTEGER, and BIGINT

A SMALLINT is a small integer number. It can be positive or negative, and ranges from -2,768 to +32,767. The small integer takes 2 bytes of storage. In DDS, you could create the analog of a small integer by specifying 2B 0 as the type of column you are creating. An INTEGER is a 4-byte number between -2,147,483,648 and +2,147,483,647. It could be represented in DDS using 4B 0. Finally, a BIGINT is an 8-byte number between -9,223,372,036,854,775,808 and +9,223,372,036,854,775,807. It could be represented in DDS using 8B 0. BIGINT is only available in OS/400 release V4R5 and above. Here is an example that creates a table containing the integer data types:

```
CREATE TABLE SQLBOOK.INTTEST
        (COL1 SMALLINT,
         COL2 INTEGER,
         COL3 BIGINT NOT NULL WITH DEFAULT)
```

Note that the NOT NULL WITH DEFAULT clause will cause COL3 to default to zero if a value is not specified when a record is inserted into the table. All numeric columns on the AS/400 will default to zero if the WITH DEFAULT clause is specified and no value is passed in. Otherwise, numeric columns will contain a NULL value if no value is passed and the column allows null data.

FLOAT and DOUBLE PRECISION

FLOAT represents a single-precision, floating-point number that takes 8 bytes of storage. DOUBLE PRECISION indicates an IEEE 64-bit floating point number and requires 16 bits of storage. These are equivalent to the DDS type of F. In order to represent a double-precision value in DDS, you would have to specify the FLTPCN keyword. The following example creates a table containing columns of these data types:

```
CREATE   TABLE SQLBOOK.FPTEST
            (COL1 REAL,
             COL2 DOUBLE)
```

COL1 is defined as REAL, which is a synonym for FLOAT. COL2 is defined as DOUBLE, which is equivalent to the DOUBLE PRECISION keyword.

DECIMAL

The DECIMAL data type represents a packed decimal field on the AS/400. This is equivalent to the DDS keyword P. When creating a decimal column, you must always specify the precision and scale of the decimal. The precision can be a value up to 31 digits and represents the total number of digits in the numeric field. The scale can be from zero up to the precision of the column you are creating. The following example creates a decimal field in a table called Y:

```
CREATE TABLE SQLBOOK.Y (A DECIMAL(15,5))
```

NUMERIC

The NUMERIC type creates a zoned decimal field within the physical file. This is equivalent to the DDS keyword S. When creating a numeric column, you must always specify the precision and scale of the number. Like the decimal, the precision of a numeric column can be from 1 to 31, and the scale can be up to the value of the precision of the column. The following statement creates a zoned decimal field in the table T:

```
CREATE TABLE SQLBOOK.T (A NUMERIC(8,2))
```

Storing Time

The AS/400 has built-in data types for the representation of dates, times, and timestamps, as shown in Table 1.3. A date field can store any legal date value and is represented internally as a 4-byte integer.

Table 1.3: AS/400 DB2 Temporal Data Types	
TIMESTAMP	A date–time field that requires 10 bytes.
TIME	A time field that can store the time of day. It requires 3 bytes.
DATE	A date field that requires 4 bytes.

Time fields can store time-of-day information and are represented internally as a 3-byte string. Each byte represents two packed-decimal digits. The first is the hour, the second is the minute, and the last is the second.

A timestamp field is the combination of a date field and a time field, but the timestamp has precision down to the microsecond level. Internally, it is represented as a 10-byte string. The first 4 bytes are the date, the next 3 bytes are the time, and the last 3 bytes represent the microsecond value.

If you use the WITH DEFAULT keywords in creating a date, time, or timestamp column, SQL will automatically insert the current date, time, or timestamp value into a record if a field's value is not specified when the record is added to the table. The following SQL statement creates a table with date, time, and timestamp fields:

```
CREATE  TABLE SQLBOOK.TIMETEST
          (F1 DATE NOT NULL WITH DEFAULT,
           F2 TIME NOT NULL WITH DEFAULT,
           F3 TIMESTAMP NOT NULL WITH DEFAULT)
```

Data Links

In OS/400 version 4, DB2 on the AS/400 introduced a new data type called DATALINK. Data links are useful if you are programming a dynamic Web system. They allow you to store the location of an external file in the SQL database, and then use SQL scalar functions to manipulate the external file or retrieve the URL to the external file. The nice thing about data links is that they can ensure that a file is not deleted if a record in the database exists that references the external file. (This is only true if the data link resides on the IFS of the AS/400 that owns the table that contains the data link.) Otherwise, the DATALINK type is of little use. If you just want to store URL information, use a VARCHAR.

Because the DATALINK type is very specialized and is at this time only supported on the AS/400 version of DB2, not many examples in this book show its manipulation. However, here is an SQL statement that will create a table that contains a DATALINK column:

```
CREATE  TABLE SQLBOOK.MYURLS
          (ID INTEGER NOT NULL PRIMARY KEY,
           LINK DATALINK LINKTYPE URL )
```

This statement creates a table called MYURLS, which contains two columns: ID and LINK. The LINK column contains data link information. Appendix B covers the functions that are available for manipulating these types of columns.

User-Defined Types

Starting with V4, the AS/400 also allows you to create your own data types to be used in the SQL database. This can be very useful for new system development, although you will probably never attempt this with your legacy systems. User-defined types are based on the built-in data types already discussed. You can create your own data type using the CREATE TYPE statement. Here is an example that creates a data type called COOL:

```
CREATE TYPE SQLBOOK.COOL AS CHAR(1) WITH COMPARISONS
```

Now that the data type is created, you can use it in a CREATE TABLE statement like the following:

```
CREATE   TABLE SQLBOOK.COOLTEST
              (ID INTEGER NOT NULL PRIMARY KEY,
               COOL SQLBOOK.COOL)
```

User-defined types are going to be great when they get all of the bugs worked out on the AS/400. But for now, I recommend that you stay far away from them. In all development situations that I have been in (through V4R4), these things have served only to complicate the SQL statements that needed to be created for data access. This is because you cannot correctly compare user-defined types to their base types. Be afraid.

Indexes and Logical Files

On the AS/400, they are called logical files; in SQL they are called indexes. Sounds simple, right? Wrong-o, daddy-o. There is a world of difference between an SQL index and an AS/400 logical file, and a world of similarity. An SQL index is implemented as an AS/400 logical file, but logical files created by DDS can have more capabilities than an SQL index logical file. I'll try to illuminate the differences by concrete examples.

An SQL index is an ordered list of a set of fields from a single SQL table. An index is created by issuing an SQL CREATE INDEX statement. Once an index is created, it will be automatically maintained by the AS/400, just like any logical file would. SQL indexes are always created with the maintenance option of *IMMED. SQL indexes are also always created with the recovery option of *AFTIPL, which means if the logical file is damaged, recovery will happen after the next system IPL. The syntax of the CREATE INDEX statement is simple:

```
CREATE <optional-UNIQUE> INDEX <index-name>
ON <table-name> (<list of columns-and-order>)
```

CREATE INDEX can take a list of one or more columns that should exist in the index, and you can optionally specify the column's sort direction. If you do not specify the sort direction, the column will be sorted in ascending order. Also, the UNIQUE keyword can be specified before the INDEX keyword. UNIQUE ensures that no rows exist with duplicate keys in the columns list.

The CREATE INDEX statement will cause a logical file to be created on the AS/400 that contains the fields specified in the statement. This logical file is implemented as a binary radix tree and contains only the fields listed in the list of columns. These fields are now called the *index key*. Here is an example CREATE INDEX statement that creates an index called PARTSPID on the table PARTS in the library SQLBOOK:

```
CREATE UNIQUE INDEX SQLBOOK.PARTSPID ON PARTS (PARTID)
```

After this statement executes, a logical file called PARTSPID exists in the library SQLBOOK. This logical file contains an ordered list of PARTID fields from the PARTS table in the library SQLBOOK. In addition, because the UNIQUE keyword was supplied, the AS/400 will ensure that no two records have an identical PARTID value.

SQL can now use this index in the satisfaction of query requests. Exactly how this is done is explained in chapters 2 and 6, but for now I will explain in broad strokes. You cannot directly read the index PARTSPID with an SQL statement, but SQL may elect to use the index when you attempt to read or use the PARTS table. For example, if you ask SQL to return rows where the PARTID column is equal to "A", SQL will probably use the PARTSPID index to search for the parts that have that part ID, in order to make the query return results faster. SQL will act just like a good programmer. A good programmer would say, "I want to get parts with a certain ID, so I will open the logical file and use CHAIN to get the part ID I want." By using the index, both SQL and the good programmer avoid reading the entire parts table in order to find the single record in which they are interested.

However, there is one big difference between SQL and programming in COBOL or RPG using record level access: SQL programmers do not have to understand what indexes are available in order to access records. If an RPG programmer needs to find a record with a certain part ID, he or she would have to know about the PARTPID logical and need to open the logical; otherwise, the entire parts file would have to be searched. An SQL programmer would just issue an SQL statement asking for the part record where the ID was equal to the desired part ID. SQL would worry about the implementation details of the query.

This can be a good thing and a bad thing. It's good because programmers only need to be concerned with the data they want from the database, not how to get the data. It is bad because the optimization (determining how to best get the data requested) is left up to a program.

Why DDS Could Be Better Than CREATE INDEX

DDS can be used to create logical files, and in some cases "indexes" created with DDS have more capabilities than the logical files created by the CREATE INDEX SQL statement. This is partly because there is a blurry line between SQL indexes, AS/400 logical files, and SQL views. (Views are discussed further later in this chapter.) An index is a binary radix tree that contains only the fields specified in the index keylist. A logical file created by DDS is also a binary radix tree that contains only the fields specified in the keylist. However, the DDS-created logical file can be made to emulate an SQL view by eliminating the field specification from the DDS file. Examine these differences by doing an example.

First, issue a CREATE TABLE statement to create a sample table in the SQLBOOK library:

```
CREATE   TABLE SQLBOOK.ITEST (PRT CHAR(10),
            COST DECIMAL(8,2), QUAN DECIMAL(6,0))
```

Next, execute the following two SQL statements to put records in the ITEST file:

```
INSERT INTO SQLBOOK.ITEST VALUES ('PART 1',10.25,6);
INSERT INTO SQLBOOK.ITEST VALUES ('PART 2',20.50,42)
```

Then, issue an SQL statement to create an SQL index over the ITEST table on column A:

```
CREATE UNIQUE INDEX SQLBOOK.ITEST1 ON SQLBOOK.ITEST (PRT)
```

You now have a logical file called ITEST1 that is an SQL index on the ITEST table in the library SQLBOOK. The logical file contains only the field PRT uniquely sorted in ascending order.

Finally, suppose you want to create a DDS logical file on the ITEST table. To do this, first create a source physical file on the AS/400 called QDSRC, using the following command:

```
CRTSRCPF FILE(SQLBOOK/QDSRC)
```

Next, use the Start Source Entry Utility (STRSEU) to enter the DDS source (shown in Figure 1.2) into a new member called ITEST2 in the file QDSCR in the library SQLBOOK.

```
A                                              UNIQUE
A               R ITEST                        PFILE(SQLBOOK/ITEST)
A               K PRT
```

Figure 1.2: This DDS creates a logical file that is indexed on the PRT column of the ITEST physical file.

Finally, use the following command to create the file ITEST2 from the DDS source:

```
CRTLF FILE(SQLBOOK/ITEST2) SRCFILE(SQLBOOK/QDSRC) SRCMBR(ITEST2)
```

The logical files ITEST1 and ITEST2 are almost identical. They have the same record length and storage utilization. The only difference can be found by using the Display File Description (DSPFD) command to display the file description report. Comparing the description line by line, you will find that the ITEST1 logical file contains one additional line of information. Under the Data Base File Attributes section of the report, you will find the line SQL File Type, which will have a value of INDEX.

This information is not in the DSPFD report on the table ITEST2. This little value keeps SQL from being able to read the logical file directly when using an SQL SE-LECT statement. It also keeps SQL from being able to delete, update, or insert records in the file. This might not seem like an important distinction now, but when you get to query optimization (chapter 6), it becomes really important.

I would recommend that you adopt a policy of always creating "indexes" by using DDS instead of the SQL CREATE INDEX command. The indexes will then be useful to RPG and COBOL programmers as well as to your SQL efforts. Indexes created by DDS are best described as crosses between real SQL indexes and SQL views.

What Not to Do with DDS

SQL cannot read multiformat logical files or use them as access paths for the resolution of a query. So, bear in mind that these are completely useless to an SQL programmer. In addition, if a logical file contains select/omit criteria, it cannot be used as an access path to a physical file in resolution of an SQL query. Stay away from these, if at all possible, as they will be of absolutely no use to you in the SQL world.

SQL Views

An SQL view is an interesting beast. The word *view* was created to describe a virtual table. See, SQL views do not actually exist. They look like logical files, but they have no records or key columns stored in them. Remember, a table is really a physical file on the AS/400, but an SQL view is merely an SQL statement pretending to be a logical file.

Before you can really understand a view, you need to understand a basic SQL statement called the SELECT statement. SELECT is how you read records from an SQL database. When you issue a SELECT statement, the AS/400 interprets the grammar of the statement and causes records to be read from one or more physical and/or logical files and returned to your application program. SELECT statements are the most powerful part of SQL and are detailed in chapter 2.

A view is created by issuing a CREATE VIEW statement. Here is its syntax:

```
CREATE VIEW <view-name> (<optional-list-of-column-names>) AS
<SQL-select-statement>
```

The view name can be any legal AS/400 table name and can consist of up to 128 characters. (However, remember that table names over 10 characters cause the AS/400 to create a system table name with the first five characters, and then append a number to the end of that string.) The optional list of columns allows you to rename the columns as they will be referenced in the view or to provide names for derived columns. The AS keyword indicates that a SELECT statement will follow, and the statement that follows the keyword describes to the AS/400 what data should be retrieved when the view is accessed.

Understanding Views by Example

This view concept is best expressed by example. First, create the table VBASE by executing the following SQL statement:

```
CREATE TABLE SQLBOOK.VBASE
        (ID CHAR(10),
        QUAN INTEGER,
        PRICE DECIMAL(8,2))
```

Next, execute the following three SQL statements to insert records into the VBASE table:

```
INSERT INTO SQLBOOK.VBASE VALUES ('ITEM1',5,12.5);
INSERT INTO SQLBOOK.VBASE VALUES ('ITEM2',20,19.95);
INSERT INTO SQLBOOK.VBASE VALUES ('ITEM3',2,4.95)
```

Now, a table called VBASE, which has three records, exists in the library SQLBOOK. Each record consists of an ID field, a QUAN field to reflect the quantity on hand, and a PRICE field to reflect the price of the item identified by ID. If you were to execute the following statement, you would receive a result similar to Figure 1.3:

```
SELECT * FROM SQLBOOK.VBASE
```

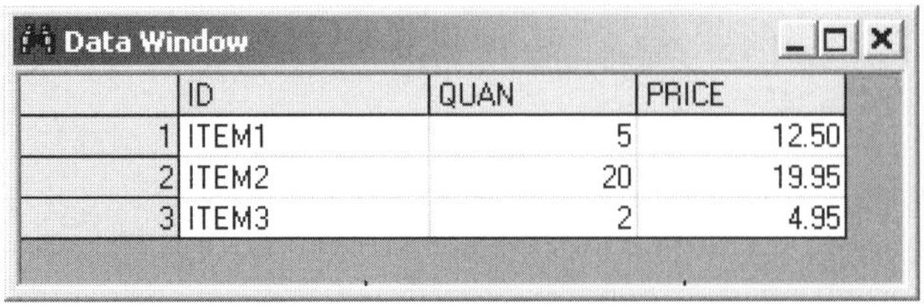

	ID	QUAN	PRICE
1	ITEM1	5	12.50
2	ITEM2	20	19.95
3	ITEM3	2	4.95

Figure 1.3: This data window shows the results of the SQL SELECT statement against the table VBASE.

The SELECT statement tells SQL to read all of the records and return all columns in each record. As you can see in Figure 1.3, SQL has returned all of the records placed into the table by the INSERT statements.

Now that you have a physical file with data in it, you can make a view. Execute the following SQL statement to create a view called VTEST:

```
CREATE VIEW SQLBOOK.VTEST (ID, QUAN, PRICE, ONHAND)
         AS SELECT ID, QUAN, PRICE, QUAN*PRICE FROM SQLBOOK.VBASE
```

Congratulations, you have a view. Let's examine the syntax of this CREATE VIEW statement. The view's name is SQLBOOK.VTEST, which means that, if the CREATE VIEW statement executes, you will have a logical file called VTEST in the library SQLBOOK. Next, the statement contains a list of column names to use in the logical file. If you choose to name the columns in a view (which I almost always do), you have the capability to rename the columns or give names to derived columns.

Note that the list of names is positional, and in no way related to the names of the fields that are coming from the database via the SELECT statement. If your SELECT statement retrieves four columns, and you decide to provide names for your fields, you must supply four column names in the list of column names.

Finally, the CREATE VIEW statement ends with the SQL SELECT statement that drives the data to be housed in the view. This statement indicates that the AS/400 should fetch the ID, QUAN, and PRICE fields from the SQLBOOK.VBASE table. In addition to those fields, the fourth field in the view is a derived field consisting of the contents of the QUAN field times the contents of the PRICE field.

Let's read the record from the VTEST view and look at the output that SQL generates. Execute the following statement:

```
SELECT * FROM SQLBOOK.VTEST;
```

You should see the output shown in Figure 1.4. To SQL, it does not matter if you are reading from a view or a table; the SQL database will treat them identically. When the statement is executed, the AS/400 looks at the target table, VTEST, and says to itself, "Oh, you're a view logical file. So, to find your data, first I need to retrieve the SQL statement that drives you and execute that statement. Then, I will take the resulting rows that you return and do any other processing that the user has asked for."

	ID	QUAN	PRICE	ONHAND
1	ITEM1	5	12.50	62.50
2	ITEM2	20	19.95	399.00
3	ITEM3	2	4.95	9.90

Figure 1.4: These are the results of selecting records from the VTEST table.

This is slightly different than if the AS/400 were selecting data from just a physical file. When the AS/400 is reading from a physical, the database says to itself, "Oh, you're a physical file. So, I just open you up and read records, and return the ones that satisfy my user's query." Almost the same, but not quite.

Why Views Are Better Than DDS Logicals

SQL views are a lot more powerful than DDS logical files in a few important areas. First, SQL views can have a richer set of derived columns than DDS logicals. In DDS, you can concatenate fields and do substring operations, but in SQL views you can do complex mathematical expressions and use SQL scalar functions to make derived values from different types of fields. This topic is examined in chapter 4, but for now, consider just a few examples of how views outperform DDS logicals. These examples refer to a table that has the following structure:

```
CREATE TABLE SQLBOOK.SALES
        (CUSTOMER CHAR(10),
        PART CHAR(10),
        QUAN INTEGER,
        PRICE DECIMAL(10,2),
        SALEDATE DATE,
        SALESMAN CHAR(3))
```

This table reflects a simple table of product sales. The following six SQL statements insert sample data into this table:

```
INSERT INTO SQLBOOK.SALES VALUES ('JOHN','PART1',6,1.95,'01/01/2000','HFA');
INSERT INTO SQLBOOK.SALES VALUES ('BILL','PART1',2,1.91,'01/03/2000','HFA');
INSERT INTO SQLBOOK.SALES VALUES ('JOHN','PART1',1,1.95,'01/09/2000','STC');
INSERT INTO SQLBOOK.SALES VALUES ('BILL','PART2',4,1.91,'01/11/2000','STC');
INSERT INTO SQLBOOK.SALES VALUES ('JOHN','PART5',91,16.95,'02/04/2000','HFA');
INSERT INTO SQLBOOK.SALES VALUES ('BILL','PART4',9,19.95,'02/04/2000','STC');
INSERT INTO SQLBOOK.SALES VALUES ('JOHN','PART3',25,6.95,'02/01/2000','HFA')
```

These sales are for parts from inventory, and salesmen HFA and STC sold them during the months of January and February in the year 2000 to customers JOHN and BILL.

Now that there is some simple example data, look at an example of how SQL scalars can be used in views. The boss wants a report of sales by month. Therefore, you create a view that has the month of the SALEDATE in one column and the total sales dollars in the other:

```
CREATE VIEW SQLBOOK.SALESV1 (MO,TD) AS
        SELECT MONTH(SALEDATE),QUAN*PRICE FROM SQLBOOK.SALES
```

You now have a view called SALESV1 in the library SQLBOOK that contains two fields, MO and TD. The MO column is the result of the expression MONTH (SALEDATE) in the view's SQL statement, and the TD column is the result of the multiplication of the columns QUAN and

	MO	TD
1	1	11.70
2	1	3.82
3	1	1.95
4	1	7.64
5	2	1,542.45
6	2	179.55
7	2	173.75

Figure 1.5: Here are the results of selecting records from the SALESV1 table.

PRICE. If you were to execute the following statement, you would see the results shown in Figure 1.5:

```
SELECT * FROM SQLBOOK.SALESV1
```

Take a look at the resulting data. The month scalar function has returned an integer that represents the month of the value of the SALEDATE column. The TD column contains the results of the multiplication of QUAN and PRICE. Now, you need only write a program that adds the values. However, SQL has the capability to do that for you. Look at a final sample statement:

```
SELECT  MO, SUM(TD)
           FROM SQLBOOK.SALESV1
           GROUP BY MO
```

Figure 1.6 shows the results of the statement. Notice that SQL has aggregated the records to produce totals for each month. This type of SQL statement is thoroughly discussed in the next chapter, but it does warrant a short explanation here. On the AS/400, you cannot use the GROUP BY keywords to cause summation on derived columns. Hiding the derived column, MO, in a CREATE VIEW statement effectively bypasses this limitation on the AS/400. The GROUP BY

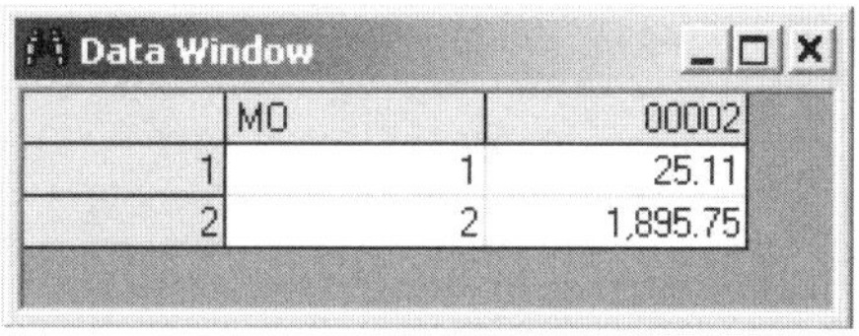

Figure 1.6: These results show how views can be used to assist in aggregating data.

clause in the example statement causes SQL to read all of the records returned by the view and aggregate them by the MO column. The SUM(TD) causes SQL to add all of the values of the field TD together.

This is really powerful. The statement is leaving the work of adding all of the values to the AS/400 and only returning summary data to the requesting program. In addition, using a statement like this would simplify the logic in the application program that needs to process the returned data.

If you do not fully understand the information on views and how they can be useful, don't panic. You will revisit them in chapters 2 and 4. Once you see them being used against real data, their value becomes apparent.

Primary Key

Files on the AS/400 can be declared using DDS to have arrival sequence, or they can be declared as having a keyed sequence. There is no way to declare a file using SQL as having a keyed sequence, because SQL is a set-based language, not a file-based language. However, an SQL table can be declared as having a primary key. The primary key is a list of one or more columns that uniquely identify a single record in an SQL table. Primary keys can be declared during the creation of the table or they can be added later using the ALTER TABLE statement.

Consider this example statement:

```
CREATE  TABLE SQLBOOK.KEYTEST
           (PARTID CHAR(20) NOT NULL PRIMARY KEY,
           CLASS SMALLINT,
           SUBCLASS SMALLINT,
           PDESC CHAR(40) NOT NULL)
```

This statement creates a table called KEYTEST in the library SQLBOOK. The table now has a primary key that consists of the PARTID column. This means that no two entries in the table can have an identical PARTID value. If you were to issue the following two SQL statements, the second would fail because it would violate the primary key clause of this table:

```
INSERT INTO SQLBOOK.PARTS VALUES ('P1',1,1,'MY DESCRIPTION');
INSERT INTO SQLBOOK.PARTS VALUES ('P2',5,6,'ANOTHER PART')
```

Figure 1.7 shows the DDS source that could be used instead of the CREATE TABLE statement. The tables created by both means would be identical, except the one created by DDS would not automatically be associated with the journal in the SQLBOOK library.

```
A                                              UNIQUE
A               R KEYTEST
A                 PARTID        20A
A                 CLASS         4B 0
A                 SUBCLASS      4B 0
A                 PDESC         40A
A               K PARTID
```

Figure 1.7: This DDS could be used instead of the CREATE TABLE statement to create the KEYTEST table.

Another way to define a primary key is to do it after the table has been created, using the ALTER TABLE statement. If you execute the following two statements, you will get a table with no primary key:

```
DROP TABLE SQLBOOK.KEYTEST;

CREATE TABLE SQLBOOK.KEYTEST
        (PARTID CHAR(20) NOT NULL,
        CLASS SMALLINT,
        SUBCLASS SMALLINT,
        PDESC CHAR(40) NOT NULL)
```

The first statement drops the KEYTEST table from the SQLBOOK library. The second creates the KEYTEST table in the library SQLBOOK. Now, executing the following statement adds a primary key to the KEYTEST statement:

```
ALTER TABLE SQLBOOK.KEYTEST
        ADD CONSTRAINT SQLBOOK.KEYTESTPK
        PRIMARY KEY (PARTID)
```

The ALTER TABLE statement first identifies the table you want to alter, then the type of alteration you are making. In this case, a CONSTRAINT called SQLBOOK.KEYTESTPK is added as a primary key. After the PRIMARY KEY keywords, you place a list of columns to include as the primary key. In the case of this table, the primary key has only one column, PARTID.

By default, declaring a primary key on a table indicates that the column(s) must be unique and must not contain null values. In addition to primary keys, you can also define additional columns in the table with the UNIQUE attribute. This ensures that no two values in that column are the same. Here is an example where you might have both a primary key and a separate column that requires unique values:

```
CREATE  TABLE SQLBOOK.EMPLOYEES
        (EMPID INTEGER NOT NULL PRIMARY KEY,
         SSN CHAR(11) NOT NULL UNIQUE,
         EMPNAME VARCHAR(40) ALLOCATE(20))
```

The above statement creates a physical file EMPLOYEES in the SQLBOOK library that has three columns, EMPID, SSN, and EMPNAME. The EMPID column is declared as the primary key of the table, and therefore there will be a keyed physical file with the key based on the EMPID column. In addition, the table now has a constraint on the SSN column; all values added to the SSN column must not already exist in the table.

If you attempt to execute the following two SQL statements, the second will fail because the SSN violates the UNIQUE constraint, even though the record does not violate the primary key constraint:

```
INSERT INTO SQLBOOK.EMPLOYEES VALUES (1,'222-34-5555','Howie Arner');
INSERT INTO SQLBOOK.EMPLOYEES VALUES (2,'222-34-5555','Carla White')
```

Foreign Key

Foreign keys are another constraint that you can place on tables. Their concept is not hard to grasp. I tend to think of them as parent–child relationships. They are best illuminated by example. Figure 1.8 shows an entity relationship diagram of the tables EMPLOYEES and TIMESHEET. These tables have a foreign key relationship based on the EMPID column. For a record to exist in the TIMESHEET table, an EMPID used in the record must exist in the parent table, EMPLOYEES. Here is the SQL that creates the TIMESHEET table:

```
CREATE TABLE SQLBOOK.TIMESHEET
        (EMPID INTEGER NOT NULL,
         WORKDATE DATE NOT NULL,
         TIMESTART TIME,
         TIMEEND TIME,
         PRIMARY KEY(EMPID,WORKDATE))
```

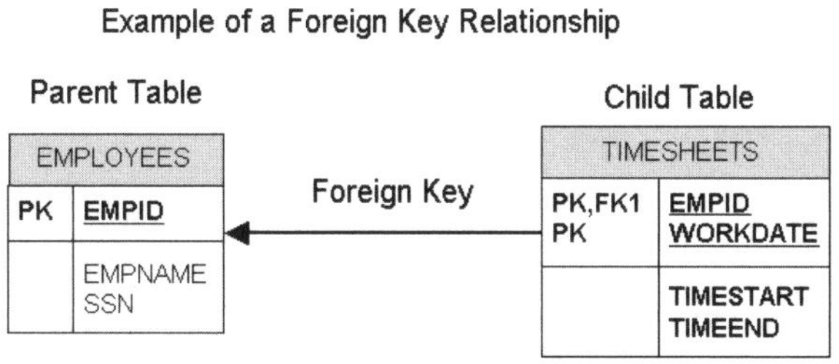

Example of a Foreign Key Relationship

Figure 1.8: This chart shows the parent–child relationship defined by foreign keys.

Notice that this table has a compound primary key that consists of the EMPID and WORKDATE fields. This means that an entry is not valid unless the combination of EMPID and WORKDATE are unique. Now that the table exists, you can add the foreign key relationship to it:

```
ALTER TABLE SQLBOOK.TIMESHEET
        ADD FOREIGN KEY (EMPID)
        REFERENCES SQLBOOK.EMPLOYEES (EMPID)
        ON DELETE CASCADE
        ON UPDATE RESTRICT
```

This FOREIGN key statement creates a relationship between the TIMESHEET table and the EMPLOYEES table created in the previous section. The foreign key places the following conditions to adding and updating records in the timesheet table:

1. The EMPID used in the record must exist in the EMPLOYEES table.

2. If you delete an employee record from the EMPLOYEES table, all timesheet entries will be removed from the TIMESHEETS table.

The first restriction is what foreign keys do by default. They ensure that there is consistency in your database by enforcing relationships between tables. The ON DELETE CASCADE grammar added to the foreign key statement enforces the second restriction. This ensures that if you delete a record from the parent table, all child records are removed.

The ON UPDATE RESTRICT grammar tells SQL to enforce the foreign key definition on updates performed to the parent table. If a programmer attempts to change an EMPID value in a record in the EMPLOYEES table, and timesheet records exist for that employee ID, SQL will not allow the update to be done until all records in the TIMESHEETS table are removed or set to a different employee ID.

Another neat thing about foreign keys is that they do not have to reference another table—they can reference themselves. Here is an example of a table that references itself:

```
CREATE TABLE SQLBOOK.FKTEST
        (EMPID INTEGER NOT NULL PRIMARY KEY,
         EMPNAME VARCHAR(40) ALLOCATE(20),
         SUPERVISOR INTEGER NOT NULL
         REFERENCES SQLBOOK.FKTEST (EMPID)
         ON DELETE RESTRICT)
```

This creates a table called FKTEST in the library SQLBOOK with the columns EMPID, EMPNAME, and SUPERVISOR. However, by adding REFRENCES SQLBOOK.FKTEST (EMPID) to the definition of the SUPERVISOR columns, a foreign key relationship that references itself has been placed against the table. This relationship enforces the rule that all employees must have a supervisor (maintained by the NOT NULL clause), and the supervisor must exist as an EMPID in the FKTEST table.

This example brings up an interesting problem. All employees must have a supervisor, but there are not employees in the table, so no records can be added. Making sure that the first record added to the table has a supervisor ID equal to its employee ID circumvents this.

Check Constraints

Another powerful weapon for database consistency in the AS/400 SQL arsenal is the check constraint. A check constraint allows you to set limits on the data that can be placed in a column of a table. A check constraint can be added to a column during creation of the table or after table creation by using an ALTER TABLE statement.

Here is an example check constraint that ensures employee ID numbers are between 1 and 1,000 in the EMPID column of the FKTEST table:

```
ALTER TABLE SQLBOOK.FKTEST ADD CHECK (EMPID <100 and EMPID >1 )
```

You can get really fancy with check constraints in your tables, and they can be a real boon to database consistency. Consider the following check constraint that I added to the TIMESHEETS table:

```
ALTER TABLE SQLBOOK.TIMESHEET
        ADD CHECK (MONTH(WORKDATE)<>12
        AND   DAYOFWEEK(WORKDATE)>1 )
```

This constraint proves what a kind-hearted soul I am. It does not allow timesheet entries where the person worked in December (provided by MONTH(WORK-DATE)<>12), and goes further by ensuring that employees work only on days other than Sunday (enforced by the DAYOFWEEK(WORKDATE)>1).

The argument to a check constraint can be any valid search condition. A search condition is an expression that returns either true or false. A check constraint will succeed only if the search condition is true. Scalar functions and other expressions can be used in the search condition. (For full details on search conditions, see chapter 2.)

Stored Procedures

Stored procedures are business logic that you can call via an SQL CALL statement. On the AS/400, stored procedures can be written in CL, C, RPG, COBOL, and any other language supported by the AS/400. They can also be written in the AS/400 stored procedure language, which is covered in chapter 7.

AS/400 stored procedures are very powerful because, with one SQL CALL statement, they can perform a lot of work. Stored procedures can return parameters, like a program call, and they can also return multiple result sets.

A stored procedure is identified to the AS/400 by the CREATE PROCEDURE statement. CREATE PROCEDURE identifies the program to call, its parameters, if it returns result sets, and the language it was written in (or in the case of SQL procedures, it contains the procedure program).

39

Uses for CREATE PROCEDURE vary, but I suggest that you explore them in detail. By using an SQL procedure, you can encapsulate business logic where it belongs, on the AS/400. Recently, I did a really large e-commerce site that involved selling HVAC parts over the Internet. The legacy application that I was interfacing with was written in RPG III and was massive. The RPG III program that calculated a price for an individual part for an individual customer was over 23,000 lines of code. By using a stored procedure declaration, I avoided rewriting the legacy code. I just called it from a Web server and it returned the price for the part. Stored procedure calls can help you build multi-platform systems quickly, which leverages the logic inherent in your AS/400 applications.

LABEL and COMMENT

SQL offers you the capability to add labels and comments to objects in the SQL database via the LABEL and COMMENT statements. The labels and comments are stored in the system catalog and can be used to document the usage of SQL columns, tables, indexes, views, procedures, functions, and user-defined types. Here is the syntax for an SQL comment:

```
COMMENT ON <object-type> <object-name>
IS <text-of-comment>
```

A comment can be up to 2,000 characters of text. Comments are useful for long-winded documentation about a column, table, index, or procedure. The *<object-type>* keyword can be any of the following: ALIAS, COLUMN, DISTINCT TYPE, FUNCTION, ROUTINE, INDEX, PACKAGE, PARAMETER, PROCEDURE, TABLE, or VIEW. The object name is the fully qualified name of the object. The comment itself is enclosed in single quotes and always follows the IS keyword.

The following statement adds a comment to the WEBTEMP table in the library SQLBOOK:

```
COMMENT ON TABLE
        SQLBOOK.WEBTEMP
        IS 'This table stored all of the web hits against
        our site in the month of October.'
```

The following statement adds a comment to the REQGEO and REQTS columns of the WEBTEMP table in the SQLBOOK library:

```
COMMENT ON SQLBOOK.WEBTEMP
           (REQTS IS 'This is the date/time of the web request',
           REQGEO IS 'This is the geographic area where the
           request came from.')
```

The LABEL ON statement is used to place a label on an ALIAS, COLUMN, TABLE, VIEW, or PACKAGE. Labels are strings up to 50 characters. The LABEL ON statement has two forms:

```
LABEL ON <label-type> <object-name> IS <label-string>

LABEL ON <label-type> <object-name> TEXT IS <label-text>
```

If the TEXT keyword is specified, the label is an OS/400 TEXT label. Otherwise, the label is a column heading.

The following statement adds column headings to the REQGEO column of the WEBTEMP table in the SQLBOOK library:

```
LABEL ON COLUMN SQLBOOK.WEBTEMP.REQGEO IS 'DATE/TIME of Request'
```

The following statement adds an OS/400 text label to the REQGEO column of the WEBTEMP table in SQLBOOK:

```
LABEL ON COLUMN SQLBOOK.WEBTEMP.REQGEO
           TEXT IS 'DATE/TIME of Request'
```

SQL Security

SQL enhances AS/400 security with some new capabilities. SQL security is controlled through the GRANT and REVOKE SQL statements. GRANT gives users rights to certain AS/400 objects, whereas REVOKE takes them away.

There are specific forms of GRANT and REVOKE that apply to tables and views, procedures, user-defined types, SQL packages, and user-defined functions. The forms for user-defined types, packages, procedures, and functions are beyond the scope of this book. However, they are defined in the *AS/400 SQL Reference,* should you be interested in using these capabilities.

Table/View Form of GRANT and REVOKE

The GRANT and REVOKE statements can be used on tables and views to control the type of operations that users can perform on them. The syntax of the statement is as follows:

```
GRANT <privilege(s)>
ON <object(s)>
TO <user-name(s) or PUBLIC>
WITH GRANT OPTION
```

Here is the syntax for REVOKE:

```
REVOKE <privilege(s)>
ON <object(s)>
FROM <user-name(s) or PUBLIC>
```

Privileges can be made up from the following keywords: ALL, ALTER, DELETE, INDEX, INSERT, REFERENCES, REFERENCES(x), SELECT, UPDATE, or UPDATE(x).

If you GRANT to PUBLIC, you are giving all users on the system the capability. If you GRANT to a specific user profile, you are only granting the list of rights to that profile.

ALL is a special keyword: It allows you to grant all table privileges to PUBLIC or the specific user profile without having to list all privileges in the statement.

ALTER controls whether the user has the capability to alter the structure of a table. REFERENCES and REFERENCES(x) allow for the capability to add referential integrity to a table (foreign keys). If REFERENCES(x) is specified, x is a list of columns in the table.

INDEX imparts the capability for the user to create indexes on the table.

INSERT, UPDATE, and DELETE grant the specified user the capability to add records to the table, update existing records in the table, or remove records from the table. The special form of update, UPDATE(x), allows you to specify a list of columns that the user is allowed to update. For example, the following statement grants user ARNER the capability to INSERT records, UPDATE specified columns, and DELETE records in the SQLBOOK.WEBTEMP table:

```
GRANT INSERT, UPDATE(REQGEO, REQTS), DELETE
        ON SQLBOOK.WEBTEMP
        TO ARNER
```

The user ARNER cannot INDEX, ALTER, or add referential integrity to the table because the user has not been granted those capabilities.

The WITH GRANT OPTION keywords gives the user(s) that you grant this authority to the capability to grant those authorities to others. Users who have WITH GRANT OPTION can only grant the authorities that they have been granted. For example, the following statement grants ALL authorities to users ARNER and HERTVICK on the WEBTEMP2 and WEBTEMP tables and allows them to grant authorities to other users on these objects:

```
GRANT ALL ON SQLBOOK.WEBTEMP, SQLBOOK.WEBTEMP2
        TO ARNER, HERTVICK
        WITH GRANT OPTION
```

The REVOKE statement allows you to take specific privileges away from a user or the public. The following statement revokes the authority from PUBLIC to add referential integrity to the REQGEO and REQTS tables or to index the WEBTEMP table:

```
REVOKE REFERENCES(REQGEO, REQTS)
        ON SQLBOOK.WEBTEMP
        FROM PUBLIC
```

Controlling What Users See via VIEWS and GRANT

Suppose you have a table of employee data, including salaries and social security numbers. This table is called EMPDATA in the SQLBOOK library. You only want public users to be able to see the EMPNAME, EMPDEPT, and EMPPHONE fields. This can be accomplished by removing all rights from the base table. You would start by creating a view of only the data you want the user to see, and then grant the specific rights you want the public to have to the new view:

```
REVOKE ALL ON SQLBOOK.EMPDATA FROM PUBLIC
```

Next, you would create a view that contains the fields that you want your users to be able to access:

```
CREATE VIEW SQLBOOK.EMPVIEW
        (EMPNAME, EMPDEPT, EMPPHONE)
        AS SELECT EMPNAME, EMPDEPT, EMPPHONE
        FROM SQLBOOK.EMPDATA
```

Finally, you would grant the SELECT rights to the view so that your users can see the data in the view:

```
GRANT SELECT ON SQLBOOK.EMPVIEW TO PUBLIC
```

The effects of this are that users can read from the EMPVIEW table, which only consists of three columns. However, users cannot do anything to the base table EMPDATA. Users selecting from EMPDATA will receive an access-violation error.

System Catalog

Tables, views, indexes, procedures, and constraints are all declared using SQL, but where is the information stored? The AS/400 maintains tables of information about your database in a system catalog. This kind of data is sometimes called *metadata*. Metadata means data about your data. The system catalogs on the AS/400 contain information about all tables, views, indexes, procedures, con- straints, etc. on your system.

When you log into an AS/400, you are given access to the system catalogs that exist in the library QSYS2. All SQL users have access to these catalogs because, without them, the system would not be able to determine what you are allowed to see or do. In addition, if the SQL collection you are accessing was created with the CREATE DATABASE or CREATE COLLECTION SQL statements, it will have copies of the system catalog available within its library. However, these copies will be limited to only the tables, views, indexes, and constraints defined within the library.

The system catalogs are almost exclusively views against the following AS/400 physical files in the library QSYS2:

- QADBXREF
- QADBPKG
- QADBFDEP
- QADBXRDBD
- QADBFCST
- QADBCCST
- QADBIFLD
- QADBKFLD

The system catalogs are detailed in appendix B. Each catalog view is defined, and its definition is accompanied by useful queries that show you how to explore your database.

Chapter Summary

In this chapter, you have been exposed to SQL concepts and how they are treated on the AS/400. New terms, such as *table*, *row*, and *column*, have been introduced. You should now have a thorough grounding in the following concepts:

- Tables are physical files on the AS/400.

- Indexes are logical files on the AS/400.

- A database can refer to all objects on the AS/400, or just objects in one library.

- A library is a collection of objects.

- The terms "library" and "collection" are synonymous.

45

- Constraints place relational and data limits on your data in tables.

- Procedures allow you to execute programs on the AS/400 via SQL.

- The system catalog is a repository of metadata about SQL objects on your AS/400.

2

SQL SELECT BASICS

So far, you've examined the structure of relational databases and how this structure relates to the AS/400. Now, you'll find out about the heart of SQL: the SELECT statement. SELECT is the most important and most useful part of SQL because it is used to retrieve data from an AS/400 table to a target program. SELECT is easy to learn, but hard to master, as the possibilities for constructing statements are endless.

Once you have learned the basics of the SELECT statement, you will be able to get data from your AS/400 into your programs and massage that data in really interesting ways. This chapter gives you the grounding on SELECT you need for the more advanced chapters that follow.

What's in a SELECT

The SELECT statement is the *who*, *what*, *when*, and *where* of grabbing data from your database. Notice, though, that it is not the *how* of grabbing data. As the programmer, you specify what data (columns) you want, where (which tables) it is to come from, and when records should be chosen, but you do not tell the computer how to retrieve the records. That is the beauty of SQL; the computer automatically decides how to best implement your query to give you the maximum performance. Table 2.1 lists the SQL SELECT clauses.

Table 2.1: SQL SELECT Clauses

Clause	Description
FROM	Identifies what tables and views are to be read to find the data.
WHERE	Specifies conditions that data must meet in order to be part of the returned set.
ORDER BY	Specifies the ordering of the returned data set.
GROUP BY	Allows you to aggregate results by columns listed in the SELECT statement.
HAVING	Allows you to specify post-aggregation record-selection conditions when you are using a GROUP BY clause. This will further reduce the result set.

The Two Most Important Words

The two most important words in a SELECT statement are SELECT and FROM. These two words specify the "what do I get" and "where does it come from" of SQL data access. A SELECT statement must always begin with the SELECT keyword, and it must always contain a FROM clause. The FROM can indicate a table, a view, or an index created by DDS. If the index was created with an SQL CREATE INDEX statement, the index cannot be referenced in the FROM clause.

Again, the key to understanding a SELECT statement is that you must specify what you want to see and from where the AS/400 is to retrieve the data. Consider the database table WEBTEMP that has been uploaded to the AS/400. (Uploading is covered in appendix C.) Here is the DDL for the WEBTEMP table:

```
CREATE TABLE WEBTEMP
         (REQGEO CHAR(20),
          REQTYPE CHAR(10),
          REQFILE CHAR(80),
          BROWSER CHAR(10),
          REQTS TIMESTAMP,
          REQSIZE INTEGER,
          REQUSER INTEGER))
```

This fictional table represents a two-month set of hits against a Web site. Each row indicates a request for a document from the Web server. The first column, WEBGEO, is the country from which the request came. It contains values like USA and CANADA. The second column, REQTYPE, indicates whether the request was a HEAD-type request, a GET-type request, or a POST request. THE REQFILE column contains the name of the document requested by the Web client, and the REQTS column contains the timestamp when the request occurred. The BROWSER column indicates the client browser platform and version making the request, and REQSIZE is the size of the data transfer in kilobytes. Finally, REQUSER is an integer that uniquely identifies the computer requesting the Web document.

This WEBTEMP table will be the basis for all SELECT statements in this chapter. Now, you can get cracking on understanding SELECTs.

Your First Query

The following SQL statement would return a list of all of the REQFILE values stored in the WEBTEMP table in the AS/400 library SQLBOOK:

```
SELECT REQFILE FROM SQLBOOK.WEBTEMP
```

The output of the query is shown in Figure 2.1.

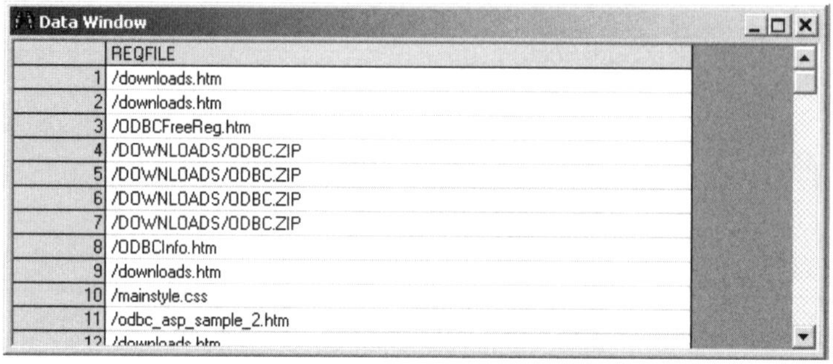

Figure 2.1: These are the results for your first SQL query. Note that the query requests only the REQFILE column from the WEBTEMP table.

Before going into detail about how that query works, do one more. The next statement would open the WEBTEMP table and read and return the values stored in the REQTS, REQGEO, and REQFILE fields.

```
SELECT REQTS, REQGEO, REQFILE FROM SQLBOOK.WEBTEMP
```

Let's take the statement apart. Immediately following the SELECT keyword, you indicate that you want the AS/400 to return the REQTS, REQGEO, and REQFILE columns. Following the list of fields, the FROM clause indicates that these fields should be read from the WEBTEMP table in the AS/400 library SQLBOOK. Simple. The output from the query is shown in Figure 2.2.

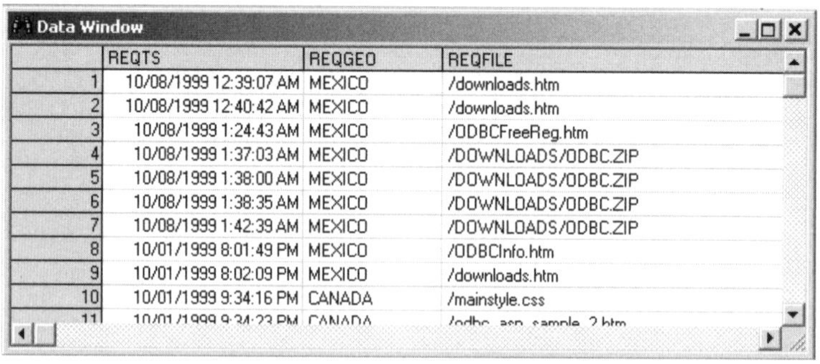

Figure 2.2: This screen shot represents the output from the second query. Note that it now displays three columns instead of one.

The List of Columns

The beautiful thing is that the list of columns does not have to contain real database fields; it can also contain *column functions* or *scalar functions*. A scalar function is a function that returns a value for each row returned by the query. It can take a column or expression as its argument. A column function can be used to aggregate values. It takes its input as a set of rows. You'll see more about column functions later. For now, here is an SQL statement that uses a column function to count the records in the WEBTEMP table:

```
SELECT COUNT(*) FROM SQLBOOK.WEBTEMP
```

This statement reads all records in the WEBTEMP table and passes them to the COUNT function. The COUNT function returns a count of how many records are in the table. Hence, the statement returns a single row as its result, and that row contains the number of rows in the WEBTEMP table, 3,035.

Here is another statement that uses a function, but in this case, it uses the scalar function UPPER to uppercase the REQFILE field:

```
SELECT REQTS, UPPER(REQFILE) FROM SQLBOOK.WEBTEMP
```

This statement returns the REQTS and REQFILE columns, but before returning the REQFILE column, it is massaged by the UPPER function to ensure that the document name is presented in uppercase. Figure 2.3 shows the output of the query.

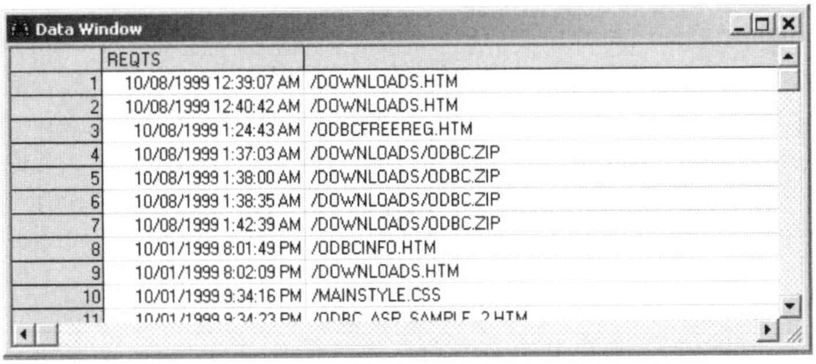

Figure 2.3: This output reflects how data can be massaged using scalar functions. The REQFILE field has been returned in uppercase.

Renaming Columns in the Column List

One important, but often overlooked, thing about the columns list is that you will usually reference columns by their column names in your application program. SQL provides a mechanism for renaming columns in the returned column list, and this capability is especially important from an application developer's perspective. Consider the following statement:

```
SELECT REQTS FROM SQLBOOK.WEBTEMP
```

The SELECT statement returns a list of rows containing the REQTS column. An application program would probably use the column name REQTS to reference the current value. In VB, it might look something like this:

```
X = MyRecordSet.Fields("REQTS").Value
```

However, what happens when you create a column that is an expression? In that case, SQL generates a column name for the virtual column, because it cannot determine the column name from the system catalogue. If SQL is generating a virtual column name, how do you reference that column by name in your code? Here is the answer:

```
SELECT COUNT(REQTS) AS MYCOUNT FROM SQLBOOK.WEBTEMP
```

The AS keyword allows you to create a column name for a column in the SELECT list at statement-execution time. If you did not supply a new column name for the above statement using the AS keyword, SQL would create a virtual column name to reference the field. By defining your own column name, you know precisely how to reference the column in your code. In addition, this gives you the capability to mask database changes from your applications.

This section explains how to provide the SELECT statement with one or more columns or functions in the columns list, and how to override the generated or actual name of a column with the AS keyword. Now that you have that concept, you can move on to controlling the data that is returned.

52

The WHERE Clause

All of the examples to this point have returned or read all of the data in the
WEBTEMP table. That's cool, but in a program, how many times do you really
want to read all of the data in a table? Most of the time, you want a subset of the
information, like this: "Show me all the employees who live in Florida," or this:
"Show me a list of WEBTEMP entries that occurred between January and February." You use the WHERE clause of the SQL statement to filter the information returned by your query.

The WHERE clause always comes after the FROM clause in an SQL SELECT statement. The WHERE keyword is always followed by a list of logical expressions
that a record must satisfy in order for that record to be returned. Here is a simple
example that returns all WEBTEMP rows that are hits from the USA:

```
SELECT * FROM SQLBOOK.WEBTEMP WHERE REQGEO='USA'
```

This sample also demonstrates the use of the * (asterisk) operator. The * indicates that SQL should return all columns from all tables referenced in the SELECT
statement. This is useful shorthand when you know you want all of the columns
returned. It keeps you from having to type the column names. The output of the
query is shown in Figure 2.4.

	REQGEO	REQTYPE	REQFILE	BROWSER	REQTS
1	USA	GET	/ODBCInfo.htm	#NULL#	10/01/1999
2	USA	GET	/mainstyle.css	#NULL#	10/01/1999
3	USA	GET	/csdlinks.htm	#NULL#	10/01/1999
4	USA	GET	/csdlinks.htm	#NULL#	10/01/1999
5	USA	GET	/mainstyle.css	#NULL#	10/01/1999
6	USA	GET	/index.htm	IE 5.0	10/01/1999 1
7	USA	GET	/mainstyle.css	IE 5.0	10/01/1999 1
8	USA	GET	/SqlthingOverview.htm	IE 5.0	10/01/1999
9	USA	GET	/mainstyle.css	IE 5.0	10/01/1999
10	USA	GET	/downloads.htm	IE 4.01	10/02/1999
11	USA	GET	/mainstyle.css	IE 4.01	10/02/1999

*Figure 2.4: These results are a subset of the entire WEBTEMP table. By using the WHERE
clause, you can retrieve hits only from the USA.*

The WHERE clause can take a list of expressions that are strung together with the AND and OR logical keywords. These types of expressions are called *search conditions*. A search condition is an expression that must be true or false. The following example query uses the logical AND to unify two search expressions. Its output is shown in Figure 2.5.

```
SELECT * FROM SQLBOOK.WEBTEMP WHERE REQGEO='USA' AND
        REQFILE='/index.htm'
```

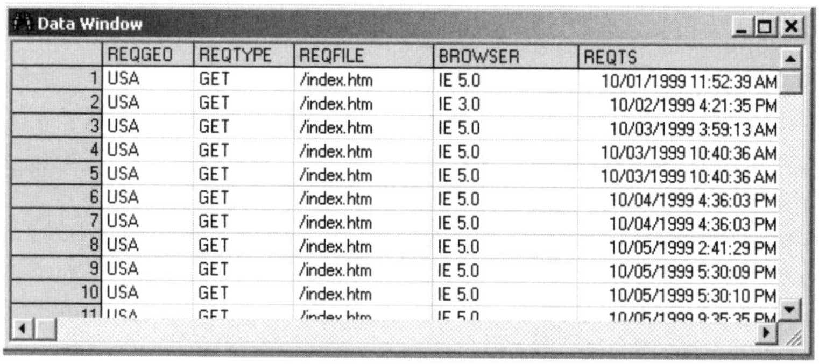

	REQGEO	REQTYPE	REQFILE	BROWSER	REQTS
1	USA	GET	/index.htm	IE 5.0	10/01/1999 11:52:39 AM
2	USA	GET	/index.htm	IE 3.0	10/02/1999 4:21:35 PM
3	USA	GET	/index.htm	IE 5.0	10/03/1999 3:59:13 AM
4	USA	GET	/index.htm	IE 5.0	10/03/1999 10:40:36 AM
5	USA	GET	/index.htm	IE 5.0	10/03/1999 10:40:36 AM
6	USA	GET	/index.htm	IE 5.0	10/04/1999 4:36:03 PM
7	USA	GET	/index.htm	IE 5.0	10/04/1999 4:36:03 PM
8	USA	GET	/index.htm	IE 5.0	10/05/1999 2:41:29 PM
9	USA	GET	/index.htm	IE 5.0	10/05/1999 5:30:09 PM
10	USA	GET	/index.htm	IE 5.0	10/05/1999 5:30:10 PM
11	USA	GET	/index.htm	IE 5.0	10/05/1999 9:35:35 PM

Figure 2.5: Here are the results when asking for records where REQGEO='USA' and REQFILE='/index.htm'.

Because AND is a logical operator, both expression 1 and expression 2 must be true. If either expression is false, the row will not be returned by SQL. In order for a record to be returned by the above query, the record must have the value USA in the REQGEO column, and the value */index.htm* in the REQFILE column. Of course, you could make a silly statement like this:

```
SELECT * FROM SQLBOOK.WEBTEMP WHERE REQGEO='USA' AND REQGEO='AFRICA'
```

This statement could never return any rows because the WEBGEO column, in a single record, cannot contain both the values USA and AFRICA.

This brings up an important point: Whenever you are debugging a query, always scrutinize the logic in your WHERE clause. Remember, the WHERE clause is a logical filter of what records you want returned, and logic errors are the predominant cause of getting the wrong result set from a query.

Expressions and Predicates in WHERE Clauses

The WHERE clause takes a list of logical expressions, but what can those expressions be? Let's look at a number of examples to give you a thorough grounding in expressions.

Simple mathematical operations are at the heart of expressions. Most of the infix operators should be familiar to you. These operators, such as +, -, *, **, and /, represent addition, subtraction, multiplication, power, and division. These infix operators can be used on numeric data types to yield a different result, which can then be compared using the comparison predicates.

You should also be aware that mathematical expressions can change the resultant data type. For example, adding the prefix operator - before a SMALLINT column to change it to a negative value results in the column begin cast to an INTEGER value. Multiplying an INTEGER column by a DECIMAL column causes the integer to be cast to a decimal and produces a decimal result. Using the ** operator results in a floating-point number. Most of these things aren't showstoppers, but it is important that you be aware of data types and that expressions can alter them. It is especially important when you are looking into query optimization problems, as comparisons between data types of differing precision can take more processor time (because they have to be temporarily cast to the same data type for comparison).

Comparison operators, like >, < , and =, can be used to yield a logical value. Note that these predicates are not just for numeric data types; they can be used to compare any SQL data types, as long as the values on the left and right of the predicate operator are type-compatible (i.e., strings compare to strings, numbers to numbers, etc.). Even if they are not type-compatible, it is sometimes possible to cast a value to a compatible data type. Table 2.2 lists a comparison of predicates that yield logical results.

Table 2.2: SQL Predicates

Predicate	Description
X<Y	True if X is less than Y.
X>Y	True if X greater than Y.
X<=Y	True if X is equal to or less than Y.
X>=Y	True if X is greater than or equal to Y.
X<>Y	True if X is not equal to Y.
X=Y	True if X is equal to Y.
X¬<Y	True if X is not less than Y. Can also be expressed as X!<Y.
X¬>Y	True if X is not greater than Y. Can also be expressed as X!>Y.
X BETWEEN Y AND Z	True if X is greater than or equal to Y and less than or equal to Z.
X NOT BETWEEN Y AND Z	True if X is not greater than or equal to Y and is less than or equal to Z.
EXISTS (SELECT statement)	True if the SELECT statement returns any rows.
NOT EXISTS (SELECT statement)	True if the SELECT statement returns no rows.
X LIKE Y	True if X is like Y. X and Y must be strings. Y can contain wildcards.
X NOT LIKE Y	True if X is not like Y. X and Y must be strings. Y can contain wildcards.
X IN Y	True if X is in the list Y. Y can be a parameterized list of constants or a SELECT statement that returns a single column.
X NOT IN Y	True if X is not in the list Y. Y can be a parameterized list of constants or a SELECT statement that returns a single column.
X IS NULL	True only if X is the null value.
X IS NOT NULL	True only if X is NOT the null value.

Temporal Expressions

In addition to numerical operations, you can do temporal expressions. Temporal expressions are math applied to date, time, and timestamp columns. The temporal operators are HOURS, MINUTES, SECONDS, MICROSECONDS, DAYS, MONTHS, and YEARS. You can only do addition and subtraction with these temporal keywords. Let's do a few example queries with simple math and temporal expressions.

Consider this query, which lists all WEBTEMP hits over 100 days old:

```
SELECT * FROM SQLBOOK.WEBTEMP WHERE REQTS < CURRENT_TIMESTAMP -
        100 DAYS
```

The query highlights two things: manipulation of timestamp values and the CURRENT_TIMESTAMP function. CURRENT_TIMESTAMP returns the current date and time on the AS/400. By subtracting 100 days from the current timestamp, the AS/400 returns all records that are over 100 days old.

The AS/400 has built-in functions for returning the hour, minute, and second of time values. The following query asks for Web hits between 10 A.M. and 1 P.M. The query relies on the HOUR scalar function, which returns a number between 0 and 23 to indicate the hour of the day:

```
SELECT * FROM SQLBOOK.WEBTEMP WHERE HOUR(REQTS)>= 10 AND
        HOUR(REQTS)<13
```

To take this example even further, let's look at Web hits that occur between 10 A.M. and 1 P.M. on Mondays and Wednesdays:

```
SELECT * FROM SQLBOOK.WEBTEMP
        WHERE HOUR(REQTS)>= 10 AND HOUR(REQTS)<13 AND
        DAYOFWEEK(REQTS) = 2 OR DAYOFWEEK(REQTS) = 4
```

This query takes advantage of the DAYOFWEEK scalar function that returns a number from 1 to 7 where 1 represents Sunday and 7 represents Saturday. Note that it uses the OR operator so that it can distinguish between DAYOFWEEK 2 and

DAYOFWEEK 4. If you included the AND operator, no records would be returned, as a single record could not have a date reflecting both Monday and Wednesday.

When using OR, consider using parentheses to better represent your logic. The previous query would read better and be easier to understand if it were expressed like this:

```
SELECT * FROM SQLBOOK.WEBTEMP
        WHERE HOUR(REQTS)>= 10 AND HOUR(REQTS)<13 AND
        (DAYOFWEEK(REQTS) = 2 OR DAYOFWEEK(REQTS) = 4)
```

The parentheses allow for grouping of logical elements, and as stated earlier, most problems with SQL statement results come from logic errors.

Finally, a third way to express this query is by using the IN operator, which takes a list of values and compares the value on the left of the IN operator to the list of values on the right. Here is the same query using IN for both expressions:

```
SELECT * FROM SQLBOOK.WEBTEMP
        WHERE HOUR(REQTS) IN (10,11,12)
        AND DAYOFWEEK(REQTS) IN (2,4)
```

Bear in mind that all of these queries return the same results. In SQL, there are always multiple ways to ask the same question, and it is your job to use the most elegant and readable form.

Another useful operator is BETWEEN, which allows you to specify two values for a field element, and is inclusive. Here is the same query, modified to use BETWEEN to return the results:

```
SELECT * FROM SQLBOOK.WEBTEMP
        WHERE HOUR(REQTS) BETWEEN 10 AND 12
        AND DAYOFWEEK(REQTS) in (2,4)
```

BETWEEN is nice, but it can sometimes make the SQL syntax confusing. I vote for using it in simple queries, but staying away from it in very complex WHERE clauses.

58

Using the LIKE *Predicate for Searching Strings*

SQL has a powerful operator for searching character-based columns, the LIKE predicate. As with IN, LIKE requires a value on the left and the right. The value on the left is usually a column, while the value on the right is a string expression. LIKE also has special operators that can appear on the right side. These operators are the % and ? symbols. The % is a wildcard character that can represent one or more characters. The ? is a wildcard character that is substituted for a single character.

Here is a query that uses the LIKE predicate and its associated wildcards:

```
SELECT * FROM SQLBOOK.WEBHITS WHERE REQFILE LIKE '/I%'
```

This query returns all records where the REQFILE column starts with the characters */I*. This query would match values like */Indexes.htm*, */I*, or */Ivan.HTM*. The % basically says that you do not care what comes after the initial string.

How about searching for a substring within a character-based column? The following query finds all records where the letters *jpg* appear in the REQFILE column:

```
SELECT * FROM SQLBOOK.WEBHITS WHERE REQFILE LIKE '%jpg%'
```

Note the use of the wildcard character. Placing the wildcard before and after the string indicates that you want all records that have *jpg* in them, regardless of whether the string starts with *jpg*, ends with *jpg*, or has *jpg* somewhere in the middle.

The ? character is used for wildcarding a single space. If you want to find all records where the letter *n* is the third character, for example, this query would do it:

```
SELECT * FROM SQLBOOK.WEBHITS WHERE REQFILE LIKE '??n%'
```

This type of pattern-matching can be useful for legacy fields that are used to represent multiple data. For example, suppose you have a work-order application with a 10-character string field called LOCATION. Whenever a work order is entered into the database, the operator enters the two-digit building number, the two-digit floor number, and the room number, separated by dashes. Using the pattern string '??-13-%' would list all work that was performed on the 13th floor of any building.

Wildcard characters are useful, but they can be a nightmare for query performance on big tables. SQL cannot use an index to speed up query execution unless you do a match on the first characters in the substring. Using '%ILE%' as the target of a LIKE clause will not use an index, whereas 'ILE%' will use an index if it is available. Be careful of LIKE on large tables.

With that said, let's look at how LIKE can be used efficiently. Suppose you created an application where data-entry personnel could identify advertisements in a newspaper. The advertiser table consists of an integer primary key and a 50-character advertiser-name field. An index called ADVERNAME has been created on the advertiser-name field. The table has over 1million rows of information. The following type of query could be executed over 100,000 times per day and return up to 500 records in less than a second:

```
SELECT ADVERNO, ADVERNAME FROM ADVERTISER
       WHERE ADVERNAME LIKE 'ABC%'
```

This query asks for all advertisers whose names start with *ABC*. By using the "starts with" type of LIKE, the ADVERNAME index is used to resolve the query. Conversely, if an operator tried the following query, the results would take over 15 seconds to display, as SQL would require a full table scan:

```
SELECT ADVERNO, ADVERNAME FROM ADVERTISER
       WHERE ADVERNAME LIKE '%ABC%'
```

Understanding how the AS/400 will implement your query can help you to design queries that will not eat all of your system resources. This topic is covered in depth in chapter 6, which covers debugging and optimizing your queries.

One last thing to understand is that an expression can exist on either side of a LIKE query. Consider the following example:

```
SELECT * FROM SQLBOOK.WEBTEMP WHERE UCASE(REQFILE) LIKE '%.JPG'
```

This query uses UCASE to capitalize the REQFILE column contents before comparing them to the LIKE expression. It would find all instances of files that have the .JPG extension.

Ordering the Results of SELECT Statements

Up to this point, you have seen how to retrieve data from SQL tables using the SELECT statement, but no attention has been paid to the order of the retrieved data. There is no guaranteed data from SQL statements will be retrieved in any set order from a table. This can be confusing. Some people assume that if a table has been defined with a key, any data read from the table should be in that order. This is not the case. Consider the following statement:

```
SELECT PARTID FROM SQLBOOK.PARTS
```

PARTID happens to be the primary key of the PARTS table. Being a primary key guarantees that there is an index over the table to ensure that no two PARTID values are the same. Because this index is required, there is a tendency to assume that the above statement would use the index to read the PARTID values, and therefore return the data in sorted order. Not so. The only way to guarantee order is to specify it, using the ORDER BY clause of the SQL statement. The following would give a list of all PARTID codes in order:

```
SELECT PARTID FROM SQLBOOK.PARTS ORDER BY PARTID
```

The ORDER BY clause can take a list of fields or numeric field identifiers to guarantee the sort order of the resulting data. Here is another example:

```
SELECT REQTS, REQPAGE FROM SQLBOOK.WEBTEMP ORDER BY 2
```

Notice the ORDER BY 2 clause. This indicates that SQL should sort the results by the second field in the select list. The second field is REQPAGE, so the resulting data set is sorted by the requested page file name. This technique comes in handy when you are using expressions in your select list. Consider this example:

```
SELECT YEAR(REQTS),MONTH(REQTS),REQFILE
       FROM SQLBOOK.WEBTEMP ORDER BY 1,2
```

This statement selects the year of the Web hit, the month of the Web hit, and the target page. Here, the ORDER BY clause indicates that the data should be sorted by columns 1 and 2 (which correspond to the year and month scalar columns). The preceding statement could also be written this way:

```
SELECT YEAR(REQTS) as YR, MONTH(REQTS) AS MO, REQFILE
       FROM SQLBOOK.WEBTEMP ORDER BY YR, MO
```

This example shows that the ORDER BY clause also can include field aliases (created by the AS operator).

Grouping Data

The hard thing to remember about SQL is that it is a set-based language, not a physical-file–based language. In a record-level–access programming language, if you wanted to make a report of Web hits by country, you would have to declare an array to hold your data, and read each record in the file. The country code of the record would be used to determine which offset of your array you would need to increment. SQL, as a set-based language, makes operations of this sort much easier because it supports aggregation through the GROUP BY function. The GROUP BY function illustrates the set-oriented features of SQL and shows how SQL can be a really powerful ally for reporting systems.

The GROUP BY keyword always follows the WHERE clause in an SQL statement, but the statement does not have to have a WHERE clause in order to use GROUP BY. GROUP BY is usually used in conjunction with COLUMN aggregate functions. Here is an example SQL statement that returns the number of hits by geography. The output of the statement is shown in Figure 2.6:

```
SELECT REQGEO, COUNT(*)
       FROM SQLBOOK.WEBTEMP
       GROUP BY REQGEO
```

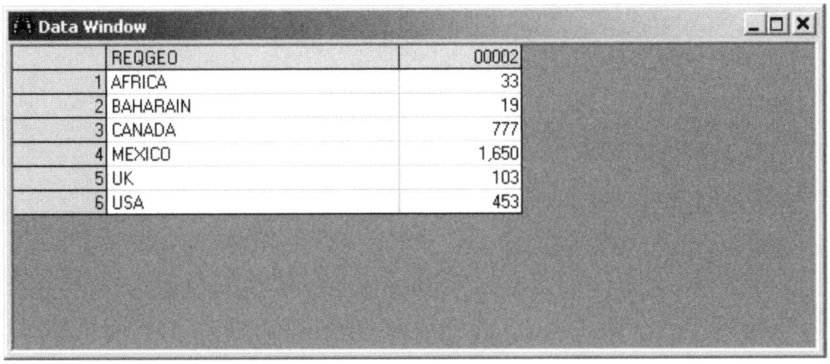

	REQGEO	00002
1	AFRICA	33
2	BAHARAIN	19
3	CANADA	777
4	MEXICO	1,650
5	UK	103
6	USA	453

Figure 2.6: This is the output returned by the GROUP BY statement. Note that SQL has aggregated the counts by the distinct values of the REQGEO field.

What's happening here is quite interesting. First, SQL reads all of the REQGEO field values from the WEBTEMP table. Then, it counts each individual value and produces the output shown in Figure 2.6. This is powerful stuff, as you can have the server do the work of totaling numeric columns for you, rather than doing complex coding on the client side.

When using a GROUP BY statement, you must always specify all columns that are not aggregate functions in your SQL statement in the GROUP BY clause. Otherwise, the statement will fail. Here is an example of a bad grouping:

```
SELECT REQGEO, BROWSER, COUNT(*)
        FROM SQLBOOK.WEBTEMP
        GROUP BY REQGEO
```

Because the BROWSER column is not part of the aggregate functions, this statement will fail. This is the correct syntax for the statement:

```
SELECT REQGEO, BROWSER, COUNT(*)
        FROM SQLBOOK.WEBTEMP
        GROUP BY REQGEO, BROWSER
```

The output for the statement is shown in Figure 2.7. Note that the output is not sorted. Again, SQL will not return sorted results unless you specifically ask it to.

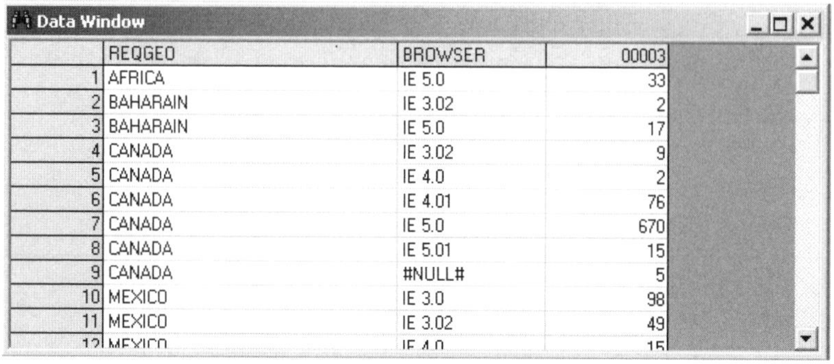

	REQGEO	BROWSER	00003
1	AFRICA	IE 5.0	33
2	BAHARAIN	IE 3.02	2
3	BAHARAIN	IE 5.0	17
4	CANADA	IE 3.02	9
5	CANADA	IE 4.0	2
6	CANADA	IE 4.01	76
7	CANADA	IE 5.0	670
8	CANADA	IE 5.01	15
9	CANADA	#NULL#	5
10	MEXICO	IE 3.0	98
11	MEXICO	IE 3.02	49
12	MEXICO	IE 4.0	15

Figure 2.7: You can group by more than one column in SQL. This output represents hits from countries aggregated by the client browser.

If a statement is using GROUP BY, the ORDER BY clause must come after the GROUP BY clause. Here is the same statement, but with sorted output:

```
SELECT REQGEO, BROWSER, COUNT(*)
        FROM SQLBOOK.WEBTEMP
        GROUP BY REQGEO, BROWSER
        ORDER BY 1,2
```

A GROUP BY statement can include a WHERE clause to restrict the data that goes into the statement. The WHERE is processed before any aggregation occurs. Here is an example that lists Internet Explorer browser hits that came only from the USA:

```
SELECT BROWSER, COUNT(*)
        FROM SQLBOOK.WEBTEMP
        WHERE BROWSER LIKE 'IE%'
        AND REQGEO = 'USA'
        GROUP BY REQGEO, BROWSER
        ORDER BY 1
```

The BROWSER column beginning with IE signifies Internet Explorer hits. Figure 2.8 shows the output from this statement.

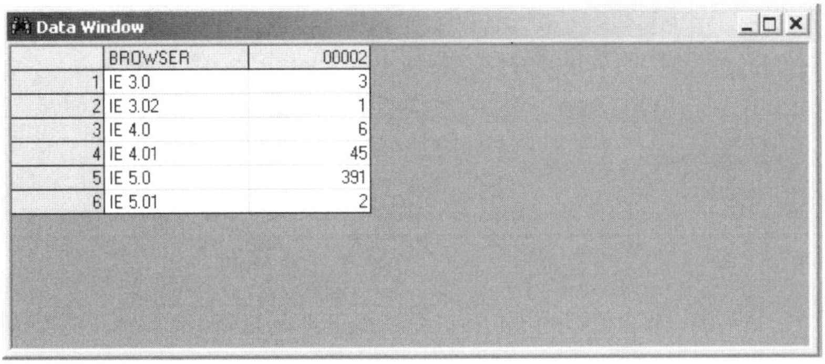

	BROWSER	00002
1	IE 3.0	3
2	IE 3.02	1
3	IE 4.0	6
4	IE 4.01	45
5	IE 5.0	391
6	IE 5.01	2

Figure 2.8: This output shows only USA hits, by only IE browsers.

Using GROUP BY, you do not have to grab just single aggregate fields as in the above examples. The following functions are available to use in GROUP BY select statements:

COUNT(x)

The COUNT function returns a count of the field or expression. COUNT optionally uses the DISTINCT argument. DISTINCT causes COUNT to count only values that are different from each other. Here is an example:

```
SELECT REQGEO, COUNT(DISTINCT REQFILE)
          FROM SQLBOOK.WEBTEMP
          GROUP BY REQGEO
```

The above statement, whose output is shown in Figure 2.9, differs from the output produced in Figure 2.6. This output reflects a count of how many different pages were viewed by country (whereas Figure 2.6 shows total number of hits by country). The DISTINCT keyword causes each page to be counted only once, even if the page occurs millions of times.

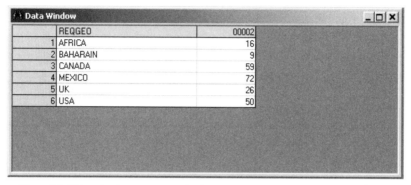

Figure 2.9: This output was generated using COUNT(DISTINCT REQFILE) as opposed to Figure 2.6, which counts all pages.

MIN(x)

MIN computes the minimum value of X, which can be a column of any data type or an expression. Here is an example of a query using MIN:

```
SELECT MIN(REQTS) FROM SQLBOOK.WEBTEMP
```

This statement returns the lower date/time value that occurs in the WEBTEMP table.

MAX(x)

MAX finds the maximum value of X, which can be a column of any data type or an expression. Here is an example of a query using MAX:

```
SELECT MAX(REQTS) FROM SQLBOOK.WEBTEMP
```

This statement returns the higher date/time value that occurs in the WEBTEMP table.

SUM(x)

SUM adds together any numeric field or expression. This can be extremely useful. For example, here is a query that finds the number of kilobytes, by geography, which a Web server sent to clients during October:

```
SELECT REQGEO,SUM(REQSIZE)
        FROM SQLBOOK.WEBTEMP
        WHERE MONTH(REQTS)=10
        GROUP BY REQGEO;
```

Avg(x)

AVG computes the average value for any numeric expression. The following SE-LECT yields the average kilobytes served by geography:

```
SELECT REQGEO,AVG(REQSIZE)
        FROM SQLBOOK.WEBTEMP
        GROUP BY REQGEO
```

Var(x) or Variance

VAR computes the variance in a set of numbers, where X can be a numeric column or numeric expression.

Stddev(x)

STDDEV computes the standard deviation in a set of numbers, where X can be a column or a numeric expression.

Putting Them All Together

You can have more than one aggregate function in a GROUP BY query. Here is an example query that uses a few functions:

```
SELECT REQGEO, MIN(REQSIZE) as MINIMUM,
        MAX(REQSIZE) AS MAXIMUM,
        AVG(REQSIZE) AS AVERAGE
        FROM SQLBOOK.WEBTEMP
        GROUP BY REQGEO
```

This query's output is shown in Figure 2.10. Note the use of the AS keyword in this query to rename the returned columns. Because of AS, the columns in Figure 2.10 have human-readable names rather than automatically generated function numbers.

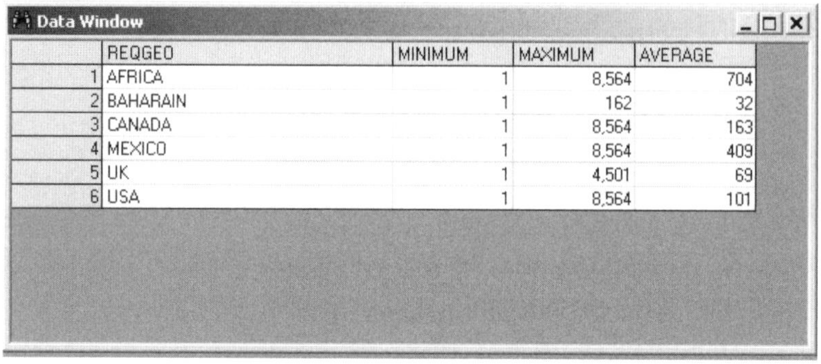

	REQGEO	MINIMUM	MAXIMUM	AVERAGE
1	AFRICA	1	8,564	704
2	BAHARAIN	1	162	32
3	CANADA	1	8,564	163
4	MEXICO	1	8,564	409
5	UK	1	4,501	69
6	USA	1	8,564	101

Figure 2.10: This example shows that you can use more than one aggregate function in a GROUP BY query.

Grouping by Scalar Functions

One limitation of the AS/400 is that it cannot group by a scalar function or derived column in versions prior to V4R3. This is not the case in other versions of the DB2 UDB database. This is a bad limitation, and I have taken IBM to task about it several times. Consider the following query:

```
SELECT MONTH(REQTS),REQGEO,COUNT(*) ,SUM(REQSIZE)
        FROM SQLBOOK.WEBTEMP
        GROUP BY MONTH(REQTS),REQGEO
```

On AS/400 systems prior to V4R3, this query would fail or return erroneous results. In order to get around this limitation, you would have to create a view and then select from the view for the aggregation. Here is the solution:

```
CREATE VIEW SQLBOOK.WEBTEST (M,G,C,S) AS
        SELECT MONTH(REQTS),REQGEO, 1, REQSIZE
        FROM SQLBOOK.WEBTEMP
```

This statement creates a view call WEBTEST in the library SQLBOOK. The WEBTEST view has four fields called M, G, C, and S. The fields contain the month of the page request, the geography of the request, the number 1 to indicate a page hit, and the size of the returned value. Now, consider the following query:

```
SELECT M,G,SUM(C),SUM(S) FROM SQLBOOK.WEBTEST
        GROUP BY M,G
```

This query is semantically the same as the previous one, but gets around the limitation of not being able to easily group by a scalar function. Summing column C, the column that always contains the value 1, has the same effect as selecting COUNT(*).

Because the capability to group by scalar functions is so new, I suggest that you use the view work-around for a while. In addition, some expressions in your SE-LECT clause can be so complex as to make your GROUP BY statements impossible to read. This view work-around can simplify your query grammar and make your SQL look less intimidating.

Using *HAVING* to Filter Groups

The WHERE clause allows you to filter data before the data makes it to the aggregation of the GROUP BY clause. HAVING allows you to filter data returned to the client after the data has been aggregated. Consider a request to create a list of Web pages that have been accessed between 100 and 200 times. The following query accomplishes this goal, as shown in the output in Figure 2.11:

```
SELECT REQFILE, COUNT(*) FROM SQLBOOK.WEBTEMP
        GROUP BY REQFILE
        HAVING COUNT(*) BETWEEN 100 and 200
```

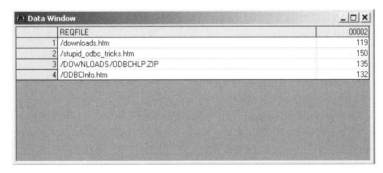

Figure 2.11: Here are the results of the HAVING query. Note that only pages that received between 100 and 200 hits are shown.

It is important to understand that the HAVING clause is not evaluated until after the data is aggregated. Here is what happens to the above query:

1. SQL retrieves all records and sorts them by REQFILE.
2. SQL creates a result set that contains the column REQFILE and its associated count by iterating through the sorted data.
3. SQL removes any records from the result set that do not satisfy the HAVING clause.

Now, consider the following query, which includes both HAVING and WHERE:

```
SELECT REQGEO, REQFILE, COUNT(*)
         FROM SQLBOOK.WEBTEMP
         WHERE BROWSER LIKE 'IE%'
         AND DAYOFWEEK(REQTS)=1
         GROUP BY REQGEO, REQFILE
         HAVING COUNT(*)<20
         ORDER BY 3 DESC
```

The result of this query is shown in Figure 2.12. The AS/400 first retrieves a result set of all records that match the WHERE criteria. In this case, that would be the geography and file name of files requested on Mondays (DAYOFWEEK(REQTS)=1), requested by only Internet Explorer browsers, (BROWSER LIKE 'IE%'). Once all records are in a temporary table, SQL aggregates the set and then removes records that have page requests greater than or equal to 20 requests (HAVING COUNT(*)<20). Finally, SQL sorts the resulting set by the third column in the result set in descending order (in this case, the count of page requests indicated by ORDER BY 3 DESC).

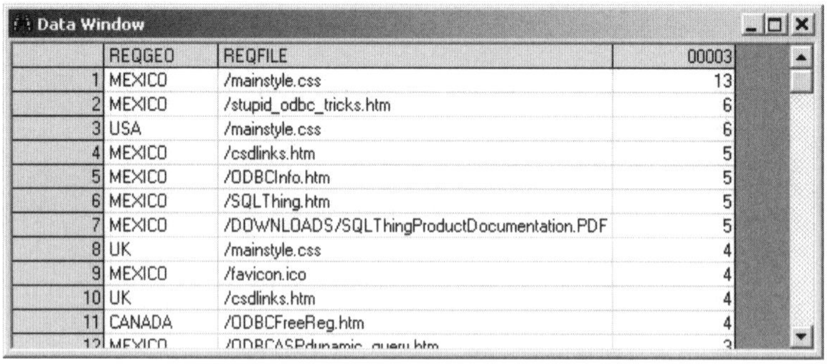
Data Window

	REQGEO	REQFILE	00003
1	MEXICO	/mainstyle.css	13
2	MEXICO	/stupid_odbc_tricks.htm	6
3	USA	/mainstyle.css	6
4	MEXICO	/csdlinks.htm	5
5	MEXICO	/ODBCInfo.htm	5
6	MEXICO	/SQLThing.htm	5
7	MEXICO	/DOWNLOADS/SQLThingProductDocumentation.PDF	5
8	UK	/mainstyle.css	4
9	MEXICO	/favicon.ico	4
10	UK	/csdlinks.htm	4
11	CANADA	/ODBCFreeReg.htm	4
12	MEXICO	/ODBCASPdynamic_query.htm	3

Figure 2.12: This example uses WHERE, HAVING, and ORDER BY to retrieve the files requested less than 20 times on Mondays by Internet Explorer browsers.

Chapter Summary

This chapter has been a whirlwind of examples of the power of the SELECT statement. By now, you should be comfortable with retrieving data from a single table in an SQL database and the basic areas of SELECT statements. In particular, here are the concepts to take away from this chapter:

- SELECT retrieves data from the database.

- The WHERE clause filters the data that you are retrieving.

- The WHERE clause is composed of logical predicate operations.

- The ORDER BY clause allows you to add order to your sets.

- The GROUP BY clause allows you to aggregate data sets.

- The HAVING clause allows you to filter aggregated sets.

3

MANIPULATING DATA IN SQL TABLES

Adatabase would not be complete without the capability to insert, modify, and remove data. Chapter 2 explains how to use the SELECT statement to retrieve records from a database. This chapter shows you how to put records into SQL tables, change the records, and then remove them. Here are the SQL statements that can be used to manipulate data in tables:

- INSERT puts one or more records into a table. INSERT also can be used to copy records from one table into another.

- UPDATE changes records currently in a table. UPDATE can have a WHERE clause that specifies which records should be updated.

- DELETE removes records from a table. DELETE can have a WHERE clause that specifies which records should be removed from the database.

Putting Data in Tables

Databases exist to hold data, and for SQL to be effective, it needs the capability to place records in physical files. This is accomplished through the SQL INSERT statement. Here is a syntax diagram for the INSERT statement:

```
INSERT INTO <table-name> (<optional-list-of-columns>)
VALUES (<list-of-column-values>)
```

The INSERT statement always starts with INSERT INTO and must be followed by a table or view name. You can also insert data into a DDS-created logical file, as long as that logical file does not have select/omit criteria or is not a multiformat logical. Also, if the logical file was created as an SQL index, you cannot insert into it.

The next argument to an INSERT statement is the optional list of columns. If you do not specify a list of columns, you are assumed to be inserting into all columns in the table, view, or index. In that case, you must supply one value for each column in the list of column values following the VALUES keyword.

Insert by Example

Issue the following SQL statement against your AS/400 to create the table SKILLS:

```
CREATE TABLE SQLBOOK.SKILLS
        (ID CHAR(4) NOT NULL PRIMARY KEY,
         DESCRIPTION CHAR(20),
         PAYRATE DECIMAL(6,2))
```

Now, execute the following SQL statement to insert a record into the SKILLS table:

```
INSERT INTO SQLBOOK.SKILLS VALUES ('HK','House Keeper',6.50)
```

Bam! You now have a record in the SKILLS table. That record has an ID of 'HK,' a description of 'House Keeper,' and the pay rate of 6.50. Note that the example statement does not name the columns to update. Because the columns are not named, the field values must all be specified, and they should be specified in the order the columns appear in the table.

You should always name your columns in an INSERT statement. Here is a better example:

```
INSERT INTO SQLBOOK.SKILLS
        (ID, DESCRIPTION, PAYRATE)
        VALUES ('PR','Programmer',30.25)
```

This statement names those columns that data is to be insert against. This is always preferable, as the underlying structure of any table could change over time. By naming your columns, you ensure that your program will work even if the table structure changes.

Here is an example to show how the INSERT code can be portable. Issue the following SQL statement to add a new column to the SKILLS table:

```
ALTER TABLE SQLBOOK.SKILLS
        ADD LASTUPD TIMESTAMP
        NOT NULL WITH DEFAULT
```

This statement adds the new column LASTUPD. It is a type of timestamp and is not allowed to be null. Because the WITH DEFAULT clause is specified, if a value for the LASTUPD column is not specified when a record is inserted, the column defaults to the current date and time. Now, execute this statement:

```
INSERT INTO SQLBOOK.SKILLS
        (ID, DESCRIPTION, PAYRATE)
        VALUES ('AN',' Analyst',50.75)
```

Note that the LASTUPD column is not specified in the INSERT statement, but the statement still works, even though the structure of the table changed. If you attempted to issue the statement without qualifying the columns, like the first example, you would receive an error.

Building Tables from Existing Data

Another way to execute the INSERT statement is to supply a set of column values, instead of individual column values, by running an SQL statement. The syntax for this is as follows:

75

```
INSERT INTO <table> (list-of-columns)
SELECT <list of columns> FROM <list-of-tables>
```

Before examining an example of this technique, let's return to the WEBTEMP database table used in the examples in previous chapters.

The WEBTEMP table contains records that represent hits against a Web site over a two-month period. However, this table is a very inefficient way to store the data. Take the column REQGEO, which represents the country where a Web hit came from. The following query returns a list of all of the different countries that requested pages (as shown in Figure 3.1):

```
SELECT DISTINCT REQGEO FROM SQLBOOK.WEBTEMP
```

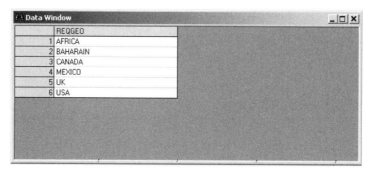

Figure 3.1: This data window shows a DISTINCT listing of different countries requesting Web files.

This query uses the DISTINCT clause to tell SQL to list only entries that are different from each other. This causes SQL to produce the output shown in Figure 3.1. Now, consider that the REQGEO field is a CHAR(20) field. That means that each entry takes 20 characters of space, or 20 bytes, since the field is not a DBCS field. With 3,000 entries in the WEBTEMP table, you would be taking 60,000 bytes of storage to store only six different country names. If you chose to represent the countries by a two-character field, which takes only 2 bytes of storage, you would be able to store the data in only 6,000 bytes. So, how do you build a table of countries that have hit the Web site?

76

The INSERT statement can be called with a SELECT statement as a substitute for a list of column values. Issue the following statement to create a table to hold the country names:

```
CREATE TABLE SQLBOOK.COUNTRIES (ID CHAR(2), NAME CHAR(20))
```

Now, issue the following INSERT statement:

```
INSERT INTO SQLBOOK.COUNTRIES (NAME,ID) SELECT DISTINCT
        REQGEO,SUBSTRING(REQGEO,1,2) FROM SQLBOOK.WEBTEMP
```

Presto chango, you now have a table of countries that is filled with the names of all of the different countries represented in the WEBTEMP table. The ID column was derived by getting a substring of the REQGEO field, specifically the first two characters. Perform the following SQL statement to view your new table (shown in Figure 3.2):

```
SELECT * FROM SQLBOOK.COUNTRIES
```

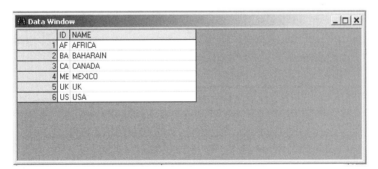

Figure 3.2: The COUNTRIES table now contains a list of each country that has visited the Web site.

Remember, the INSERT statement can take a list of columns or can be driven by the results of a SELECT statement.

Updating Data

Another must-have for SQL is the capability to update data in a database. This is accomplished via the SQL UPDATE statement. The UPDATE statement has the following syntax:

```
UPDATE <table-name> SET <column-name>=<value>
WHERE <where-clause>
```

This statement can take one or more column names in the SET portion. Here is an example UPDATE that changes the description and pay rate of a skill in the SKILLS table:

```
UPDATE SQLBOOK.SKILLS
        SET DESCRIPTION='Neo Programmer',PAYRATE=18.98
        WHERE ID='PR'
```

The WHERE clause in an UPDATE statement acts just like a WHERE clause in a SELECT statement. It can contain any list of expressions that must be satisfied in order to find the record(s) to update. In the case of the above statement, you are instructing UPDATE to change only records where the ID field is equal to PR. Because the ID field is a primary key, this statement can change only one record.

The list of columns to update is a comma-separated list. The preceding example instructs SQL to set the DESCRIPTION column to the value 'Neo Programmer,' and to set the PAYRATE column to the value 18.98.

It is important to remember that the WHERE clause of the UPDATE statement is what restricts the set of records to be updated. Consider the following statement:

```
UPDATE SQLBOOK.SKILLS SET PAYRATE=PAYRATE*1.10
```

This statement gives all skills a 10 percent raise. Because the statement was not qualified with a WHERE clause, it updates *all* records in the database.

You need to be really careful with the UPDATE statement. Setting up a WHERE clause incorrectly can cause a lot of havoc. Let me relate an experience that illustrates the pain that UPDATE can cause. I worked at a shop where people classified advertisements in local newspapers. Each newspaper had between 20 and 400 ads per issue. Sometimes, a data-entry person would accidentally enter an issue under the wrong date or the wrong newspaper number. Our supervisory personnel would then use the SQL UPDATE statement to change the issue date from one date to another with a statement like this:

```
UPDATE ADS SET IDATE = '01/01/1999' where PAPERNO=281 and
        IDATE='01/04/1999'
```

This statement would change all occurrences of paper 281, date 01/04/1999 to reflect the date 01/01/1999, a simple change that saved having to re-enter the data. One day, though, a supervisor was not paying attention and issued the following query:

```
UPDATE ADS SET IDATE='01/01/1999' where PAPERNO=281 and
        IDATE<>'01/04/1999'
```

The <> means not equal, so this person set all records in the database for paper 281 to the date 01/01/1999 *except* the ads that had the incorrect date 01/04/1999. This changed over 500,000 records in the database and forced us to restore the data from a backup. Please be careful with UPDATE.

Changing the WEBTEMP Table

Earlier in this chapter, you saw that the WEBTEMP table was inefficient, as it was storing the country name in 20 characters. Let's do some "surgery" on the table to make it more relational. Begin by executing the following SQL statement to create a new table called WEBTEMP2:

```
CREATE TABLE SQLBOOK.WEBTEMP2
        (REQGEO CHAR(20),
        REQTYPE CHAR(10),
        REQFILE CHAR(80),
        BROWSER CHAR(10),
        REQTS TIMESTAMP,
        REQSIZE INTEGER,
        REQUSER INTEGER,
        GEOID SMALLINT)
```

Note that this copy of the table includes a new column called GEOID that is a small integer. This column will hold the new geography identifier that you are about to create. Now, issue the following SELECT statement to copy all of the data from the WEBTEMP table into the WEBTEMP2 table:

```
INSERT INTO SQLBOOK.WEBTEMP2
        (REQGEO, REQFILE, REQTYPE, BROWSER, REQTS, REQSIZE,
        REQUSER)
        SELECT REQGEO,REQFILE, REQTYPE, BROWSER, REQTS, REQSIZE,
        REQUSER FROM SQLBOOK.WEBTEMP
```

You now have a table called WEBTEMP2 that has all of the data that was in WEBTEMP, with the addition of a column called GEOID. You could have altered the base table WEBTEMP to add the column GEOID, but I would rather expose you to the concept of copying data. Also, notice that the GEOID column was not named in the INSERT statement's list of columns, nor is there a value supplied in the list of columns in the SELECT list. Because no value was supplied, the GEOID column in the table now contains the null value for each row in the table.

Execute the following query and scroll to the right of the results table. You should see output like that shown in Figure 3.3. SQLThing uses #NULL# to represent a field that contains the null value.

```
SELECT * FROM SQLBOOK.WEBTEMP2
```

	REQTS	REQSIZE	REQUSER	GEOID	
1	10/08/1999 12:39:07 AM	3	114	#NULL#	
2	10/08/1999 12:40:42 AM	3	114	#NULL#	
3	10/08/1999 1:24:43 AM	2	131	#NULL#	
4	10/08/1999 1:37:03 AM	4,501	131	#NULL#	
5	10/08/1999 1:38:00 AM	4,501	131	#NULL#	
6	10/08/1999 1:38:35 AM	4,501	131	#NULL#	
7	10/08/1999 1:42:39 AM	4,501	131	#NULL#	
8	10/01/1999 8:01:49 PM	12	149	#NULL#	
9	10/01/1999 8:02:09 PM	3	149	#NULL#	
10	10/01/1999 9:34:16 PM	1	199	#NULL#	
11	10/01/1999 9:34:23 PM	54	199	#NULL#	

Figure 3.3: This is how the WEBTEMP2 table should look after you copy the data. Note that the GEOID column contains #NULL#, which is how SQLThing indicates that the value of the column is a null, not spaces.

Next, let's prepare a table to contain the geography identifiers. Execute the following statement:

```
CREATE TABLE SQLBOOK.GEOIDS
        (GEOID SMALLINT NOT NULL PRIMARY KEY,
        GEONAME CHAR(20) NOT NULL)
```

You now have a table on the AS/400 that can hold geography relations. Next, execute the following six SQL statements to insert the data into the GEOIDS table:

```
INSERT INTO SQLBOOK.GEOIDS VALUES (1,'AFRICA');
INSERT INTO SQLBOOK.GEOIDS VALUES (2,'BAHARAIN');
INSERT INTO SQLBOOK.GEOIDS VALUES (3,'CANADA');
INSERT INTO SQLBOOK.GEOIDS VALUES (4,'MEXICO');
INSERT INTO SQLBOOK.GEOIDS VALUES (5,'UK');
INSERT INTO SQLBOOK.GEOIDS VALUES (6,'USA')
```

Execute the following SQL statement, and you should see a table similar to the one shown in Figure 3.4:

```
SELECT * FROM SQLBOOK.GEOIDS
```

Figure 3.4: This is how your GEOIDS table should look after inserting all of the records.

Now you have a table on the AS/400 called GEOIDS, in the SQLBOOK library, which contains six rows. These rows relate to the geographic area that requested a Web page. You'll need to perform a very special UPDATE request to set the GEOID field in the WEBTEMP2 table to relate back to the GEOIDS table:

```
UPDATE SQLBOOK.WEBTEMP2 A
        SET GEOID = (SELECT GEOID FROM SQLBOOK.GEOIDS B
        WHERE B.GEONAME = A.REQGEO)
```

After this query is finished, all 3,035 rows of the WEBHITS2 table will have the GEOID field correctly filled in with the code that refers to the correct entry in the GEOIDS table. Execute the following query to see the updated data (shown in Figure 3.5):

```
SELECT * FROM SQLBOOK.WEBTEMP2
```

Figure 3.5: After executing the UPDATE statement, WEBTEMP2 has the GEOID field filled in. It can now be related back to the GEOIDS table.

How Does This Work?

The above query has what is called a *subselect* in it. A subselect is a special kind of SELECT statement that only returns one value and one row. Let's walk through the query so you will understand what is happening.

First, the query is targeting table SQLBOOK.WEBTEMP2 in the UPDATE statement. Notice the letter *A* after the table name. This is a temporary alias that will be used later in the query to refer to any columns in the WEBTEMP2 table. Next, the UPDATE statement indicates that the target column for updating is the GEOID field. To the right of the equal sign is the subselect that will get the value for SQL to use in updating the record. This subselect tells SQL to read the GEOID value from the table SQLBOOK.GEOIDS. The WHERE clause of the subselect tells SQL to only read the GEOID value where the GEONAME field (in table GEOIDS) equals the A.REQGEO field. Now, A is an alias for the SQLBOOK.WELTEMP2 table, so in effect the subselect is saying, "Give me the GEOID from the GEOIDS table where the GEONAME field is equal to the GEOREQ field of the current record that I am positioned on in the WEBHITS table."

So, although SQL is a set-based language, subselects offer the capability to process records in a set one record at a time. For each record that is read from the WEBHITS2 table, the subselect query will be executed to find the matching GEOID from the GEOIDS table, where the GEONAME matches the GEOREQ from the current record.

Now that the WEBTEMP2 table has the GEOID field, there is no longer a need for the data in the REQGEO field. Execute the following statement to remove the column:

```
ALTER TABLE SQLBOOK.WEBTEMP2 DROP COLUMN REQGEO
```

The WEBTEMP2 table now is a more relational table and takes less space. (Chapter 4 explains how to use the relational features of the SELECT statement to join the tables together.)

Deleting Data

Sometimes data has just got to go, and DELETE is the SQL way to remove records. DELETE is very simple, as it takes only DELETE FROM *<table-name>* to remove all data from a table. Optionally, you can supply a WHERE clause to limit the deletion of records to just a subset of the records in the table.

The following query would delete only the skill PR from the SKILLS table.

```
DELETE FROM SQLBOOK.SKILLS WHERE ID='PR'
```

The WHERE clause of the DELETE statement takes a list of expressions, just like the WHERE clause of a SELECT statement. Here is an example of a DELETE statement that uses a subselect in its WHERE clause:

```
DELETE FROM SQLBOOK.SKILLS
          WHERE PAYRATE > (SELECT AVG(PAYRATE) FROM SQLBOOK.SKILLS)
```

The subselect in this query returns a single value that represents the average rate of pay for all skills in the table SKILLS. The DELETE statement will delete all skills that have a rate of pay higher than the average rate of pay.

Be very careful with the DELETE statement. If you incorrectly specify your WHERE clause, you could accidentally delete records.

Positioned UPDATE and DELETE Operations

Using record-level access, you can position a file pointer to a record, and then update or delete the record. In SQL, this can be accomplished via a construct called a *cursor*. A cursor is like a pointer to a record. Cursors are discussed in detail in chapters 5 and 7. You can only use cursors from an application programming language. They cannot be directly manipulated from interactive SQL.

Chapter Summary

Because INSERT, UPDATE, and DELETE are very simple and straightforward operations, this chapter is short but sweet. By now, you should know how to do the following:

- Insert records into a physical file using the VALUES lists.

- Insert records into a physical file using a SELECT statement.

- Update records in a physical file.

- Update records using a subselect.

- Delete records from a physical file.

- Use subselects in WHERE clauses of statements.

In addition, you should understand that WHERE clauses in the UPDATE and DELETE statements are the same as WHERE clauses in SELECT statements.

4

ADVANCED SELECT STATEMENTS

This chapter takes you beyond the simple SELECT statements discussed in previous chapters to introduce you to the concept of joining tables, using the CASE statement, performing complex manipulation of data, creating unions, and more. This chapter is full of examples and neat tricks, and its goal is to show you some of the more obscure and powerful features of SQL.

Union

A union is the marriage of one or more sets of SQL data. It is used between SQL statements to add the results together. By default, a union is a distinct list of records in the new, combined set. Optionally, you can specify UNION ALL to get a complete list of all records from both sets, including duplicates. In order to use UNION, all SELECT statements that are to be "unioned" together must have the same number of columns, and each column must be of a compatible data type.

Union is a hard concept to explain. Let's make some data and do some example unions. Execute the following statement to make a simple inventory table called UT1:

```
CREATE TABLE SQLBOOK.UT1
        (ID INTEGER NOT NULL PRIMARY KEY,
         DESCRIPTION CHAR(20),
         PRICE DECIMAL(8,2))
```

Now, insert the following data into the table:

```
INSERT INTO SQLBOOK.UT1 VALUES (1,'HEATER',1000.95);
INSERT INTO SQLBOOK.UT1 VALUES (2,'AIR CONDITIONER',495.20);
INSERT INTO SQLBOOK.UT1 VALUES (3,'COIL',20.57);
INSERT INTO SQLBOOK.UT1 VALUES (4,'SPRING',0.99)
```

With this table called UT1, which has four sample records, consider the following statement:

```
SELECT * FROM SQLBOOK.UT1 WHERE ID<3
```

This returns a set of rows where the ID is less than three. Now, how about this statement:

```
SELECT * FROM SQLBOOK.UT1 WHERE ID>=3
```

This statement returns the set of rows where the ID is greater than or equal to three. How about this statement:

```
SELECT * FROM SQLBOOK.UT1 WHERE ID<3
        UNION
        SELECT * FROM SQLBOOK.UT1 WHERE ID>=3
```

In this case, the UNION operator puts the output of both queries together into one set. That set is then returned to the calling application. The output for the query is shown in Figure 4.1.

This is a really stupid union, but it probably gives you an idea of how UNION puts sets together.

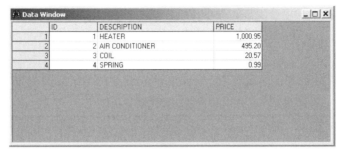

Figure 4.1: This is the output of the UNION statement.

Let's look at some other things that UNION does. First, execute this statement:

```
SELECT * FROM SQLBOOK.UT1
```

This gives a list of all four records in the UT1 table. Now consider the following union:

```
SELECT * FROM SQLBOOK.UT1
          UNION
          SELECT * FROM SQLBOOK.UT1 WHERE ID<3
```

The output of this statement is the same as shown in Figure 4.1. What you might have thought was going to happen did not happen. The union did not produce an output of six records, the combination of the records from the first SELECT plus a repeat of the first two records produced by the second SELECT. This is because, by default, UNION removes duplicates from the result set.

Let's try one more "baby" union:

```
SELECT * FROM SQLBOOK.UT1
          UNION ALL
          SELECT * FROM SQLBOOK.UT1 WHERE ID<3
```

The result of this statement, as shown in Figure 4.2, is six rows because UNION's default behavior was overridden by the ALL keyword. The resulting set now has duplicate data.

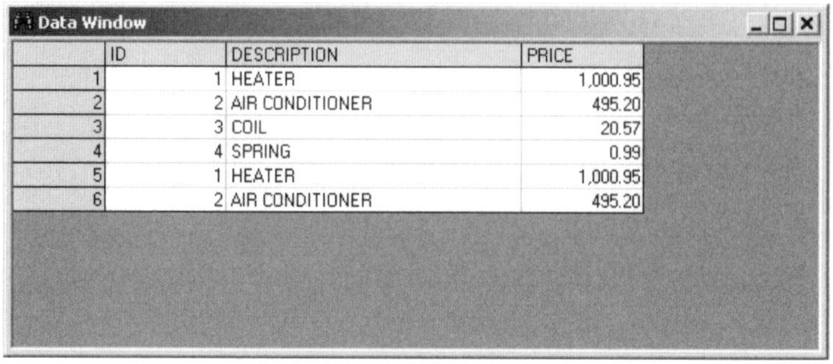

	ID	DESCRIPTION	PRICE
1	1	HEATER	1,000.95
2	2	AIR CONDITIONER	495.20
3	3	COIL	20.57
4	4	SPRING	0.99
5	1	HEATER	1,000.95
6	2	AIR CONDITIONER	495.20

Figure 4.2: This is the result of using UNION ALL.

Joins and Unions

The previous examples were pretty trivial, but they serve to give you the basics of UNION. To see something practical from UNION, execute the following statement to create a table called UTW:

```
CREATE TABLE SQLBOOK.UTW
         (WAREHOUSE CHAR(1),
         PID INTEGER REFERENCES SQLBOOK.UT1 (ID),
         ONHAND INTEGER,
         PRIMARY KEY (WAREHOUSE, PID))
```

The table UTW (which stands for "union test warehouse") contains the columns WAREHOUSE, PID, and ONHAND. These columns represent where inventory is, the part ID of the inventory item, and its onhand quantity. In this silly inventory, if an item is not on hand at the warehouse, there is no record for that part at the warehouse. The PID will be used to relate to the ID field in the UT table. Add the following data to your table:

```
INSERT INTO SQLBOOK.UTW VALUES ('A',1,5);
INSERT INTO SQLBOOK.UTW VALUES ('B',1,22);
INSERT INTO SQLBOOK.UTW VALUES ('A',2,19);
INSERT INTO SQLBOOK.UTW VALUES ('B',2,11);
INSERT INTO SQLBOOK.UTW VALUES ('A',3,19);
INSERT INTO SQLBOOK.UTW VALUES ('B',4,2)
```

Before getting any deeper into unions, you need to understand *joins*. A join allows you to combine tables based on a common key value. For example, table UT1 has a list of items that are available in inventory, and its primary key is the column ID. Table UTW has a list of items, the warehouse they are located in, and the on-hand quantity. This table has a foreign key reference to UT1. You can combine these tables so that you can select columns from either table in one SELECT. Consider the following SQL statement, which produces the results shown in Figure 4.3.

```
SELECT ID, DESCRIPTION, PRICE, WAREHOUSE, ONHAND
        FROM SQLBOOK.UT1, SQLBOOK.UTW
        WHERE ID=PID
```

	ID	DESCRIPTION	PRICE	WAREHOUSE	ONHAND
1	1	HEATER	1,000.95	A	5
2	1	HEATER	1,000.95	B	22
3	2	AIR CONDITIONER	495.20	A	19
4	2	AIR CONDITIONER	495.20	B	11
5	3	COIL	20.57	A	19
6	4	SPRING	0.99	B	2

Figure .4.3: This is the result of joining tables UT1 and UTW.

This SELECT tells SQL that you want the columns ID, DESCRIPTION, PRICE, WAREHOUSE, and ONHAND. The FROM clause specifies that the data is to come from tables UT1 and UTW. The WHERE clause instructs SQL to retrieve data only where the ID column from table UT1 is equal to the PID column of table UTW. In effect, for each record that SQL reads from UT1, it will use the ID value to look up the fields it needs from UTW.

Now, back to UNION. Let's use JOIN and UNION to solve a simple business problem. As mentioned earlier, in this inventory, if an item is not on hand at the warehouse, there is no record for that part at the warehouse. However, the tyrannical inventory manager wants an item list with quantities on hand for warehouse B. If an item is not on hand, the manager wants the item to show with a quantity of zero. Consider the following query:

```
SELECT ID, DESCRIPTION, PRICE, WAREHOUSE, ONHAND
       FROM SQLBOOK.UT1, SQLBOOK.UTW
       WHERE ID=PID AND WAREHOUSE = 'B'
```

This query would yield the results shown in Figure 4.4. The type of join performed in this query is called an *equi-join* or *inner join*. An equi-join returns only records that satisfy the equality relationship. In other words, it returns only records where the part in UT1 has a corresponding record in the UTW table for warehouse B.

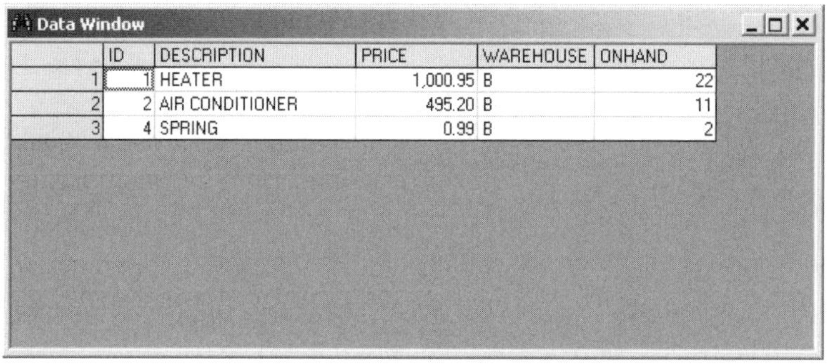

Figure 4.4: This query shows the results of selecting from tables UT1 and UTW, restricted only to items in warehouse B.

The problem is that the manager wants a list of all items. If an item is not stocked in inventory, he wants the report to record it without the on-hand quantity. The following statement can be used to list parts that are not available in warehouse B:

```
SELECT ID, DESCRIPTION, PRICE
       FROM SQLBOOK.UT1
       WHERE ID NOT IN
       (SELECT PID FROM SQLBOOK.UTW WHERE WAREHOUSE='B')
```

This query uses a subselect to return a list of items that exist in warehouse B. The ID NOT IN tells SQL that you want a listing of parts where the part ID is not in the list of parts coming from the subselect, which is a list of parts not stored at warehouse B. If you use the following UNION statement to combine the results of the two SELECTs, you will get the results that the manager wants (shown in Figure 4.5):

```
SELECT ID, DESCRIPTION, PRICE, WAREHOUSE, ONHAND
        FROM SQLBOOK.UT1, SQLBOOK.UTW
        WHERE ID=PID AND WAREHOUSE = 'B'
        UNION
        SELECT ID, DESCRIPTION, PRICE, 'B', 0
        FROM SQLBOOK.UT1 where ID NOT IN
        (SELECT PID FROM SQLBOOK.UTW WHERE WAREHOUSE='B')
```

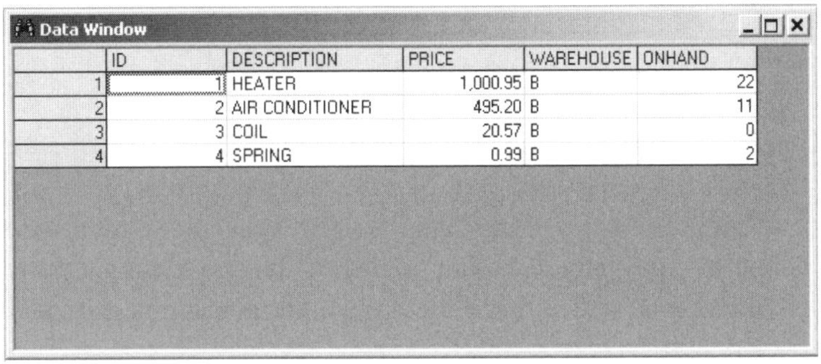

	ID	DESCRIPTION	PRICE	WAREHOUSE	ONHAND
1	1	HEATER	1,000.95	B	22
2	2	AIR CONDITIONER	495.20	B	11
3	3	COIL	20.57	B	0
4	4	SPRING	0.99	B	2

Figure 4.5: The result of the union shows all parts, regardless of whether they are in warehouse B.

This type of union is almost the equivalent of an *outer join*. However, an outer join would return nulls in the warehouse and on-hand columns for the records where the parts did not exist in warehouse B. In contrast, the union enables you to return values.

Left Outer Joins

Joins can be fun or joins can be trouble. When they are trouble, it is usually either because of performance problems or because they do not return the results you want. If they do not return the results you want, it might be because you do not understand the join process. Let's look at some more queries to get a thorough grounding in joins.

You saw the equi-join in the previous section. The next type of join you need to understand is the outer join. Look at the following example:

```
SELECT ID, DESCRIPTION, PRICE, WAREHOUSE, ONHAND
        FROM SQLBOOK.UT1 LEFT OUTER JOIN SQLBOOK.UTW
        ON ID=PID and WAREHOUSE='B'
```

This statement causes the table UT1 to be read. For each part in UT1, SQL attempts to find a record in UTW where the PID field is equal to the ID field and the warehouse is B. This is called the *join condition*. If a record does not exist in the UTW table, all columns from UTW in the select list will be returned as null values. This is an outer join.

The SQL-92 specification and other versions of DB2 Universal support syntax for both *left* and *right* outer joins. DB2 on the AS/400 only supports the left join at this time. The LEFT keyword indicates that the table on the left is the table that should control the outer join behavior. You should always include the LEFT keyword, even though it is optional and the default, because in the future the AS/400 will support the RIGHT keyword also.

The output for the example outer join query is shown in Figure 4.6. Notice that this output is very similar to the output from the UNION query shown in Figure 4.5. Before SQL invented the outer join concept, unions were used to simulate the outer join behavior. The point of an outer join is that you want all records from the left table, and a record from the right table if it exists, or all columns from the right table to be expressed as null values if no matching record is found.

	ID	DESCRIPTION	PRICE	WAREHOU	ONHAND
1	1	HEATER	1,000.95	B	22
2	2	AIR CONDITIONER	495.20	B	11
3	3	COIL	20.57	#NULL#	#NULL#
4	4	SPRING	0.99	B	2

Figure 4.6: In the results of this outer join, part 3 has null values for the WAREHOUSE and ONHAND columns because there is no entry for part 3 in the UTW table.

Outer join behavior can get really tricky when combined with a WHERE clause. To demonstrate this, consider the following query:

```
SELECT ID, DESCRIPTION, PRICE, WAREHOUSE, ONHAND
        FROM SQLBOOK.UT1
        LEFT OUTER JOIN SQLBOOK.UTW ON ID=PID
        WHERE WAREHOUSE='B'
```

This looks very similar to the last query, but the results tell the tale. You might think that you would get the same results as shown in Figure 4.6. Figure 4.7 shows, though, that the AS/400 did not perform the outer join as you might have expected (returning nulls where the rows did not exist in B). Nevertheless, the AS/400 did exactly what you told it do.

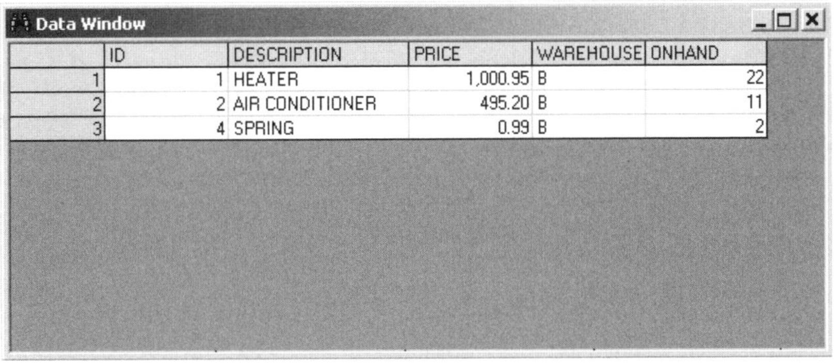

Figure 4.7: This query should have a record for part 3 because of the outer join specification. Joins and WHERE clauses can have subtle results.

Because the WHERE clause specifies that the warehouse value should be B, only records from the UTW table with B are used to join to the UT1 table. So, the outer join makes a record with null values for the WAREHOUSE and ONHAND columns to perform the outer join in the case of a record with an ID of 3. However, you asked for records where the warehouse column is B, and null is not equal to B, so SQL excludes the record from the resulting set because it did not fit your WHERE criteria. SQL did all of the outer join work, and then your WHERE clause excluded the result. Outer joins can be really subtle.

The full syntax of the outer join statement is as follows:

```
<source-table> LEFT OUTER JOIN <target-table> ON <join-condition>
```

Join conditions can be any expression that you might use in a WHERE clause.

Remember, outer joins can be done with unions, as shown in Figure 4.5. I think that unions are much better than outer joins, as you can feed values other than null into a union. However, sometimes an outer join will perform better than a union. If you do not mind getting null columns, then outer joins are for you. At least you have a choice in the matter!

Inner Joins

Another name for the equi-join is an inner join. These joins can be accomplished via the WHERE clause or in join specifications in the FROM clause. Consider the following statement:

```
SELECT ID, DESCRIPTION, PRICE, WAREHOUSE, ONHAND
       FROM SQLBOOK.UT1, SQLBOOK.UTW
       WHERE ID=PID AND WAREHOUSE = 'B'
```

This produced the output shown in Figure 4.4. The following query will produce the identical output. The major difference is that this example uses the SQL JOIN syntax:

```
SELECT ID, DESCRIPTION, PRICE, WAREHOUSE, ONHAND
       FROM SQLBOOK.UT1 INNER JOIN SQLBOOK.UTW ON ID=PID
       WHERE WAREHOUSE = 'B'
```

The full syntax for inner joins is as follows:

```
<source-table> INNER JOIN <target-table> ON <join-condition>
```

Finally, you could elect to put the entire WHERE criteria in the inner join syntax. Here is an example:

```
SELECT ID, DESCRIPTION, PRICE, WAREHOUSE, ONHAND
        FROM SQLBOOK.UT1 INNER JOIN SQLBOOK.UTW ON ID=PID
        AND WAREHOUSE = 'B'
```

Remember, inner joins return rows only where the join criteria is satisfied. Outer joins return all records from the left table and column data from the right table when the join criteria is satisfied, and null values for the columns from the right table if no record matches the current record on the left side.

Cartesian Product or Cross Joins

When I began programming in SQL, I thought that cross joins (sometimes called the *Cartesian product*) were one of the most useless types of joins. You will rarely use cross joins in your programming, but you need to understand the concept, as it can come in handy in certain situations. A cross join is where you return each record from the source table with all records from the target table. Let's look at an example of a cross join.

The easiest way to generate a cross join is to specify two tables in your FROM clause and then not specify join criteria in your WHERE clause. Here is a simple cross join of the UT1 table to the UTW table:

```
SELECT * FROM SQLBOOK.UT1, SQLBOOK.UTW
```

SQL will satisfy this query by reading a row from the UT1 table. Then, SQL will read every record in the UTW table, join that record to the UT1 record, and return the row in the result set. Once SQL has returned each pairing of the first row with each row in UTW, it will move to the next record in UT1. Because UT1 has four rows and UTW has six rows, the cross join would return 24 rows (4*6).

You can also use SQL's JOIN syntax to invoke a cross join. Here is the same query using cross join syntax:

```
SELECT * FROM SQLBOOK.UT1
        CROSS JOIN SQLBOOK.UTW
```

The output for both statements is shown in Figure 4.8, as they produce the same effect.

	ID	DESCRIPTION	PRICE	WAREHOUSE	PID	ONHAND
1	1	HEATER	1,000.95	A	1	5
2	1	HEATER	1,000.95	A	2	19
3	1	HEATER	1,000.95	A	3	19
4	1	HEATER	1,000.95	B	1	22
5	1	HEATER	1,000.95	B	2	11
6	1	HEATER	1,000.95	B	4	2
7	2	AIR CONDITIONER	495.20	A	1	5
8	2	AIR CONDITIONER	495.20	A	2	19
9	2	AIR CONDITIONER	495.20	A	3	19
10	2	AIR CONDITIONER	495.20	B	1	22
11	2	AIR CONDITIONER	495.20	B	2	11
12	2	AIR CONDITIONER	495.20	B	4	2

Figure 4.8: This is the output from a cross join of tables UT1 and UTW.

One of the more creative uses that I have found for the cross join came from a friend who called me about a reporting problem. He was running a report on a single table of data, but he wanted the SQL result set to have columns for the start-date and end-date range for which the report was requested. In that way, the report-writing program would have access to the date range that was requested, and then use the date range in calculations within the report writer. An additional complicating factor was that the SQL statement was doing GROUP BY operations. Therefore, the start and end dates could not be passed as parameters into the list of columns that were to be selected from the database.

His program was a report server that basically sat there querying a table, looking for unsatisfied report requests. That table had, among other columns, a REQUESTID column that was the primary key, and STARTDATE and ENDDATE columns that indicated the range of the report. When an entry was placed in the report request table, his program would read a transaction file based on the start date and end date, and make aggregate sums of parts sold. The program then created an ActiveX data object and sent it to the report writer. So, how could he elegantly add columns that contained the start and end dates to the output of the aggregated SQL statement?

The answer was to use a Cartesian product (cross join). Suppose he picked up a report with REQUESTID equal to A. The following query would join the RE-QUESTS table to the TRANSACTIOS table and return the PARTID, STARTDATE, ENDDATE, and the sum of the PRICE column times the QUANTITY column. (Note that this query is for demonstration purposes. Data is not supplied to make it work as an example for this book.)

```
SELECT A.PARTID, B.STARTDATE, B.ENDDATE,
       SUM(PRICE*QUANTITY)
       FROM TRANSACTIONS A, REQUESTS B
       WHERE A.TRANSDATE>=B.STARTDATE AND
       A.TRANSDATE<=B.ENDDATE AND B.REQUESTID = 'A'
       GROUP BY A.PARTID, B.STARTDATE, B.ENDDATE
```

This only works because the requests table has only one record that satisfies the WHERE clause. Suppose there were 25,000 transactions within the time period. Because there is only one row in the REQUESTS table that satisfies the WHERE clause, the number of rows returned by the cross join query would be 1*25,000, or 25,000 rows. Then, the GROUP BY clause causes the records to be aggregated, and you end up with a list of part ID, the single start date, the single end date, and the sum of the price times the quantity field. Because the start date and end date is always the same, the effect is a result set grouped by just part ID.

However, this would not have worked if the REQUESTS table's ID column was not unique. Suppose that the REQUESTS table had two records with a request ID of A. SQL would have returned 2*25,000, records or 50,000 rows, which is not the result intended. The totals would have been doubled. The use of Cartesian product only works in this situation because the REQUESTS table will only ever return one row.

I have to admit, I was mighty impressed with myself for finding a use for Cartesian products. The queries presented at the end of this chapter also make creative use of cross joins.

Self Joins

Besides joining a table to another table, sometimes it is useful to join a table to itself. For example, suppose you wanted to find all users who visited both the Web pages index.htm and stupid_odbc_tricks.htm on the same day. The following query will answer this question; its output is shown in Figure 4.9:

```
SELECT A.REQUSER,COUNT(*)
        FROM SQLBOOK.WEBTEMP A, SQLBOOK.WEBTEMP B
        WHERE A.REQUSER = B.REQUSER AND
        DATE(A.REQTS)=DATE(B.REQTS) AND
        A.REQFILE='/index.htm' AND B.REQFILE =
        '/stupid_odbc_tricks.htm'
        GROUP BY A.REQUSER
```

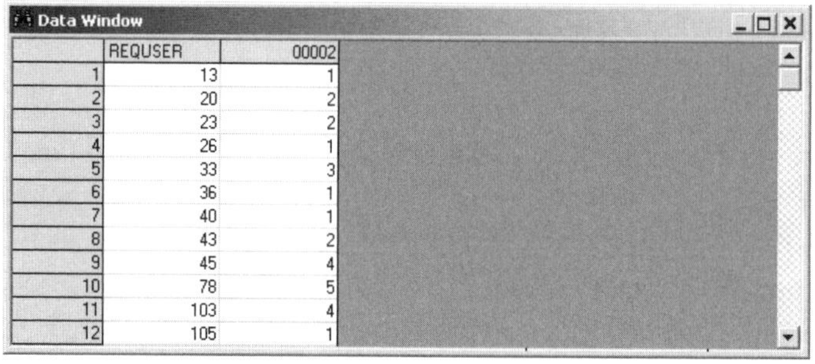

	REQUSER	00002
1	13	1
2	20	2
3	23	2
4	26	1
5	33	3
6	36	1
7	40	1
8	43	2
9	45	4
10	78	5
11	103	4
12	105	1

Figure 4.9: Here are the results of the self join. The second column represents the number of times a user visited both pages in a single day.

The key to this query is that the database performs a self join. Note the WHERE clause of the query, which indicates that SQL should read from the WEBTEMP A table and the WEBTEMP B table. To SQL, the query is referencing two different copies of the WEBTEMP table, one referred to as A and the other as B. Looking at the WHERE clause, you will see that the two tables are being joined where the REQUSER columns are equal and where the date value portions of the timestamp column REQTS are equal. Table A is a listing of hits against the REQFILE value of /indexes.htm. Table B is a listing of hits against the REQFILE value of /stupid_odbc_tricks.htm.

SQL gets the results of the first select, and then joins the results of the second select in a self-join operation. Because the self join is an equi-join rather than an outer join, rows are returned only when the REQUSER and DATE(REQTS) fields exist in both sets of data. The count is the number of times that this situation exists.

So, in the data represented in Figure 4.9, user 13 visited the page combination on one day, but user 20 visited the combination more than one time.

Self Joins Using EXISTS

An alternate way to represent the self-join query would be to use the EXISTS predicate. The following query is equivalent to a self-join:

```
SELECT REQUSER,COUNT(*) FROM SQLBOOK.WEBTEMP A
        WHERE REQFILE='/index.htm' AND
        EXISTS (SELECT B.REQUSER
        FROM SQLBOOK.WEBTEMP B
        WHERE B.REQUSER = A.REQUSER AND
        B.REQFILE='/stupid_odbc_tricks.htm' AND
        DATE(B.REQTS) = DATE(A.REQTS))
        GROUP BY REQUSER;
```

This query yields the same results as those in Figure 4.9. The EXISTS predicate returns a value of true if at least one row is returned by the subselect on the right side of EXISTS. The subselect is fired for each row returned in the parent select query. It is effectively passing in the values of the current row in the parent query. This EXISTS statement is looking for rows where the REQFILE value is equal to /stupid_odbc_tricks.htm that were viewed by the current user in the parent query on the same date as the current row of the parent query. Whether to use a self join or EXISTS is up to you when doing this type of query. Both will optimize with similar execution plans, further illustrating that there is always more than one way to ask the same question with SQL.

Exception Joins

An exception join can be used to find records where the join criteria are not met. For example, suppose you wanted to find records where the user viewed the /index.htm Web page, but did not view stupid_odbc_tricks.htm on the same day. You could express that relationship using the following exception join:

```
SELECT A.REQUSER,COUNT(*)
          FROM SQLBOOK.WEBTEMP A EXCEPTION JOIN SQLBOOK.WEBTEMP B
          ON A.REQUSER = B.REQUSER AND DATE(A.REQTS)=DATE(B.REQTS)
          AND A.REQFILE='/index.htm' AND
          B.REQFILE = '/stupid_odbc_tricks.htm'
          GROUP BY A.REQUSER
```

The output of this query is shown in Figure 4.10. Note that user 1 visited /index.htm on 12 occasions without visiting /stupid_odbc_tricks.htm. The exception join only returns results where a row exists in the first table, but no corresponding row exists in the second table. If the exception join is used to return columns from both tables, the columns from the second table will be represented by null values, as they do not exist.

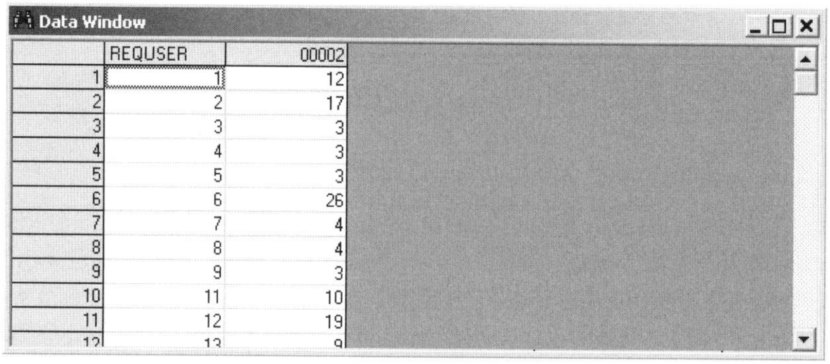

	REQUSER	00002
1	1	12
2	2	17
3	3	3
4	4	3
5	5	3
6	6	26
7	7	4
8	8	4
9	9	3
10	11	10
11	12	19
12	13	9

Figure 4.10: Here are the results of an exception join.

The CASE Statement

The AS/400 introduced the SQL-92 CASE statement in V4R1. CASE is a way to transform data before returning it to the client. It can be used wherever an expression can be used. There are two supported forms of CASE. Here is the syntax for the first form:

```
CASE <expression>
  WHEN <value> THEN <result>
  WHEN <value> THEN <result>
  ELSE <result>
END
```

In this syntax, *expressions* is any legal expression that results in a value. *Value* can be an expression, column, or literal. The CASE statement evaluates the expression to determine a value, then tests the value against each WHEN clause to determine which to execute. *Result* can be an expression, a column, or a literal value, but each result must be of the same compatible data type.

The second form of CASE is as follows:

```
CASE WHEN <expression> THEN <result>
WHEN <expression> THEN <result>
ELSE <result>
END
```

The main difference is that each expression is evaluated, and the first expression that returns true causes the result to be returned. As in the case of the first form, each result must yield a value of the same data type, and this result can be an expression, a literal, or a column.

Suppose you wanted to make a table of Web hits by day of the week, but label the days of the week with their text equivalent. The following query returns the total number of hits and average number of hits by day of the week, using the DAYOFWEEK scalar function:

```
SELECT DAYOFWEEK(REQTS) AS "Day of Week",
        COUNT(*) AS "Pages Served",
        AVG(REQSIZE) AS "Average Transfered",
        SUM(REQSIZE)  AS "Total Transfered"
        FROM SQLBOOK.WEBTEMP
        GROUP BY DAYOFWEEK(REQTS)
```

This query returns output like that shown in Figure 4.11. (I added the column headers using the AS function to avoid those ugly SQL-generated column names.)

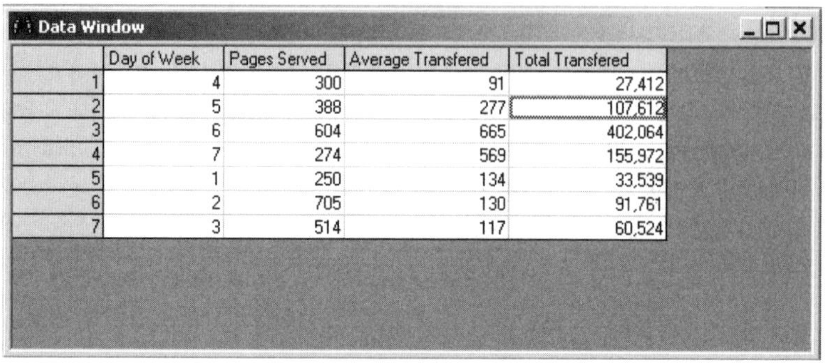

	Day of Week	Pages Served	Average Transfered	Total Transfered
1	4	300	91	27,412
2	5	388	277	107,612
3	6	604	665	402,064
4	7	274	569	155,972
5	1	250	134	33,539
6	2	705	130	91,761
7	3	514	117	60,524

Figure 4.11: These are the results of the day-of-week query.

The query is fine, but you want to see the days of the week as string values to make the query more readable. In a perfect world, the following statement would do what you want:

```
SELECT CASE DAYOFWEEK(REQTS)
         WHEN 1 THEN 'Sunday'
         WHEN 2 THEN 'Monday'
         WHEN 3 THEN 'Tuesday'
         WHEN 4 THEN 'Wednesday'
         WHEN 5 THEN 'Thursday'
         WHEN 6 THEN 'Friday'
         WHEN 7 THEN 'Saturday'
         END AS "Day of Week",
         COUNT(*) AS "Pages Served",
         AVG(REQSIZE) AS "Average Transfered",
         SUM(REQSIZE)  AS "Total Transfered"
         FROM SQLBOOK.WEBTEMP
         GROUP BY DAYOFWEEK(REQTS)
```

However, we live in an imperfect world, and the above statement will not work on the AS/400 because of limitations on grouping by the output of scalar functions. To get the statement to work, you would need to create a view:

```
CREATE VIEW SQLBOOK.DOWVIEW (Dowstring,Downumber,CntVal,BytesTrans)
        AS
        SELECT CASE DAYOFWEEK(REQTS)
        WHEN 1 THEN 'Sunday'
        WHEN 2 THEN 'Monday'
        WHEN 3 THEN 'Tuesday'
        WHEN 4 THEN 'Wednesday'
        WHEN 5 THEN 'Thursday'
        WHEN 6 THEN 'Friday'
        WHEN 7 THEN 'Saturday'
        END,
        DAYOFWEEK(REQTS), 1, REQSIZE
        FROM SQLBOOK.WEBTEMP
```

Now you have a virtual table called DOWVIEW in the SQLBOOK library that contains four columns: the day of the week as a string, the day of the week's number, the number 1, and the size of the request. Figure 4.12 shows what the records look like in the virtual table. It was created by the statement SELECT * FROM SQLBOOK.DOWVIEW.

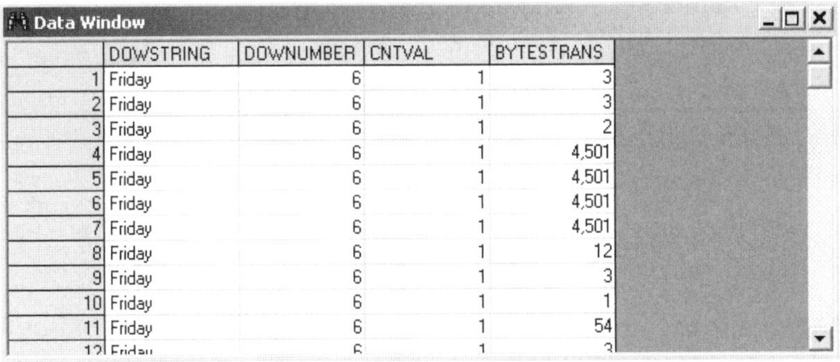

	DOWSTRING	DOWNUMBER	CNTVAL	BYTESTRANS
1	Friday	6	1	3
2	Friday	6	1	3
3	Friday	6	1	2
4	Friday	6	1	4,501
5	Friday	6	1	4,501
6	Friday	6	1	4,501
7	Friday	6	1	4,501
8	Friday	6	1	12
9	Friday	6	1	3
10	Friday	6	1	1
11	Friday	6	1	54
12	Friday	6	1	3

Figure 4.12: This is what the data in the virtual table DOWVIEW looks like.

Now that you have a view with good column names, you can use the following statement to create the sorted report (shown in Figure 4.13):

```
SELECT DOWSTRING as "Day of Week",
        SUM(CNTVAL) as Hits,
        AVG(BYTESTRANS) as "Average Transfered",
        SUM(BYTESTRANS) as "Total Transfered"
        FROM SQLBOOK.DOWVIEW
        GROUP BY DOWSTRING
```

Data Window

	Day of Week	HITS	Average Transfered	Total Transfered
1	Friday	604	665	402,064
2	Monday	705	130	91,761
3	Saturday	274	569	155,972
4	Sunday	250	134	33,539
5	Thursday	388	277	107,612
6	Tuesday	514	117	60,524
7	Wednesday	300	91	27,412

Figure 4.13: Here are the results of selecting from DOWVIEW with a GROUP BY. However, the results are not sorted correctly.

Everything looks hunky-dory, except that the output is not sorted correctly. To see the output in the traditional manner, execute the following new version of the statement:

```
SELECT DOWSTRING as "Day of Week",
        SUM(CNTVAL) as Hits,
        AVG(BYTESTRANS) as "Average Transfered",
        SUM(BYTESTRANS) as "Total Transfered",
        DOWNUMBER as "Day Number"
        FROM SQLBOOK.DOWVIEW
        GROUP BY DOWSTRING,downumber
        ORDER BY "Day Number"
```

The result of the statement is shown in Figure 4.14. This statement also illustrates what I call a "stupid AS/400 trick." In almost all other SQL systems, renaming a column using AS allows you to refer to the column by its original name in the ORDER BY portion of the statement. Notice the ORDER BY in the above statement had to refer to the DOWNUMBER column by the name it was renamed to, "Day Number." If you did not do this, the SQL statement would fail. Kudos, IBM for making a weird AS/400 platform-specific change to SQL! (Can you feel the sarcasm dripping from that last statement?)

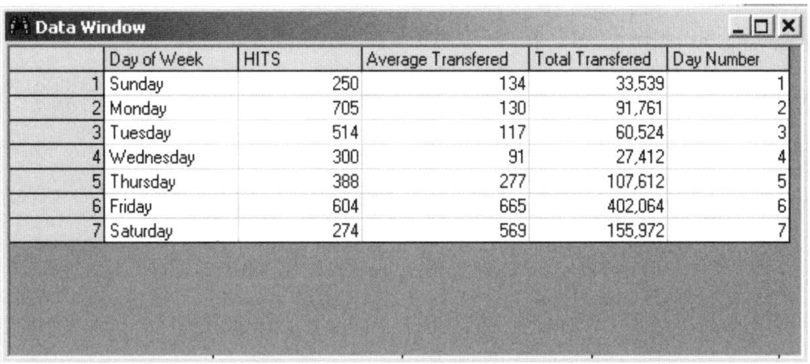

	Day of Week	HITS	Average Transfered	Total Transfered	Day Number
1	Sunday	250	134	33,539	1
2	Monday	705	130	91,761	2
3	Tuesday	514	117	60,524	3
4	Wednesday	300	91	27,412	4
5	Thursday	388	277	107,612	5
6	Friday	604	665	402,064	6
7	Saturday	274	569	155,972	7

Figure 4.14: By adding the DOWNUMBER field to the SELECT, you can sort the results by day number.

A few final observations are in order. You will notice that to get the desired sort order, you had to add the DOWNUMBER column to the result set. In some SQL dialects, you can order by a column that is not in the select list. In the AS/400 SQL dialect, a column must be in the select list to be used in the ORDER BY portion of the statement.

Secondly, notice that the DOWNUMBER field is the last field in the query. A lot of people mistakenly think that a GROUP BY statement must start with the columns you want to group by, then include the summary columns. However, SQL defines no order that the columns must appear in for a statement that uses GROUP BY. Most people choose to place the grouped columns first, then the aggregates.

Advanced Date Arithmetic

You can get really creative with timestamp columns in SQL. SQL has a variety of scalar functions that return portions of a timestamp or are useful for transforming strings into dates and times. Table 4.1 lists some of these. You'll see lots of example date/time queries in this section, as I feel temporal manipulation is the neatest part of SQL.

Table 4.1: Scalar Functions for Date, Time, and Timestamp	
CURDATE	Returns the current date.
CURTIME	Returns the current time.
DATE(X)	Returns X as a date data type. Equivalent to CAST X AS DATE.
DAYOFWEEK(X)	Returns an integer between 1 and 7 representing the day of the week for the date or timestamp value X, where 1=Sunday.
DAYS(X)	The number of days that have elapsed since 1-1-0001 and the date represented by X as an integer.
DAY(X) DAYOFMONTH(X)	Returns the day part of the date or timestamp value X.
DAYOFYEAR(X)	Returns a number between 1 and 366 representing the day of the year of the date or timestamp X.
HOUR(X)	Returns the hour portion of the timestamp or time type X.
MICROSECOND(X)	Returns the microseconds portion of the timestamp X.
MINUTE(X)	Returns the minute portion of time or the timestamp type X.
QUARTER(X)	Returns an integer between 1 and 4 representing the quarter that the date or timestamp X exists in.
SECOND(X)	Returns the seconds portion of the time or timestamp X.
TIME(X)	Returns X as a time data type. Equivalent to CAST X AS TIME.
TIMESTAMP(X)	Returns the timestamp representation of X, if X can be converted to a timestamp.
WEEK(X)	Returns the week, 1 to 52, that the date or timestamp X falls in.
YEAR(X)	Returns the year part of the date or timestamp value X.

Web Hits by Date and Hour

The query below uses the DATE scalar function to return the date portion of the timestamp REQTS, the hour portion of REQTS, and then a count of hits. Because of the GROUP BY clause, this results in a set showing hits by date and hour.

106

```
SELECT DATE(REQTS) as DATE,
         HOUR(REQTS) as HOUR,
         COUNT(*) AS HITS
         FROM SQLBOOK.WEBTEMP
         GROUP BY DATE(REQTS), HOUR(REQTS)
```

Output results for the statement are shown in Figure 4.15. Note that GROUP BY references the grouped columns by their select names and not by the column aliases created using the AS operator.

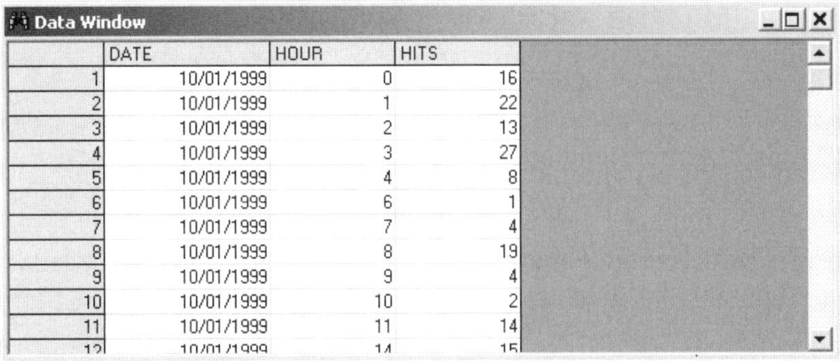

	DATE	HOUR	HITS
1	10/01/1999	0	16
2	10/01/1999	1	22
3	10/01/1999	2	13
4	10/01/1999	3	27
5	10/01/1999	4	8
6	10/01/1999	6	1
7	10/01/1999	7	4
8	10/01/1999	8	19
9	10/01/1999	9	4
10	10/01/1999	10	2
11	10/01/1999	11	14
12	10/01/1999	14	15

Figure 4.15: Here are the results of selecting Web hits by date and hour.

Showing Hits by 15-Minute Increments

Because it relies on several scalar functions to produce the results, a query to show hits by 15-minute increments is tricky. Because this formula is really complex, the AS/400 cannot GROUP BY the formula unless it is named in a view. Create the following view:

```
CREATE VIEW SQLBOOK.WEBHITV
         (Hitdate, Countbase, KBSent, TimeInc) AS
         SELECT DATE(REQTS),1,REQSIZE,
         SUBSTRING( DIGITS(( HOUR(REQTS) * 100) +
         ( INTEGER(  MINUTE( REQTS) / 15) * 15)),7,4)
         FROM SQLBOOK.WEBTEMP
```

This view selects the date of the REQTS column, the number 1 (which will be used as the basis of a count), the number of kilobytes sent, and then a complex time formula. The time formula will return the time by 15-minute increments throughout the day. Figure 4.16 shows how the formula works.

```
Assume that the time portion of the timestamp represents 8:21 AM
The first function executed is HOUR(REQTS), which returns 8
Next, 8*100 returns 800
MINUTE(REQTS) yields 21
21/15 yields 1.4
INTEGER(1.4) yields 1, as INTEGER truncates decimal places
800+15 yields 815
DIGITS(815) yields '0000000815'
SUBSTRING('0000000815',7,4) = 0815
```

Figure 4.16: This step-by-step breakdown explains the formula for calculating the 15-minute increment of a Web hit.

The result is a nice string representation of the day part that a query falls into. Execute the following statement to get the results shown in Figure 4.17:

```
SELECT * FROM SLQBOOK.WEBHITV
```

	HITDATE	COUNTBASE	KBSENT	TIMEINC
1	10/08/1999	1	3	0030
2	10/08/1999	1	3	0030
3	10/08/1999	1	2	0115
4	10/08/1999	1	4,501	0130
5	10/08/1999	1	4,501	0130
6	10/08/1999	1	4,501	0130
7	10/08/1999	1	4,501	0130
8	10/01/1999	1	12	2000
9	10/01/1999	1	3	2000
10	10/01/1999	1	1	2130
11	10/01/1999	1	54	2130
12	10/01/1999	1	3	2130

Figure 4.17: This is what the data in the view WEBHITV looks like.

Now that a view is in place, you can execute a query with a GROUP BY against the view to aggregate the data.

```
SELECT HITDATE, TIMEINC,
        SUM(KBSENT) AS "KB Sent", SUM(COUNTBASE) AS HITS,
        SUM(KBSENT)/SUM(COUNTBASE) AS "AVERAGE SENT"
        FROM SQLBOOK.WEBHITV
        GROUP BY HITDATE, TIMEINC
        ORDER BY 1,2
```

The output of the query is shown in Figure 4.18. Note that the output does not have a colon separator in the TIMEINC column. For fun, reformulate the query so that it does. (Yes, I could have told you to use the AVG function to calculate the average kilobytes sent, but I wanted to show that you could do math with the results of an aggregate function.)

	HITDATE	TIMEINC	KB Sent	HITS	AVERAGE SENT
1	10/01/1999	0000	127	3	42
2	10/01/1999	0015	104	3	34
3	10/01/1999	0030	136	7	19
4	10/01/1999	0045	28	3	9
5	10/01/1999	0100	75	4	18
6	10/01/1999	0115	42	4	10
7	10/01/1999	0130	59	7	8
8	10/01/1999	0145	79	7	11
9	10/01/1999	0200	147	9	16
10	10/01/1999	0215	35	4	8
11	10/01/1999	0300	22	1	22
12	10/01/1999	0345	425	26	16

Figure 4.18: This is the grouped output from the WEBHITV view.

Using Common Table Expressions to Avoid Views

The previous query was really cool, but needed a view to get around the limitation of GROUP BY on the AS/400. There is a way to make a temporary view that only lasts until the processing of a query is finished. This temporary view is called a *common table expression*. It looks like a SELECT statement in the FROM clause of a query. Here is an example of the common table expression grammar:

```
(SELECT <columns> FROM <table> WHERE <conditions>) AS <Table-Name>
```

Once you use one of these, you can reference any column returned by a common table expression in the rest of your query. Another advantage of common table expressions is that they allow for parameters to be referenced in column expressions (which is a no-no in a regular SELECT statement).

Examine the previous query implemented as a common table expression. Here is the query:

```
SELECT HITDATE, TIMEINC,
        SUM(KBSENT),
        SUM(CNT),SUM(KBSENT)/SUM(CNT)
        FROM (SELECT DATE(REQTS) as HITDATE,REQSIZE AS KBSENT,1 as
        CNT,
        SUBSTRING( DIGITS(( HOUR(REQTS) * 100) + ( INTEGER(
        MINUTE( REQTS) / 15) * 15)),7,4) AS TIMEINC
        FROM SQLBOOK.WEBTEMP) as T
        GROUP BY HITDATE, TIMEINC
        ORDER BY 1,2
```

First, the query selects HITDATE , SUM(KBSENT), SUM(CNT), and SUM(KBSENT) /SUM(CNT). It looks like normal SQL so far, but pay close attention to the FROM clause. Instead of naming a table, the FROM clause is passed a SELECT statement!

Take a look at this SELECT to see what is actually happening here. The statement says SELECT DATE(REQTS) AS HITDATE, REQSIZE AS KBSENT, 1 AS CNT, and then gives the formula for calculating the day part as TIMEINC. It goes on to specify that the data should be read from and then closes the parenthesis and names the table T. Effectively, the query is creating a virtual table T with the columns HITDATE, KBSENT, CNT, and TIMEINC. Then, the outer SELECT reads this virtual table T and aggregates the results.

If you execute this query, you will see the results that are shown in Figure 4.17. This query is exactly the same as creating the view, selecting from it, and aggregating the results (as we did in the last query). The advantage, though, is that no view was created.

Now, let's take this a step further and add some parameter markers to the query to really spice it up:

```
SELECT HITDATE, TIMEINC, SUM(KBSENT),SUM(CNT),SUM(KBSENT)/SUM(CNT)
      FROM (SELECT DATE(REQTS) as HITDATE,REQSIZE AS KBSENT,1 as CNT,
      SUBSTRING( DIGITS(( HOUR(REQTS) * 100) +
      ( INTEGER(  MINUTE( REQTS) / ?) * ?)),7,4) AS TIMEINC
      FROM SQLBOOK.WEBTEMP) as T
      GROUP BY HITDATE, TIMEINC
      ORDER BY 1,2
```

The query is exactly the same, but both 15s in the TIMEINC formula have been re-placed with parameter markers. Remember, the 15s are there so that the formula breaks the data into 15-minute increments. Now, at runtime you will be prompted for the value by which the query should aggregate.

Run the query and supply the value 30 for both prompts. Bingo! The query now returns the results by 30-minute increments instead of 15-minute increments. Figure 4.19 shows the results of running the query with 30 as the parameter.

	HITDATE	TIMEINC	00003	00004	00005
1	10/01/1999	0000	231	6	38
2	10/01/1999	0030	164	10	16
3	10/01/1999	0100	117	8	14
4	10/01/1999	0130	138	14	9
5	10/01/1999	0200	182	13	14
6	10/01/1999	0300	22	1	22
7	10/01/1999	0330	425	26	16
8	10/01/1999	0400	21	1	21
9	10/01/1999	0430	33	7	4
10	10/01/1999	0600	1	1	1
11	10/01/1999	0730	51	4	12
12	10/01/1999	0800	443	19	23

Figure 4.19: These results are from the query with the common table expression. Its advantage is that you can specify the time increment as a parameter.

The big difference is that the formula accepts parameter markers (?) in place of the number 15. This supports selecting Web hits by alternate time periods.

Common table expressions are really neat things, and the best part is you can use more than one common table expression in a query.

Converting Legacy Dates
to Date and Timestamp Data Types

Sometimes legacy tables are just plain ugly. Create the following table to represent ugly legacy data:

```
CREATE TABLE SQLBOOK.LEGACY
        (ORDERNUM INTEGER,
         ORDCENT DECIMAL(2,0),
         ORDYR DECIMAL(2,0),
         ORDMO DECIMAL(2,0),
         ORDDA DECIMAL(2,0),
         CUSTOMER CHAR(10))
```

The table is meant the represent the order header records, obviously without all of the required data fields, of a legacy application. Wow, it's Y2K compliant, as it has a century flag! In this case, the century data contains a 19 if the century of the date is 1900 and a 20 if the century of the date is in 2000.

Insert the following records into the table:

```
INSERT INTO SQLBOOK.LEGACY VALUES (1,19,99,1,13,'JOHN');
INSERT INTO SQLBOOK.LEGACY VALUES (2,19,99,2,23,'JOHN');
INSERT INTO SQLBOOK.LEGACY VALUES (3,20,0,2,2,'JOHN');
INSERT INTO SQLBOOK.LEGACY VALUES (4,19,99,6,1,'BILL');
INSERT INTO SQLBOOK.LEGACY VALUES (5,20,0,1,10,'BILL')
```

Execute the following SQL to see how ugly your creation is (as shown in Figure 4.20):

```
SELECT * FROM SQLBOOK.LEGACY
```

The following query will convert the data in the respective date fields into an SQL date:

```
SELECT CUSTOMER, ORDERNUM,
        DATE( TRIM( CHAR( ORDMO )) || '/' ||
        TRIM( CHAR( ORDDA )) || '/' ||
        TRIM( CHAR(( ORDCENT * 100 ) +ORDYR)))
        FROM SQLBOOK.LEGACY
```

Data Window

	ORDERNUM	ORDCENT	ORDYR	ORDMO	ORDDA	CUSTOMER
1	1	19.00	99.00	1.00	13.00	JOHN
2	2	19.00	99.00	2.00	23.00	JOHN
3	3	20.00	0.00	2.00	2.00	JOHN
4	4	19.00	99.00	6.00	1.00	BILL
5	5	20.00	0.00	1.00	10.00	BILL

Figure 4.20: Here are the results of selecting data from the ugly legacy table.

The results of this query are shown in Figure 4.21. The function works by using the CHAR function to turn the DECIMAL(2,0) columns into character columns, and then concatenates the columns together into the string representation of a date. (The || operator is equivalent to the CONCAT function.) The DATE function is then used on the resultant string to transform the string into an AS/400 date data type. You could use this function within a view, and then perform aggregations over the resulting columns in the view.

Data Window

	CUSTOMER	ORDERNUM	00003
1	JOHN	1	01/13/1999
2	JOHN	2	02/23/1999
3	JOHN	3	02/02/2000
4	BILL	4	06/01/1999
5	BILL	5	01/10/2000

Figure 4.21: You can transform legacy dates to AS/400 date types.

SQL Durations

As shown in chapter 2, timestamps and dates can be added and subtracted from each other using SQL. The result is something truly awful called a *duration*. A duration represents the duration between timestamps in the form years, months, days, hours, minutes, seconds, and microseconds. IBM loves the duration, but most other SQL databases return this value as a floating-point value, where the left side of the decimal represents the number of days between the timestamps and the right side represents the day part difference in microseconds. Although I like this form better because you can get a lot more creative with it, you can still do a lot of stupid date tricks with durations. Table 4.2 shows the scalar functions that deal with durations.

Table 4.2: Duration Scalar Functions	
DAY(X-Y)	Returns the difference in days between the date or timestamp values X and Y as an integer.
MONTH(X-Y)	Returns the difference in months between the date or timestamp values X and Y.
YEAR(X-Y)	Returns the difference in years between the date or timestamp values X and Y.
HOUR(X-Y)	Returns the difference in hours between the time or timestamp values X and Y.
MINUTE(X-Y)	Returns the difference in minutes between the time or timestamp values X and Y.
SECOND(X-Y)	Returns the difference between the time or timestamp values X and Y in hours.
MICROSECOND(X-Y)	Returns the difference between the time or timestamp values X and Y in microseconds.

Before looking at any more queries, consider how durations are internally represented. If both data types are dates in an expression, a duration is returned as a DECIMAL(8,0) number. The first 4 bytes represent the number of years between the dates, the next 2 bytes are the number of months between the dates, and the last 2 bytes are the number of days between the dates.

If both data types are times, a time duration is returned. A time durations is a DECIMAL(6,0) number, where the first 2 bytes represent hours between the data, the next 2 bytes are minutes between the data, and the last 2 bytes are the seconds

114

between the data. Finally, if either data type is a timestamp, then the duration is returned as a timestamp duration. A timestamp duration is a DECIMAL(20,6) number, which is the result of a date duration concatenated with a time duration. The six positions after the decimal point represent the number of microseconds between the durations.

Now that you know this, consider how to put it to use. Here is a query that returns the number of minutes a visitor spent at a Web site within one date (as shown in Figure 4.22):

```
SELECT REQUSER, DATE(REQTS) AS VIEWDATE,
          ( ( SECOND( MAX(REQTS) - MIN(REQTS) ) )  / (60 * 1.00 ) )
          + MINUTE(MAX(REQTS) - MIN(REQTS) )
          + HOUR( MAX(REQTS) - MIN(REQTS) ) * 60 AS "TOTAL TIME"
          FROM SQLBOOK.WEBTEMP
          GROUP BY REQUSER, DATE(REQTS)
```

	REQUSER	VIEWDATE	TOTAL TIME
1	1	10/04/1999	0.15
2	1	10/07/1999	0.38
3	1	10/15/1999	32.67
4	2	10/01/1999	0.07
5	2	10/05/1999	1.88
6	2	10/08/1999	0.00
7	3	10/08/1999	0.62
8	4	10/09/1999	1,130.68
9	5	10/12/1999	0.77
10	6	10/14/1999	2.28
11	6	10/18/1999	780.15
12	6	10/19/1999	52.23

Figure 4.22: In this output of the duration query, the third column indicates the number of minutes and (decimal) seconds the user spent on the site for the day value in column 2.

This query has some problems. If a user visits twice in one day, the query calculates the time from the first hit in the day to the last hit in the day. If there were a session identifier in the table that uniquely identified the user session, the query could be based on the combination of the user and the session identifier to accurately time an individual's visits. However, the query does show you how to manipulate differences between timestamps as durations.

Because the query is grouped by REQUSER, then by DATE(REQTS), the MIN and MAX functions used are always grabbing the minimum and maximum timestamp within a one-day duration for a single user. MIN(REQTS) – MAX(REQTS) results in a timestamp duration. The SECOND( ) function recognizes that the value passed to it is a duration, not a timestamp, and correctly returns the number of seconds between the durations. The number of seconds is then divided by 60/1.00 to yield a decimal number. The 60/1.00 is a dodge to turn the number 60 into a decimal representation of 60. However, the SECOND function returns an integer. Therefore, if it is divided by 60, you will lose the decimal part of the division because both numbers are integers. (You could have used the DECIMAL( ) scalar function rather than dividing by 1.00.)

Next, the MINUTE scalar gets the number of minutes between the timestamps. Finally, the HOUR scalar yields the number of hours between the timestamps. This value is then multiplied by 60 to yield minutes, which are then added to the minutes and seconds. Bang. You have the time in minutes from first hit to last hit in one day! Cool.

Percent-to-Total Calculations

Managers love to see percent-to-total reports. Using common table expressions, you can effectively do these reports without resorting to creating a view. This query is another useful implementation I can think of for a cross join.

Suppose you get a request to do a report on warehouse inventory as a percent-to-total inventory. The following query will do that, using the UT1 and UT2 tables from the join examples. The results are shown in Figure 4.23.

```
SELECT WAREHOUSE, E.TOTAL AS TOTAL,
       SUM(ONHAND*PRICE) AS THISWAREHOUSE,
       SUM((ONHAND*PRICE)/E.TOTAL*100) AS PCTTOTAL
       FROM SQLBOOK.UTW,
       (SELECT SUM(ONHAND*PRICE) AS TOTAL FROM SQLBOOK.UT1,SQLBOOK.UTW
        WHERE ID=PID) AS E,
       SQLBOOK.UT1 AS F
       WHERE ID=PID
       GROUP BY WAREHOUSE, E.TOTAL
```

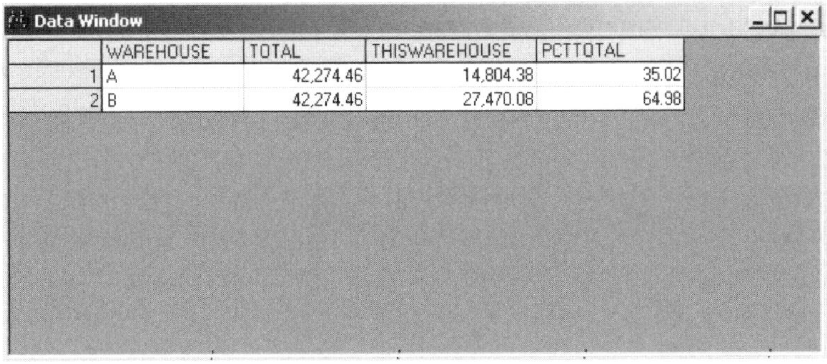

	WAREHOUSE	TOTAL	THISWAREHOUSE	PCTTOTAL
1	A	42,274.46	14,804.38	35.02
2	B	42,274.46	27,470.08	64.98

Figure 4.23: These are the results of the warehouse percent-to-total query.

This query implements a common table expression in order to derive TOTAL, which is the total dollars on hand in both warehouses. The TOTAL column is then used to show each warehouse total expressed as a percentage of the total on-hand dollars in all warehouses. Let's walk through this step by step.

First, if you executed the following query, you would receive the total on-hand dollars in all warehouses:

```
SELECT SUM(ONHAND*PRICE)
        FROM SQLBOOK.UTW, SQLBOOK.UT1
        WHERE ID=PID
```

This query joins the UTW warehouse table to the UT1 parts table on part ID, and sums the values of the ONHAND column times the PRICE column, resulting in the value 42,274.46, which is the total dollars of inventory on hand in all warehouses.

Next, you execute the following query to get the total dollars in each warehouse:

```
SELECT WAREHOUSE SUM(ONHAND*PRICE)
        FROM SQLBOOK.UTW, SQLBOOK.UT1
        WHERE ID=PID
        GROUP BY WAREHOUSE
```

This query returns two rows, one for warehouse A and one for warehouse B, by again joining the UTW and UT1 tables on the part ID columns, aggregating the sum of ONHAND times PRICE, and grouping the sum by the warehouse column. The results are 14,804.38 for warehouse A and 27,470.08 for warehouse B.

The percent-to-total calculation is quite simple (WAREHOUSETOTAL/ GRANDTOTAL)*100. So, the percent-to-total for warehouse A is 35.02 (148804.38/42,274.46) * 100, and the percent-to-total for warehouse B is 64.98, (27,470.08/42,274.46) * 100.

Using the common table expression, SQL is mimicking what you just walked through. First, SQL creates a table with only one row, which is the total on-hand dollars at all warehouses, and calls that table E. (This is done by the common table expression in the WHERE clause.) Next, SQL joins the files UT1 and UTW on the part ID column to produce a table that has columns from the warehouse and parts tables so that the statement can total the on-hand dollars for each warehouse. Finally, SQL joins the results of the two joined tables to the single row returned from the common table expression so that the TOTAL field can be included in each row returned by the query.

Notice that this is the other use for a Cartesian product (cross join). Because no criteria are specified to join the rows from UT1 and UTW to the E table, each row from E is joined to each row in the UT1, UTW join. This query only works because E only returns one row.

Play with this one a while and it will sink in.

Using a Three-Way Join with a Cross Join

Well, the boss loves your percent-to-total report, but now she wants to see each item in the warehouse, its percent to the total on-hand in the warehouse, and then its percent to the on-hand total of all warehouses. No problem.

To execute this query, you need information on total on-hand dollars for all warehouses, total on-hand dollars for this warehouse, and total on-hand dollars for each part. The following statement gets the total dollars for all parts at all warehouses:

```
SELECT SUM(ONHAND*PRICE) AS GT
        FROM SQLBOOK.UT1,SQLBOOK.UTW
        WHERE ID=PID
```

In order for the query to work, the GT column (which contains the total for all warehouses) needs to exist in each row of the query for the calculation.

The next query gets the total on hand for each warehouse:

```
SELECT WAREHOUSE AS WHN,SUM(ONHAND*PRICE) AS WT
        FROM SQLBOOK.UT1,SQLBOOK.UTW
        WHERE ID=PID
        GROUP BY WAREHOUSE
```

This query returns two rows: one for warehouse A and one for warehouse B. Notice that the query returns the WAREHOUSE column as a column named WHN. Finally, both of these queries can be combined as common table expressions within a query that will perform the required percent-to-total operations. Here is the final statement, with the results shown in Figure 4.24:

```
SELECT WAREHOUSE, DESCRIPTION,
        SUM(ONHAND*PRICE) AS PARTTOTAL,
        SUM((ONHAND*PRICE)/GTOTAL.GT*100) AS PCTGLOBAL,
        SUM((ONHAND*PRICE)/WHTOTAL.WT*100) AS PCTWAREHOUSE
        FROM SQLBOOK.UTW,
        (SELECT SUM(ONHAND*PRICE) AS GT
            FROM SQLBOOK.UT1,SQLBOOK.UTW
            WHERE ID=PID)
          AS GTOTAL,
        (SELECT WAREHOUSE AS WHN,SUM(ONHAND*PRICE) AS WT
          FROM SQLBOOK.UT1,SQLBOOK.UTW
          WHERE ID=PID
          GROUP BY WAREHOUSE)
          AS WHTOTAL,
        SQLBOOK.UT1 AS F
        WHERE ID=PID AND WHTOTAL.WHN=WAREHOUSE
        GROUP BY WAREHOUSE, DESCRIPTION
```

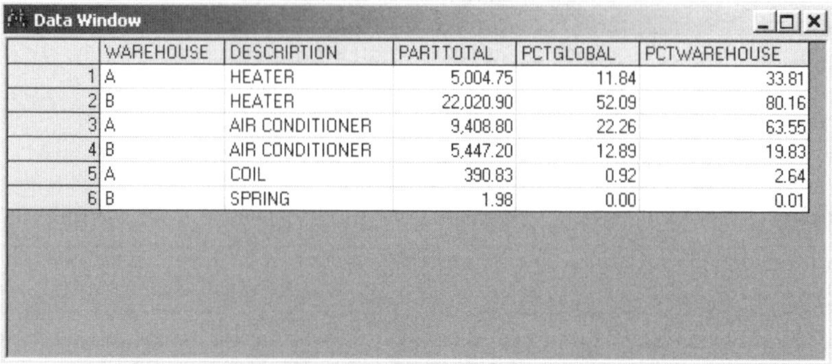

Data Window

	WAREHOUSE	DESCRIPTION	PARTTOTAL	PCTGLOBAL	PCTWAREHOUSE
1	A	HEATER	5,004.75	11.84	33.81
2	B	HEATER	22,020.90	52.09	80.16
3	A	AIR CONDITIONER	9,408.80	22.26	63.55
4	B	AIR CONDITIONER	5,447.20	12.89	19.83
5	A	COIL	390.83	0.92	2.64
6	B	SPRING	1.98	0.00	0.01

Figure 4.24: Here are the results of the warehouse/part percent-to-total. Notice HEATER in warehouse B is 52.09% of the global inventory onhand and 80.16% of warehouse B inventory onhand.

In essence, the query creates a table called WHTOTAL with two fields, one for the warehouse and one for the total on hand for that warehouse. It joins WHTOTAL to the UTW table, where the WHN (the renamed WAREHOUSE column) is equal to the WAREHOUSE column. Then, the results of that join are joined to the UT1 table where the part ID columns are equal. Finally, for each row resulting from that join, a cross join is implemented with the GTOTAL table, which places the GT column (the grand total of all the warehouses) in each resultant row. The results are then aggregated and should produce the data shown in Figure 4.24.

Creating Ranks from Data

One last neat thing that can be done with common table expressions is ranks. Suppose you want to categorize the activity on your Web site into three groups: LOW for days where hits are less than 100; MEDIUM for days where the hits are greater than 100 but less than 300; and HIGH for days where the activity is at or above 300. The following query with a common table expression will do this:

```
SELECT HITDATE,
         CASE WHEN TEMPRANK < 100 THEN 'LOW'
              WHEN TEMPRANK < 300 THEN 'MEDIUM'
              ELSE 'HIGH'
         END AS RANK
         FROM ( SELECT DATE(REQTS) AS HITDATE,COUNT(*) AS TEMPRANK
          FROM SQLBOOK.WEBTEMP2
           GROUP BY DATE(REQTS)) AS A
         ORDER BY 1
```

This query uses a common table expression to make a temporary table called A containing two columns (HITDATE and TEMPRANK). These columns are the date of the REQTS timestamp column and the sum of Web hits for that date. The outer query takes these results and uses a CASE statement to return the value LOW, MEDIUM, or HIGH based on the sum of hits (TEMPRANK) for the given day. Then, the outer query names this column RANK. The output looks like the results shown in Figure 4.25.

Data Window

	HITDATE	RANK
1	10/01/1999	MEDIUM
2	10/02/1999	MEDIUM
3	10/03/1999	MEDIUM
4	10/04/1999	MEDIUM
5	10/05/1999	MEDIUM
6	10/06/1999	MEDIUM
7	10/07/1999	MEDIUM
8	10/08/1999	MEDIUM
9	10/09/1999	LOW
10	10/10/1999	LOW
11	10/11/1999	MEDIUM
12	10/12/1999	MEDIUM

Figure 4.25: These are the results of the rank query. Notice that CASE enables aggregation for a set of values.

However, say the boss wants to know how many days you had each type of activity. Again, you can use the power of common table expressions and nest them to aggregate the results of the above query. Execute the following:

```
SELECT RANK,COUNT(*) AS NUMDAYS FROM
          (SELECT HITDATE,
          CASE WHEN TEMPRANK <100 THEN 'LOW'
               WHEN TEMPRANK <300 THEN 'MEDIUM'
               ELSE 'HIGH'
          END AS RANK
          FROM ( SELECT DATE(REQTS) AS HITDATE,COUNT(*) AS TEMPRANK
           FROM SQLBOOK.WEBTEMP2
            GROUP BY DATE(REQTS)) AS A) AS B
          GROUP BY RANK
```

This query takes the output of the inner query, ranks each output value, and passes it to the higher query. The higher query, in turn, counts each time the rank values occur and aggregates the data to produce the output shown in Figure 4.26

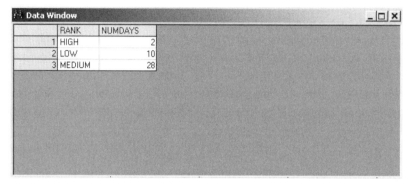

Figure 4.26: The result of the nested rank query shows the number of days the Web site experienced each rank of traffic.

Chapter Summary

This chapter has exposed you to the concepts of joins, unions, and some really cool queries. These queries should give you ideas on how you can use SQL at your own shop. Here are the concepts to take away from this chapter:

- Tables can be joined to other tables of similar data types.

- The AS/400 supports inner, outer, exception, and cross joins.

- UNION is used to put the results of two SELECT statements together.

- UNION ALL is the only way to avoid retrieving distinct data from a union.

- Dates and times can be used in arithmetic and can return durations.

- Scalar functions can be used in GROUP BY, but sometimes you need a view due to AS/400 SQL limitations.

- Common table expressions can be used as temporary views.

- Ranks can be generated using common table expressions.

5

CURSORS, TRANSACTIONS, JOURNALS, AND LOCKING

Before you can understand locking and transaction control, you need to know about *cursors*. A cursor is like a pointer to the row where an SQL statement is currently positioned. In some programming environments, like CLI, ODBC, JDBC, or OLEDB, you can move the cursor forward and backward through the results returned from an SQL SELECT statement. In addition, you can perform an operation called a *positioned update*. A positioned update instructs DB/2 to change the record at the current position of the cursor. There is more information on cursor manipulation in chapter 7, but all you need to know is the basic concept for now. Cursors are important because they affect record-locking behavior in an SQL application. Let's examine cursors by walking through how they can be used.

Cursors

Suppose you are creating a program that debits funds from budget accounts. Your budget table has columns for the account number, the name of the account, and the current balance. You need to enforce the rule that a budget account can never contain a negative number. The best way to enforce this rule is through a constraint on the current balance column. In this example, pretend that your boss, Bluto, is afraid of constraints and wants you to do it programmatically.

This requires you to read the record, determine if funds are available for the debit, and then update the record. You can do this most efficiently via a cursor. In your host-programming environment, you can set up the SQL SELECT statement that will read the record and name the statement CURSOR1. Executing that statement causes the record to be read and, as a side effect, a cursor points at the current row position on the AS/400. You can then verify that the funds are available and issue the following SQL statement to update the row:

```
UPDATE <budget-table-name> SET <balance-column> = <new-balance>
        WHERE CURRENT OF CURSOR1
```

This statement will perform the update to the target table against the current position of the SQL statement identified as CURSOR1. This process is outlined in Figure 5.1.

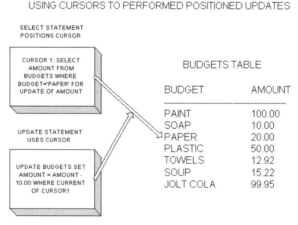

Figure 5.1: A positioned update can be accomplished with a cursor.

A statement qualifies for a positioned update if it doesn't use aggregate functions. For now, that's it for cursor information. It's a pointer to the current row in a SELECT. You also can use cursors to position DELETE statements. Here's the syntax for a positioned delete:

```
DELETE FROM <table-name> WHERE CURRENT OF CURSOR1
```

Transaction Control on the AS/400

To be considered an SQL database, the database must provide for transactions against its tables. In IBM speak, a transaction is called a *unit of work*. If an error is encountered during the processing of a unit of work, the programmer can elect to issue a ROLLBACK statement. The ROLLBACK causes all database changes since the beginning of the unit of work to be backed out of the database. If the unit of work is successful, the programmer issues a COMMIT statement to cause all of the database changes to become permanent. COMMIT and ROLLBACK help ensure that a set of changes to a database has integrity.

Journals and Receivers

On the AS/400, transactions against the database are accomplished via the use of journals. If you used CREATE DATABASE or CREATE COLLECTION to create a library on your AS/400, a journal called QSQJRN was created in the library. All tables created in the library are automatically journaled to the QSQJRN journal. Even if a library on the AS/400 was not created using CREATE DATABASE or CREATE COLLECTION, tables would be automatically journaled if a journal called QSQJRN existed in the library.

If you have a legacy library and want to add journaling, you can create a journal in the library called QSQJRN using the Create Journal command (CRTJRN). Once the journal is created, any new tables created in the library will automatically be journaled to it. To make legacy tables journaled, you need to execute the Start Journal Physical File command (STRJRNPF) against each file that you want to journal. Conversely, you can turn off journaling for a file using the End Journaling Physical File command (ENDJRNPF) against that file.

For journals to work, they need special files called *journal receivers*. A journal receiver contains records for all changes made to all files associated with the journal to which it is attached. Another use for journal receivers is as *audit files*. Because all changes are recorded in them, they can be reviewed when you need to find who made database changes and when those changes were made. Figure 5.2 shows the output of the Display Journal command (DSPJRN). The screen is limited to only journal entries made against the LOCKTEST table in the SQLBOOK library. The following command invokes the display:

```
DSPJRN JRN(SQLBOOK/QSQJRN) FILE((SQLBOOK/LOCKTEST))
```

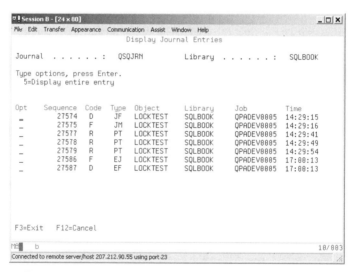

Figure 5.2: Here are all of the journal entries for the LOCKTEST table. Using option 5, you can inspect the database changes that were made.

Definition of a Transaction

In SQL, a transaction consists of all events that take place between COMMIT and ROLLBACK statements. When a program starts, the first time it touches something in the database, whether just reading or changing data, is considered the beginning of a transaction. This moment is called a *checkpoint*. Changes from one checkpoint to the next checkpoint are not made permanent until a COMMIT is executed. If a ROLLBACK is received during the processing of the transaction, all changes will be undone by backing out the journal entries from that moment to the last checkpoint. A ROLLBACK is also considered a checkpoint.

A side effect of COMMIT and ROLLBACK is that all record locks that have been created by the database manager are released. Before you can really understand transactions, the subject of record locks and how SQL controls those locks must be dealt with. SQL controls record locking through the isolation level of the program.

Isolation Levels and Locking

One of the really nice things about SQL is that you do not have to worry about placing record locks on table rows; SQL does this automatically for you. The way that SQL places record locks on rows in tables depends on the isolation level that was in place when the SQL statement was invoked. The isolation level determines how SQL statements from your program "get along" with the other programs and statements concurrently running on the AS/400. In fact, this is called *concurrency* in SQL lingo.

There are five isolation levels available on the AS/400. Here they are, in order, from least restrictive to most restrictive:

- No Commit (NC)
- Uncommitted Read (UC)
- Cursor Stability (CS)
- Read Stability (RS)
- Repeatable Read (RR)

At the most restrictive level, everything your program reads is locked until you issue a COMMIT or ROLLBACK. At the lowest isolation level, locks are released as soon as the data is read, and no commitment control is allowed (COMMIT and ROLLBACK have no effect) because changes are committed as soon as the statement completes execution. In fact, you can only change non-journaled tables if your SQL statement is executed in the lowest isolation level (NC).

As a programmer, you have to choose the appropriate level of isolation that your program needs in order to successfully operate. Choosing an isolation level too low will not allow you to roll back changes to the database or might cause your program to fail because data changes between the time you read it and the time you update a record. Conversely, choosing an isolation level too high might result in other applications not being able to read records from the database because your program has the records locked. Using isolation levels correctly is an art. Let's look at each isolation level to see when and how you might use it.

No Commit (NC)

NC is the bottom of the totem pole as far as isolation levels go. Also, using No Commit means that you have no transaction control whatsoever. Each SQL statement is committed as soon as the statement finishes execution. Programs that use this isolation level should not expect the data to be consistent from one read to the next.

When would you use this isolation level? The answer is almost never. Because shared locks are thrown only when a row is read and then immediately released, you have no guarantee that some other program might not change data between the time you read the record and when you chose to update it. Therefore, this isolation level is inappropriate for any reports that require table consistency.

However, there is one important use of this isolation level, as far as the AS/400 is concerned. It is the only isolation level that allows you to update, insert, or delete records in non-journaled tables. Because you will be dealing with legacy tables that might not be journaled, you will have to use this isolation level if you want to change data in these tables. If consistency does not matter to a report or query, then this isolation level is appropriate, as it offers the least contention.

Uncommitted Read (UR)

The UR isolation level is one step up the ladder from No Commit. It does not lock any records that you read from the database, but it does allow you to have transactional control (support of COMMIT and ROLLBACK). It also has a nasty side effect: You can read changes that others have made to database tables even if those changes have not been committed by other applications. In SQL, these are called *dirty reads*. Let's consider how they can affect your program.

Say you are writing a transaction-processing program for a bank. The program will transfer money from one account to another. For the transaction to be successful, enough money must exist in the account from which the money is coming. Let's say your program is going to remove $25 from account A and place it in account B. Account A currently has a zero balance. Now, suppose that some application program credits account A the sum of $50, but has not yet committed the transaction. Your program is running in UR isolation. So, when it reads the account information, it sees that $50 is available (even though the transaction of the other program is not committed). This can be a bad thing if you need information to be consistent.

UR should only be used if you need transaction support, but do not need consistency between database reads.

Cursor Stability (CS)

Cursor stability is where you start getting serious about consistency and record locking. Using CS isolation guarantees that you won't get dirty reads. In addition, the row that any SQL SELECT statement is currently positioned at is locked by the database, as long as the SQL statement qualifies for positioned update.

In addition, CS ensures that you do not read records that have not been committed by other applications. Finally, CS makes sure that you cannot read records that have been locked by other applications.

When do you use CS? I use it any time I need to look up and lock an individual record (not a set of records). For example, suppose you have a table of sequence numbers called SEQID in the library SQLBOOK. You can use the table to generate unique identifiers for records in your database. The table has two columns, ID and VAL, where ID is a character sequence identifier and VAL is the current sequence number as an integer. You might use the SQL and pseudocode shown in Figure

5.3 to retrieve the next number and lock the record, and then issue the next statement to update the value.

```
<make connection and select cursor stability as isolation level>

SET TRANSACTION ISOLATION LEVEL CS

<prepare the following SQL statement>

SELECT VAL+1 FROM SQLBOOK.SEQID WHERE VAL='WORKORDER'
FOR UPDATE OF VAL WITH CS

<name SQL statement C1>
<Execute SQL statement C1>
<Fetch value of first column>
<prepare another SQL statement>

UPDATE SQLBOOK.SEQID SET VAL=? WHERE CURRENT OF C1

<Bind parameter value into the parameter marker>
<Execute statement>

COMMIT
```

Figure 5.3: This pseudocode might be executed to get the next sequence number from a table of sequence numbers.

This logic would, of course, have to be executed in some programming language like C or RPG. It also could be done from another platform like a PC running an Excel macro. The point of the example is that it locks minimal resources in getting the next ID number. Chapter 7 descibes a stored procedure that retrieves ID numbers from a database and uses CS isolation.

Read Stability (RS)

Read Stability goes a little further than cursor stability by locking every row that you read with an SQL statement. This ensures that any row you read cannot be changed by another application until after your transaction is committed. Like CS, it also ensures that you cannot read uncommitted changes made by other applications. The only downside to CS and RS isolation levels is that they both still allow *phantom rows*.

A phantom row occurs when you read a set of data, someone adds a record to the set, and then your application rereads the set of data and sees the new record. This is not usually a problem in application design, but you should be aware that it could happen.

When I am programming crucial sections of code and need to ensure that no one changes the data that I have read, I use the RS isolation level. It gives me locking assurance but does not throw table locks like the RR isolation level does.

Repeatable Read (RR)

Repeatable Read is the most restrictive isolation level. Everything you read is locked by SQL automatically placing a table lock on any tables you touch. Phantom rows cannot exist in RR because nobody can insert data into the table until your transaction finishes. You need to be really careful using RR isolation because of how locks are thrown in it. I almost never use RR in my application development. If I do, I ensure that the transaction is initiated and then committed quickly so as not to interfere with other users and programs on the box.

Changing Isolation Levels and Controlling Locks

Now that you have the concept of transactions and isolation levels, I'm going to show you some tricks on how to control record-locking behavior regardless of your isolation level. But first, how do you change the isolation level? This can be accomplished in several ways, depending on where you are running your SQL application. For example, a PC program using ODBC to connect to the AS/400 could use the ODBC functions that control the ODBC environment to change isolation level. Alternatively, the programmer could forgo those functions and issue the following SQL statement to cause the isolation level to change:

```
SET TRANSACTION ISOLATION LEVEL CS
```

A program written in RPG on the AS/400 could be compiled to use an isolation level of RR, but then execute the above statement during runtime and cause the isolation level to change.

On the AS/400, isolation level can be changed only at a *commitment control boundary*. This is the time between issuing a COMMIT or ROLLBACK and the subsequent touching of the database. Once you touch the database, you are in another transaction and cannot change isolation level until the next commit boundary. Figure 5.4 illustrates the concept of commitment control boundaries.

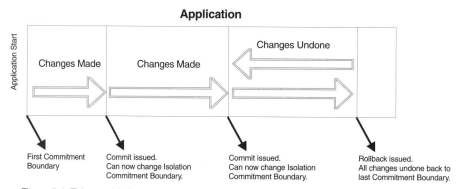

Figure 5.4: This graphic illustrates how COMMIT and ROLLBACK affect commitment control boundaries.

However, you can change the isolation level on an individual statement level and influence locking behavior by using extensions to the SQL grammar. The first extension is the FOR UDPATE OF clause that you can add to a SELECT statement.

Example of Locking Records

To see how record locks work, start by creating a table called LOCKTEST in the library SQLBOOK on your AS/400. The table should have two columns: A, a CHAR(1) column, and B, an integer. The following statement will create the table:

```
CREATE TABLE SQLBOOK.LOCKTEST
            (A CHAR(1), B INTEGER);
```

Insert the following rows into your table:

```
INSERT INTO SQLBOOK.LOCKTEST VALUES ('A',1);
INSERT INTO SQLBOOK.LOCKTEST VALUES ('B',2)
```

Finally, go to the options panel in SQLThing (by choosing Environment, then Options Panel), clear the Auto Commit check box, and click Save Options. This will ensure that you can use transactions by turning off the ODBC Auto Commit feature. Auto Commit means that after each statement is executed in the SQL Editor window, a COMMIT is automatically issued by ODBC. Because I want to show you how locks are managed through commitment boundaries, this feature needs to be disabled.

Type in the following SQL statement to move to the CS isolation level:

```
SET TRANSACTION ISOLATION LEVEL CS
```

Next, issue the following SQL statement to ensure a lock is thrown on the record you are reading:

```
SELECT * FROM SQLBOOK.LOCKTEST
           WHERE A='A'
           FOR UPDATE OF B
```

Now, from a 5250 terminal-emulation session, issue the following command to see the locks on the LOCKTEST file (as shown in Figure 5.5):

```
DSPRCDLCK FILE(SQLBOOK/LOCKTEST)
```

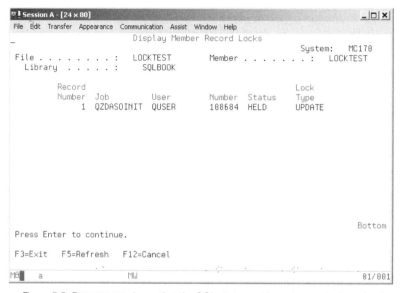

Figure 5.5: DSPRCDLCK shows that the SQL statement has placed a lock on the first record in the LOCKTEST table

This lock will stay active until the next commitment boundary. Flip back to SQLThing and select Environment→Commit to cause ODBC to issue a COMMIT. Then, switch back to your 5250 session and press F5 to refresh the screen. You will notice that the lock that was issued against the first record in the LOCKTEST table has now been released. Locks are always released at commitment-control boundaries unless you use the KEEP LOCKS statement.

More on Controlling Isolation Levels

Suppose your program is in NC or NS isolation, but you need to throw a lock on a record so that you can ensure that it is not changed. The following statement reads a record from the table LOCKTEST and ensures a lock is placed:

```
SELECT * FROM SQLBOOK.LOCKTEST
          WHERE A='Z'
          FOR UPDATE OF A
```

If you want, after executing the statement, you could run the Display Record Locks command (DSPRCDLCK) to view the locks placed against records in the table.

Say your application is in RR isolation, and you need to read values out of a table, but do not want to throw locks on the records you read. Adding FOR READ ONLY to the end of a SELECT statement will ensure no locks are thrown. In addition, if any records are locked in the target table, you will be able to read them because of the FOR READ ONLY clause.

Another extension that can be added to the end of a SELECT is the WITH clause. WITH allows you to change the isolation level for the duration of the statement. Here is an example:

```
SELECT * FROM SQLBOOK.LOCKTEST
        WHERE A='Z'
        WITH CS
```

This statement would be executed using CS isolation, even though the application is in NC isolation. In addition to the WITH clause is the capability to specify the keywords KEEP LOCKS. KEEP LOCKS causes all read locks to be held for the duration of the SQL statement. It can only be used with isolation levels CS and above. Here is an example:

```
SELECT * FROM SQLBOOK.LOCKTEST
        WITH CS KEEP LOCKS
```

A side effect of the execution of this statement is that all records in the table will be locked. Even though CS isolation implies that only the record at the current cursor position is locked, KEEP LOCKS causes record locks to be retained until the next commitment boundary.

Designing Applications with Commitment Control

The most important thing about designing SQL-based applications is dealing with locking and transaction issues. The system is always a tradeoff between access and resource contention issues. More restrictive isolation levels cause more resource contention among programs. This can lead to user frustration. Less restrictive isolation levels can cause data in the database to become invalid due to phantom rows or dirty reads. All of these issues need to be taken into account when designing an application.

The main thing to keep in mind is that transaction span should be kept as short as possible when in higher isolation levels. Look at the application and decide where the crucial processing points are. Only use the higher isolation levels if the application absolutely must have them. By keeping the time your application spends in the higher isolation levels to a minimum, you will get better throughput and more satisfied users.

Designing Applications without Commitment Control

Because you might have to deal with a legacy application that does not use commitment control, a discussion of that topic is appropriate at this point. The problem with journals is that they were not originally part of the AS/400. Therefore, many legacy applications do not use journaling against their physical files.

Also, most RPG and COBOL AS/400 legacy applications were written with the idea that the code could not fail. This is due in part to the AS/400 being such a robust platform. Those systems are all hosted on a single integrated platform and multiple database writes from terminal emulation sessions are usually batched during a single program process. The terminal data was probably good, because programmers wrote code to ensure that any parts added to orders existed in the parts table, or that quantities were positive numbers, etc. Programmers also had a lot of control over the order in which operations were performed. They could ensure that the user performed step A, then B, and finally C.

In the Web world, you don't have control over the order of operations that the client initiates. Also, clients can bookmark pages and jump past steps you might want them to perform. Whether your SQL applications are client/server, Web, or n-tiered, you are now running from multiple platforms and adding points of failure to your system. What if the TCP/IP link goes down during a transaction? What if the Web server crashes during order posting? What if a user turns off the

PC while writing an order? These were not questions you had to answer when writing legacy applications, but they are things you have to deal with under the Web and client/server models. (Big posterior pain problem, if you ask me.)

All is not lost, as there are ways you can design interfaces to your legacy system to minimize the fact that you have no commitment control. It takes a little forethought, but the process is not that hard. To show you one possible way, let's look at a simple order entry system without commitment control, discuss the failure points, and then see how to minimize them.

The Victim Application

Our "victim application" is a legacy order-entry system that does not support journaling. The following files are on the system: order header, order detail, and branch item master. This is a batch-oriented system for updating accounting and other tables, but some quantity information is adjusted at the time an order is placed into the system. The legacy terminal application allows a user to define an order, add items to the order, and then post the order. During posting, the order header is written, and then each item on the order is posted to the order detail table. As each item is posted, the quantity on hand in the warehouse-item master table is debited by the quantity ordered. It is a really simple system, but very effective, and has served the company well for over 10 years.

The Trouble with Web Apps

Suppose you had to design a Web interface to this system. Web interfaces can present you with a lot of problems. A Web application is usually multiplatform; it might be running on a Linux box, an AIX box running WebSphere, Windows 2000 using Internet Information Server, etc. The simple fact is that it is probably not running on the AS/400. Even if it is, that does not make it immune to failure.

Also, the Web application might be running in Java or using technology like Active Server Pages and communicating via SQL. There can be inadvertent bugs in the application code that can cause it to crash, unexpected record-locking issues that can cause it to halt, or communication-link failures that can cause half an order to be written. These are all bad news. Remember that Web applications are new and have not been time-tested like the legacy system. You are putting more moving parts between your data and your user. More moving parts add up to more points of failure. If you had commitment control, these would not be an issue because a half-posted order would automatically be rolled back by the AS/400. But that is a perfect world and this is not.

Design of the Application

The first design of the Web order-entry system that interfaces with the legacy system would probably store the parts a user is selecting in a database table on the AS/400. Because Web applications have no inherent state, items that a user selects must be written in a physical file so that the application can remember what the user has selected for purchase. As the user selects items and specifies quantities, the items are written to the table under that user's ID, but no quantity adjustments are made. (This is just like the legacy application, except that the legacy system probably does not write to a file on the AS/400. It just keeps them in memory.)

When the user finally is finished working on the order, either today or next week, he or she presses a button to initiate processing of the order. The Web code validates each part, and then writes the order header record to the target physical file using SQL INSERT statements. It then proceeds to write each item detail to its respective physical file and adjusts the warehouse-item master quantities. All this is done by executing SQL statements. When all parts are processed, the Web app deletes all of the parts from the table used to keep order state, as those parts are now part of an order. If this code completes, you have a good order posted to the host system and are ready for the user to do another.

However, if you have a failure at any time during this crucial processing, there is no way to undo the order. What if the router goes down during the writing of the detail records? What if the server runs out of memory and halts? What if the order is posted, but the state table is not cleaned up, and the user processes the order again? You have no control in these situations; you are relying on the "byte gods" to ensure that your data gets where it is going. Bad design. This is a vital area of processing that has multiple modes of failure waiting to swoop down and wreck your evening.

You need to identify the crucial failure portions of your application. Then, you have to look at how to minimize the communications required to perform the operations. You want to have one point of call to cause the order to be processed. Once that call is made, you are ensured that the order is either posted completely or nothing happens at all.

Minimizing Failure

My approach to this problem effectively removes all failure points in the process of posting the order. The biggest point of failure is during the writing of the order records to the physical files and updating the quantities. The solution is to write to empty copies of the physical files in QTEMP, and then call a stored procedure for final processing. These QTEMP targets can be made using COPY FILE. It doesn't matter if you are using JDBC, ODBC, or ADO from the client application, as you can always execute any AS/400 command as if it were a stored procedure. (Chapter 7 has more about stored procedures.)

Executing the following command would cause an empty copy of the order header file to be written to QTEMP:

```
CPYF FROMFILE(SQLBOOK/ORDHDR) TOFILE(QTEMP/ORDHDR) CRTFILE(*YES)
```

Executing the command again creates copies of the detail tables and other required tables in the QTEMP library. After making the empty copies, the Web application posts the order header and detail records to the QTEMP copies using the same INSERT statements it would have used to write to the target physical files. Finally, the Web application calls a stored procedure on the AS/400. This stored procedure could be written in CL, RPG, or COBOL. The stored procedure's goal is to update the quantities on hand in the warehouse-item master table, and then copy the data from the QTEMP physical files to the target physical files in the production system. Moving the data could be accomplished with a simple copy/append operation using the CPYF command. Finally, the AS/400 program removes the state records from the state table so that the user is in a clean, new order. Once the procedure is finished, it returns a variable to the calling application to let it know that the operation is complete (possibly returning the order number for the new order).

The beauty of this approach is that the only point of crucial failure now resides on the AS/400. Using this method, if your application fails during the writing of temporary files, who cares? The temporary files will be automatically deleted by the AS/400 because they are in QTEMP. What if the application call writes all of the temporary files, and then calls the stored procedure, but fails before the procedure completes and returns control to the calling program? No problem; the procedure will complete, and then it will attempt to return data to the calling program. The data return will fail, but the results of the procedure will still be complete.

Living without commitment control is like living without coffee or Jolt cola. It can be done, but it takes some adjustments to your mode of thinking. Chapter 7 outlines how to create a program on the AS/400 that can be called via SQL. If you need to interact with legacy data, I suggest you give this chapter careful consideration.

Chapter Summary

In this chapter, you learned about record locking, transactions, and isolation levels on the AS/400. You should understand the following:

- SQL automatically issues locks. Locks depend on the isolation level of the program.

- Isolation levels cannot be changed except on a commitment boundary.

- Locks are released when a COMMIT or ROLLBACK occurs.

- NC is the only isolation level that can change non-journaled tables.

- Transactions in high isolation levels should be as short as possible.

- Stored procedures can be used to encapsulate business logic.

6

DEBUGGING SQL STATEMENTS AND ENHANCING PERFORMANCE

This chapter introduces you to the AS/400 query optimizer and explains how to inspect its output. The query optimizer controls how the AS/400 gets the data you ask for in queries. It is usually a smart feature, but sometimes it makes mistakes. You'll see how to interpret what the optimizer says and discover techniques for enhancing SQL performance based on that data. In addition, other performance issues are discussed, along with tips on garnering the most performance from your SQL applications.

The Query Optimizer—Fundamentals

Ever wonder what's going on when your SQL statement is executed? How does the AS/400 turn your statement into a program that gets the data efficiently from the database? The answer is the query optimizer.

SQL is an interpreted language. When you execute an SQL statement, a parser takes apart the statement to determine the files you want to access, the columns you want to retrieve, and the search conditions you want to satisfy. The parser then uses the query optimizer to examine available access paths to determine the best way to get your data. Understanding how the optimizer works is a key to diagnosing SQL performance problems.

The AS/400 employs a *cost-based optimizer*. This means that the optimizer looks at each different way to access the data and makes a metric called *implementation cost*. Once the optimizer has looked at all ways to get the data, it chooses the method with the smallest implementation cost.

Access Paths

Access paths are ways that the AS/400 can get to your data. Three different access paths are possible on the AS/400:

- Find records by reading the table directly (table scans).
- Find records by using an index (a logical file).
- Find records using Encoded Vector Indexes.

As you know from chapter 1, an index is a logical file on the AS/400. An Encoded Vector Index (EVI) is a new entity that was introduced in V4R3. For now, just think of EVIs as another type of logical file. The main point is that the AS/400 has only three ways to get at data when a query is run. The optimizer will choose one of these access paths and then choose an access method appropriate for that access path. The following sections review the access methods available to each access path, and describe their pluses and minuses.

Table Scans

The table-scan method requires reading all of the data in the file. If the file is not large, this is not a problem. However, if the file contains a lot of records, this is not the preferred access method. Typically, the optimizer will choose to use the table scan if it estimates that the query will return more than 20 percent of the records in the physical file.

Table scans can be really efficient because they minimize I/O when selecting large amounts of data. It sounds backwards, but it is true because database rows are stored in pages. The AS/400 will retrieve a page in one I/O request and, therefore, have all of the rows on that database page in memory. In addition, table scans allow the AS/400 to use asynchronous I/O to efficiently load the pages into RAM. This really boosts the performance of a table-scan query in getting the data into the processing area.

Remember, the heart of a table scan is the fact that you have to read each record in the database, examine the record, and if it meets the selection criteria, move it into a storage area. Once the scan is complete, you copy the records in the storage area back to the client as a result set. Note that you are using temporary storage to hold the intermediate result set until it is ready for the client application.

To understand query performance and resource utilization during a table scan, you need to understand how the AS/400 decides if the records it just read need to be in the result set or not. The AS/400 uses two algorithms during the record examination process: *derived selection* and *dataspace selection*. The dataspace selection algorithm is really efficient, while derived record selection can take a lot of processor and I/O resources (so you should avoid it if possible). Derived selection is required when the selection criteria contain information that must be derived from database columns. Here is when derived selection will be used:

- If the query uses selection criteria values that contain scalar operations, such as WHERE MONTH(DATECOL)=1.

- If the query is evaluating numeric values of different data types, such as WHERE INTEGERCOL = DECIMALCOL.

- If the query is evaluating a substring of a character column, such as WHERE SUBSTRING(CHARCOL),1,3)='HFA'.

- When VARCHAR columns are mentioned in the selection criteria, such as WHERE VARCHARCOL = 'FRED'.

- If, in comparing character columns to parameters, the length of the parameter passed is greater than the column length, such as WHERE CHAR2COL = 'OU '.

These are all situations to avoid if at all possible. Sometimes, it is possible to change your query so that the derived selection algorithm is not needed.

Parallel Table Prefetch

A parallel table prefetch is almost exactly the same as a table scan, except the AS/400 will use multiple input streams to read the table into RAM for processing. Remember that the query optimizer has a number that represents the time it thinks the query will use on CPU processing and also the time the query will spend reading records from the database (the input time). If the input time is greater than the CPU time, the AS/400 could elect to use parallel table prefetch to get the data.

However, several factors control whether the query actually gets to use this advanced method. This method causes the AS/400 to optimize the use of multiple disk arms in retrieving the data from the disks. It also uses more memory than a regular table scan. Therefore, having a lot of queries running at the same time as this method could have a negative impact on your performance. The AS/400 controls which queries are eligible for this method by examining the query options for the job and for the AS/400 system. The QQRYDEGREE system value controls whether this option can be used. Changing whether a job can use this method is invoked by using the CHGQRYA command and setting DEGREE to *ANY.

This option is great for nasty queries that need to read really big tables. Be very careful about its use, especially if your system is already tight on I/O. In addition, make sure that the expert object cache is set to on (*CALC) for the memory pool in which your database server or job is running.

The Role of Indexes

Indexes play an important role in SQL performance. They provide keyed access paths to get at data in a physical file. To the DB/2 optimizer, indexes are considered for record selection when a query uses table joins and result-set sorting or because of record-selection criteria in the queries where clause-matching fields are available in an index.

When the optimizer looks at the available indexes, it determines the selectivity of the index as it relates to your query. The selectivity of an index is a number that represents how many choices there are for each distinct key. The optimizer uses this number to estimate how many records will match your WHERE clause, and that helps determine the cost of using a particular index.

For example, let's say you have a transaction table of about 200,000 records. It has a CHAR(1) column called TRANSTYPE indicating whether each transaction is I (for *in*) or O (for *out*), and a CHAR(2) column called STATE indicating the state where the transaction occurred. If an index were created on the TRANSTYPE value alone, it would not be very selective, as it only has two possible values for the set of 200,000 records. An index created with the STATE column plus the TRANSTYPE column would be more selective because it would have 100 possible values for selectivity (two possible transaction types and 50 possible state values).

The AS/400 uses the selectivity of the index to determine if that index will result in finding the data quicker than doing a table scan. The higher the selectivity of the index, the more weight that index gets when the optimizer selects it. Of course, the optimizer is also considering whether the keys of the index match the selection, join, or ordering criteria of the query.

It is important to understand a few key facts about the optimizer and DDS-created logical files being considered as indexes. First, if the DDS-based logical uses SELECT OMIT criteria, it might not be able to be used by the optimizer for retrieving results from the base table unless the SELECT OMIT coincides with the selection criteria in the WHERE clause. Second, if the DDS logical file is a multiformat logical file, it cannot be used by the optimizer or even read by an SQL SELECT statement.

Out of the logical files that are left, the optimizer examines the logicals in *creation descending order*. This means that the index created most recently is evaluated first. The AS/400 examines the columns available in the index to see if they match the sorting, grouping, or selection criteria of the query, and then calculates the selectivity factor and cost values for that index. The optimizer then moves to the next available index in the list and evaluates it until the list is exhausted or the optimizer runs out of time. As the AS/400 processes each index, it compares its cost to the previous index and keeps the best selection as its current access method.

When looking for performance problems, it is important to understand the optimizer time limit. The query optimizer has an internal time limit that controls how much time it will spend trying to figure out how to implement your query. If there are a lot of logical files attached to a physical file, the optimizer might exceed the allotted time before it has finished examining each available index. This might mean that an index that would make the query run really fast is not selected because the optimizer never got to it. (This causes the optimizer to fully evaluate all access paths for any SQL statements.)

The AS/400 could elect to create a temporary index for processing your query. It could also elect to make a temporary index derived from another logical file. There are many ways that the AS/400 can use indexes to retrieve data from your tables. Because it's outside the scope of this book, refer you to the IBM manual *DB2 UDB for AS/400 Database Performance and Query Optimization*, specifically chapter 2, "Data Access Paths and Methods." This manual is available online from the IBM AS/400 Web site.

Encoded Vector Indexes

With the advent of V4R3, a new type of index has been added to your arsenal of query response-time weapons, the Encoded Vector Index (EVI). A logical file, or regular index, on the AS/400 is always a binary radix tree. An EVI index is a bitmap of key values. These indexes are useful when executing a query, which could return a large number of values, because they can be scanned more efficiently.

The AS/400 will use an index only if it determines that the query will return less than 20 percent of the total number of records in the physical file. EVI indexes are useful for queries that will return or access between 20 percent and 60 percent of the data in a file. Above 60 percent, the AS/400 usually will elect to table scan. So, EVIs fill an important performance niche on the AS/400.

The heart of the EVI is a bitmap of values that represent whether the database record at that offset contains the value or not. Use the data in Table 6.1 as an example.

Table 6.1: Transactions in Physical File			
TRANSNUM	STATE	QUANTITY	PARTID
0001	FL	22	AB21
0002	FL	32	KL32
0003	TN	91	AB19
0004	FL	13	KL32
0005	FL	21	AB01
0006	TN	9	AB32
0007	WY	2	AB01

Table 6.1 contains seven rows of data. If a bitmap index were created on the STATE column, the result would conceptually look like Figure 6.1.

Notice the values in the bitmap column for the FL key. The first bit has a value of one, indicating that the record at offset 1 in the table has the key value. The third bit is zero, indicating that the record at offset 3 in the table does not have the key value. If you were to query the database for records where STATE equaled FL, the AS/400 could retrieve the bitmap and know the offsets for each FL record in the database.

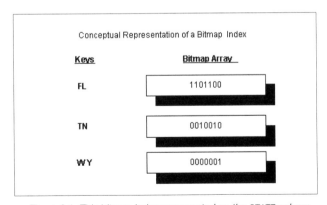

Figure 6.1: This bitmap index was created on the STATE column.

In addition, the bitmaps can be combined via a logical OR to find records with multiple values. For example, querying for a state equal to FL OR WY would return a bitmap of 1101101, which indicates that the records at offsets 1, 2, 4, 5, and 7 should be retrieved.

The problem with bitmap structures is that they take a lot of space. Let's say the example transaction table had 200,000 records, where all 50 states are referenced. The storage requirement for that bitmap index would be 10,000,000 bits (200,000 * 50). This can get unwieldy when you have a large number of distinct key values in a bitmap index. Bitmap structures also cause problems in updating data, as the index consists of X number of arrays of bits, where X is the number of distinct key values. Adding a lot of data to the database causes the arrays to be re-dimensioned and extended continually.

Enter the Vector

An advancement from IBM, EVI indexes allow all of the benefits of a bitmap index but do not have the storage overhead. Instead of using an array of bits for each key value, the AS/400 stores a single array of 1-, 2-, or 4-byte vectors. The number of vectors in the array is equal to the number of records in the table. Each distinct value in the database is given a vector as it is encountered, and each offset in the array contains the vector value that represents the column value stored in that record in the table. So, an EVI index is a combination of a table that maps keys to vectors and a single array representing the vector locations in the database.

Figure 6.2 shows a conceptual vector table for the transaction data in Table 6.1. When the AS/400 needs to find records using this index, it reads the table of vectors to retrieve the vector key for the column values it is searching, and then compares those values to each element in the vector array. This is quite speedy.

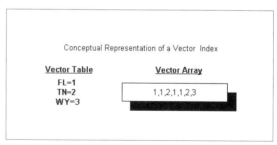

Figure 6.2: This represents the conceptual view of an EVI index over the data in Table 6.1.

The number of bytes required to represent the column data is directly related to the number of distinct values in the column. If the number of distinct values is less than 256, each vector will be only 1 byte. If the number of values is less than 32,768, each value can be represented using only 2 bytes. Database columns having more than 32,768 distinct values will be represented by 4-byte vectors.

The point of the EVI methodology is that it takes less space than the traditional bitmap index. In addition, the EVI is maintainable in a production environment, whereas bitmap indexes are notorious for causing problems. Another advantage of EVI indexes is that the AS/400 can combine multiple EVI indexes in memory when resolving a database query.

Suppose you have two EVI indexes on the transaction table shown in Table 6.1. The first index is on PARTID and the second is on STATE. Now, imagine executing the following query:

```
SELECT * FROM TRANSACTIONS WHERE STATE IN ('FL','MO','HI','CA')
             AND PARTID IN ('AB21', '2T36',"K201")
```

The query optimizer could choose to merge the two indexes together to get the result set. This merge can be very fast for statements that retrieve large numbers of records. Therefore, you need to play with EVI indexes on your large tables.

Creating EVI Indexes

EVI indexes can be created only through SQL or using Operations Navigator in Client Access. There is no way to create an EVI using DDS. Here is the syntax for creating a VCI index:

```
CREATE ENCODED VECTOR INDEX <IXNAME>
ON <TABLENAME> (<LIST-OF-COLUMNS>)
WITH <X> DISTINCT VALUES
```

The *<IXNAME>* will be replaced with the name of the index, *<TABLENAME>* will be replaced with the name of the table to index, and *<LIST-OF-COLUMNS>* will be replaced with a list of columns to index. The *<X>* should be replaced with a number that represents the distinct values you think this index will have. This number allows the AS/400 to determine the size of the vector required in the index ahead of time.

Getting Optimizer Information

At this point, you should have a basic understanding of what the optimizer does: It picks the way it is going to retrieve and process the data required to satisfy your query. It has many choices for how it can do this, and it tries to pick the best access path and method. Once it has chosen an access path and method, it stores this method and calls it an *access plan*.

Most of the time, the AS/400 query optimizer does a fine job creating access plans. Sometimes, though, it can be downright stupid. After all, it's just a program and does not have the intuitive knowledge of a human. Part of your job in SQL is to monitor the optimizer and deliver corrections when performance is not optimal. I call these situations "evil optimizer quirks." Several tools can help you root out evil optimizer quirks. Which ones you use depends on the type of program you are debugging.

The Print SQL Information utility (PRTSQLINF) can print the statements and optimization information from a program that was created using an SQL precompiler (like RPG, C, or COBOL). If you are diagnosing problems in a precompiler-based application, or just checking on optimization decisions, this is definitely the utility to use. The utility takes the name and library of the program to print, and creates a spool file of SQL statement and optimization messages.

PRTSQLINF also can be used to print SQL statements stored in SQL *package files*. Package files are created for client/server programs if the Enable Extended Dynamic box is checked on the configuration pages of the ODBC connection the client is using. Packages also are created for JDBC and OLEDB access and can be created for embedded SQL applications, too. Package files contain all of the queries that the application issued and the access plans for the queries. Again, the PRTSQLINF command will create a spool file describing the implementation of the queries stored in the package.

More information about statement optimizations can be obtained from the Start Debug (STRDBG) command. STRDBG causes all query optimizer messages to be written to the job log, which can then be viewed using the Display Job Log (DSPJOBLOG) command. This technique works particularly well for debugging ODBC, JDBC, and OLEDB client-server jobs. (Later in the chapter, you will see an example that uses STRDBG as a stored procedure so that optimizer information can be read.)

Another tool is the Start Database Monitor (STRDBMON) command, which will cause information collection on all SQL statements in all running programs to be written to a table. This table can then be viewed and sorted to retrieve optimization information and access path suggestions. I find this method is useful only when trying to diagnose overall system performance in shops that have large numbers of interactive query users. If you know the application causing the performance problem, one of the previous methods is better.

There is an interactive database monitor that you can navigate via Operations Navigator in Client Access Express. It basically gives all of the information that the STRDBMON process does, but the information is available as API calls. Therefore, you could write a custom program for viewing and interpreting the results. (This is not for the weak of heart, as "some assembly is required.")

Another tool to consider, and to watch in future releases of OS/400, is Visual Explain. Visual Explain is available via Operations Navigator's Run SQL Scripts function. This can be a neat way to graphically see the implementation of your query and get a lot of other useful information about query execution. This feature is available beginning in V4R5, and should be considered beta quality at this point.

Routinely, Visual Explain finds my queries too complex to explain or has trouble because I am using SQL features that are not implemented in Visual Explain. In addition, because Run SQL Scripts doesn't support parameterized queries, you might get incorrect optimization information from Visual Explain when using literals in your queries rather than parameter markers or host variables as you would in your production application. Incorrect optimization information won't always result, but keep the possibility in mind when using the tool.

Even with these drawbacks, there are some merits to using Visual Explain. Figure 6.3 shows a screen shot of the Visual Explain window after the Run SQL Scripts function digests a query that I fed to it. Note that the screen plainly shows that the target table will be accessed via an Index Scan with Key Positioning. Right-clicking on the Index Scan icon allows me to navigate to information about the queries target table, the index used, and query environment settings. Also, the windowpane to the right of the graphical icons represents a host of information that I would have to pore through the job log to ascertain about the implementation and timing of the query that I just executed.

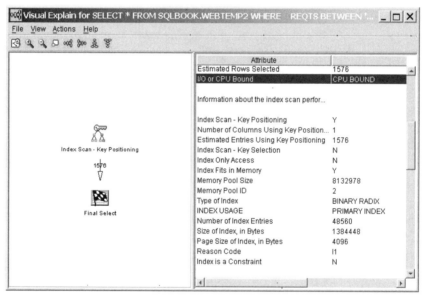

Figure 6.3: Visual Explain can help you understand the implementation of a query, but the AS/400 Job Log often yields more useful information.

This is a very promising tool, but I believe it's not quite ready to be your only information resource about query execution and optimization. In future releases of Operations Navigator, I am sure IBM will work to overcome some of the deficits of the Run SQL Scripts environment and continue to improve the Visual Explain interface. For now, you should learn how to interpret Job Log informational messages to gain insight into query performance and optimization.

Another tool worth mentioning is Database Essentials from Centerfield Technology. This tool interfaces with the database monitor and proprietary extensions on the AS/400 to gather information about runtime SQL usage.

Using the AS/400 Job Log

The AS/400 job log is my favorite source for information on how a query is processed. When a job is placed into debug mode, a wealth of information is kept in this area. I want to share with you a quite effective way to work with job log information that goes back to how I develop and test my SQL statements. I use a PC client interface like SQLThing. I basically use the tool to develop the statements, and it helps me diagnose performance problems by telling me how long the statement took to prepare, execute, and fetch records. I typically go through an interactive process of trying the statement, viewing the job log, and then retrying the statement with variations to see if I can influence the query optimizer.

Of course, for simple statements you might not do all of this, but let's walk through several queries so that you can take advantage of this technique. As you go through the returned optimizer information, you'll see how the query could be improved. After you have done a few of these exercises, you will begin to understand how to interpret the information in the job log and also gain insight in how queries are implemented on the AS/400. You also will see that the way you ask the question can be very important.

Getting Started

Before you can begin, make sure you have completed all of the steps in appendix C on loading the sample data and installing the SQLThing tool. In addition, you should have completed chapter 5, specifically where the WEBTEMP table is used to create the more relational table WEBTEMP2. Finally, these examples require more than just the 3,000 or so rows in the WEBTEMP2 table. To create more rows for optimization testing, issue the following SQL statements:

```
INSERT INTO SQLBOOK.WEBTEMP2
    SELECT REQTYPE, REQFILE, BROWSER,
    REQTS + 1 MONTH, REQSIZE, REQUSER, GEOID
    FROM SQLBOOK.WEBTEMP2;

INSERT INTO SQLBOOK.WEBTEMP2
    SELECT REQTYPE, REQFILE, BROWSER,
    REQTS + 2 MONTHS, REQSIZE, REQUSER, GEOID
    FROM SQLBOOK.WEBTEMP2
```

Your WEBTEMP2 table will now have about 12,000 rows of data. With this amount, you can begin to explore query performance issues.

If you have completed all of these tasks, you should be able to bring up the SQLThing program. Log into your AS/400 using the ODBC data source you set up by following the instructions in appendix C. Now open the File menu and select New to get a blank SQL interactive window. You are ready to begin.

Finding and Displaying Your Job

The first hurdle in getting to the job log is finding your job number. If you connect to the AS/400 through ODBC, JDBC, or OLEDB, your job is running in the QSERVER subsystem and has a job name of QZDASOINIT. Unfortunately, all of the QZDASOINIT jobs in the QSERVER subsystem have the same user name: QUSER. This makes using the Work Active Jobs (WRKACTJOB) command difficult to use in finding your target job.

Take a look at Figure 6.4, which is the output of the WRKACTJOB SBS(QSERVER) command. This command causes a listing of all jobs currently running in the QSERVER subsystem. Note that there are several QZDASOINIT jobs for user QUSER. This is because there is one job for each ODBC, OLEDB, and JDBC program currently connected to the AS/400. To actually find the job you are interested in, you would need to use option 5, to work with the job, then option 10 to see the actual AS/400 user profile that is logged in. You would have to repeat this for all listed jobs until you found the one you wanted. This is further complicated by the fact that many Web-based programs use the same user profile to connect to the AS/400 for all of their data requests. You could potentially have hundreds of jobs with the same user profile listed in the job log.

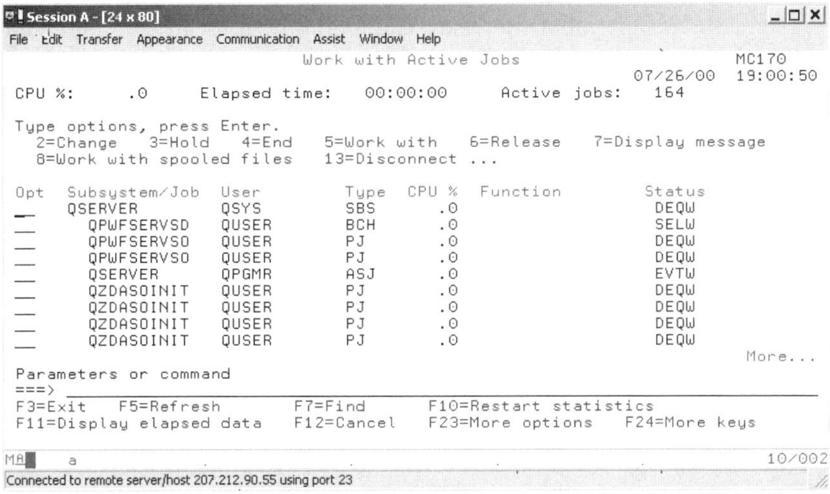

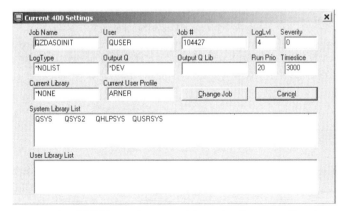

Figure 6.4: Finding client server jobs can be very difficult when large numbers of users are logged in simultaneously.

SQLThing makes finding your job easier by allowing you to invoke a stored procedure on the AS/400 that will retrieve your job number and other information. Go to the Environment menu and then select Display AS/400 Job Information. You should see a screen like the one shown in Figure 6.5.

Figure 6.5: SQLThing retrieves your job number for you, making debugging easier.

This screen contains the job name, user, and job number for the job SQLThing is using to execute your statements on the AS/400. Now, start up a terminal emulation session and type the following command:

```
WRKJOB <job-number>/QUSER/QZDASOINIT
```

This will cause a screen like Figure 6.6 to appear. From this screen, you can access information about what files the SQL statement is using, record locks, logical files, and the job log of the job.

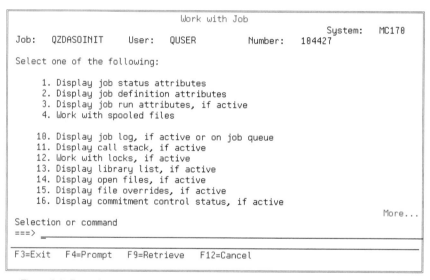

```
                              Work with Job
                                              System:   MC170
 Job:   QZDASOINIT     User:   QUSER        Number:   104427
 Select one of the following:

     1. Display job status attributes
     2. Display job definition attributes
     3. Display job run attributes, if active
     4. Work with spooled files

    10. Display job log, if active or on job queue
    11. Display call stack, if active
    12. Work with locks, if active
    13. Display library list, if active
    14. Display open files, if active
    15. Display file overrides, if active
    16. Display commitment control status, if active
                                                        More...
 Selection or command
 ===> _

 F3=Exit   F4=Prompt   F9=Retrieve   F12=Cancel
```

Figure 6.6: From the WRKJOB screen, you can get all sorts of useful information about your SQL statements.

Starting Debug

The next challenge is to start debugging this job. Of course, now that you know the job number, you could start a service job and issue the Start Debug (STRDBG) command from the command line. I have made it easier by adding these functions to SQLThing. If you choose Environment Options Panel, you will see the screen shown in Figure 6.7. By checking the AS/400 Debug option and then clicking Save Options, you cause the SQLThing program to call the AS/400 Start Debugc ommand. Because it is calling the command from the current connection to the AS/400, the AS/400 job associated with SQLThing is now in debug mode, and query optimizer messages are being written to the job log.

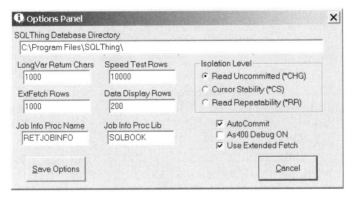

Figure 6.7: Checking the AS/400 Debug option and pressing Save Options will cause your job to enter debug mode.

Reading the Job Log

The environment is now set up, and you are ready for some query debugging action! Now that you are back at the interactive window, type the following query and execute it:

```
SELECT * FROM SQLBOOK.WEBTEMP2 WHERE
        REQTS BETWEEN '1999-10-01-00.00.00.000000'
        AND '1999-10-01-23.59.59.999999'
```

The query is stupid, but that's not the point. The point is that if you go to the terminal emulation window you have open, and select option 10, you should see a screen like the one shown in Figure 6.8.

```
                              Display Job Log
                                                    System:    MC170
 Job . . :    QZDASOINIT    User . . :    QUSER        Number . . . :    104427

 _    Job 104427/QUSER/QZDASOINIT started on 07/26/00 at 17:52:21 in subsystem
        QSERVER in QSYS. Job entered system on 07/26/00 at 17:52:21.
      Servicing user profile ARNER.
      Servicing user profile ARNER from client 208.61.173.33.
      Unable to retrieve query options file.
      Unable to retrieve query options file.
      Arrival sequence access was used for file WEBTEMP2.
      Access path suggestion for file WEBTEMP2.




                                                                    Bottom
 Press Enter to continue.

 F3=Exit    F5=Refresh    F10=Display detailed messages    F12=Cancel
 F16=Job menu              F24=More keys
```

Figure 6.8: This screen shows the job log for your SQLThing ODBC connection. Note that there is an access path suggestion for the query.

First, look at the top of the job log. It says that it is serving user profile ARNER, and gives the time I logged in and my IP location. Next, the log has an annoying message about the query options file. Ignore any of these for now; you will find out more about query option files later in this chapter. The next line says that the arrival sequence was used in processing the query. This message indicates that a table scan is being performed in order to implement this query. However, the really important message is the next one, "Access path suggestion for file WEBTEMP2." This is the AS/400's way of telling you it thinks you should create an index. See, the AS/400 is already giving helpful advice!

Move your cursor over the access-path suggestion message and press the F1 key. You should see a screen similar to Figure 6.9.

```
                        Additional Message Information
 -
Message ID . . . . . . :   CPI432F      Severity . . . . . . . :    00
Message type . . . . . :   Information
Date sent  . . . . . . :   07/27/00     Time sent  . . . . . . :    16:43:29

Message . . . . :    Access path suggestion for file WEBTEMP2.
Cause . . . . . :     To improve performance the query optimizer is suggesting a
  permanent access path be built with the key fields it is recommending. The
  access path will access records from member WEBTEMP2 of file WEBTEMP2 in
  library SQLBOOK.
    In the list of key fields that follow, the query optimizer is recommending
  the first 0 key fields as primary key fields. The remaining key fields are
  considered secondary key fields and are listed in order of expected
  selectivity based on this query. Primary key fields are fields that
  significantly reduce the number of keys selected based on the corresponding
  selection predicate. Secondary key fields are fields that may or may not
  significantly reduce the number of keys selected. It is up to the user to
                                                                      More...
Press Enter to continue.

F3=Exit   F6=Print   F9=Display message details   F12=Cancel
F21=Select assistance level
```

Figure 6.9: This is the detail of the access-path suggestion message.

This shows the detail of the access-path suggestion message. Most of the message is bull-dada boilerplate disclaimer. If you scroll the screen to see the rest of the message, however, you will find that the optimizer provides a list of columns that it thinks should be in the access path. In this case, the optimizer suggests the REQTS field be included. Press F12 on the terminal emulation session to get back to the main job log display.

Creating an Index to Boost Performance

Make the AS/400 happy by creating an access path using the requested field. To do this, execute the following statement:

```
CREATE INDEX SQLBOOK.WTREQTS
       ON SQLBOOK.WEBTEMP2 (REQTS ASC)
```

Now, re-execute the first query, and then press F5 on your terminal emulation screen to see a refresh of the job log. Your screen should be similar to Figure 6.10.

```
                          Display Job Log
                                                     System:   MC170
  Job . . :   QZDASOINIT   User . . :   QUSER      Number . . . :   104427

  _    Job 104427/QUSER/QZDASOINIT started on 07/26/00 at 17:52:21 in subsystem
          QSERVER in QSYS. Job entered system on 07/26/00 at 17:52:21.
       Servicing user profile ARNER.
       Servicing user profile ARNER from client 208.61.173.33.
       Unable to retrieve query options file.
       Unable to retrieve query options file.
       Arrival sequence access was used for file WEBTEMP2.
       Access path suggestion for file WEBTEMP2.
       Unable to retrieve query options file.
       The OS/400 Query access plan has been rebuilt.
       Access path of file WTREQTS was used by query.


                                                                   Bottom
  Press Enter to continue.

  F3=Exit    F5=Refresh    F10=Display detailed messages    F12=Cancel
  F16=Job menu           F24=More keys
```

Figure 6.10: The last message in the job log indicates that the WTREQTS index was used to satisfy the query.

There are two important pieces of information in the updated job log. The message "OS/400 Query access plan has been rebuilt" indicates that some change has occurred that caused the AS/400 to have to reoptimize the SQL statement. Move your cursor over that message and press F1 to see the full explanation of why the access plan was rebuilt. In this case, it was rebuilt because of reason code 5. Reason code 5 indicates that the optimizer chose to rebuild because a new index or access path was available.

Watch your job log for these messages. If the messages are being created for reasons other than new access paths being available, a problem query might need to be investigated. In this case, however, the message is appropriate.

The next message of interest is "Access path of file WTREQTS was used by query." This message tells you that the query did, in fact, use the new index that you created. Press F1 while your cursor is over the message to see the message details. In this case, the index was used because it was appropriate to the record-selection criteria of the query.

The query optimizer can use the new index to make the query return records much faster than the table-scan method. Always look for access-path suggestions in your job logs, as they point to potential increases in query performance.

Effects of Static vs. Dynamic SQL

At this point, you have an idea of how the optimizer works and how to interrogate its decisions. Now you need to go through the application design and development tools that can affect the performance of your code. The first concept to be covered is static versus dynamic SQL.

When you issue an SQL statement, the optimizer decides on an access path and then implements your query. If you issue static SQL statements, this process happens for the query only the first time the query is seen by the optimizer. After the access plan is created, it can be stored in a special object called a *package*. Then, if the optimizer sees the same query again, it will not have to optimize the query. Instead, the optimizer will retrieve the stored plan from the package file.

Dynamic SQL statements are typically constructed on the fly by putting a query string together in memory and then passing the string to DB2. The optimizer will create an execution plan, but not put the plan in a package file. Instead, the optimizer will store the plan for the duration of the program and, if the exact statement is executed again, the optimizer will reuse the plan. Once the application terminates, however, the plan goes into the bit bucket. If the application starts again, the statement will be reoptimized.

So, what's the point of all this? So far, the only thing that looks advantageous about package files is that a statement is only optimized the first time it is used. That is the point. Optimization takes time, especially for a complex join or when there are a lot of logical files on the physical files referenced in the query. In addition, you can do ugly things in SQL (such as selecting from a view that is a

161

view of a view of a join). Optimizing that kind of query requires the optimizer to repeatedly hit the system catalogs for information about the view, the next view, the next view, and finally the underlying tables. Remember, this isn't magic. It's a program that has to look at what you want, how you want it, and then hit the system catalog to look for available indexes, column data types, etc. Also, it has to evaluate each available logical file and the selectivity of the keys in the logical file.

Optimization takes time and processor resources. It also takes I/O resources because of the lookups against the system catalog files. If you have a way to reuse data from the optimizer, you should use it to increase overall system throughput. While static SQL and packages give you this capability, to take advantage of it you need to create reusable statements.

Reusable SQL Statements via Parameters

Think about an inventory system that has a parts master file. The order entry screen probably allows someone to look up a part by its ID code. An item master screen might also allow someone to look up a part by its ID. Even if this lookup statement is only used in one place, it is probably executed many times a day. It's a function that operators need to perform over and over. Take a look at the following query:

```
SELECT DESCRIPTION FROM PARTS WHERE PARTID='123'
```

This statement would theoretically return the description of a part whose ID value is 123. Most likely, there is an index on part ID. The optimizer would select the index and return the description quickly. Now, look at the next statement:

```
SELECT DESCRIPTION FROM PARTS WHERE PARTID='9901'
```

Again, this statement will return the description of a part whose ID value is 9901. However, the optimizer doesn't realize that both of these statements are intended for the same purpose: to return an item description. It sees that the statement lengths are different and chooses to select the appropriate access path to find the data, again. Let's say that optimizing this statement takes 0.20 seconds. If you implemented this method in your program and the operators looked up 20,000 part descriptions a day, you would have wasted 66 minutes of programming operations redoing the same thing.

The key to making the statement reusable is to use parameter markers or host variables for the part of the statement that will change. A host variable is only used in languages on the AS/400—like C, RPG, and COBOL—that support embedded SQL. A parameter marker is used when you are programming from an ODBC, JDBC, OLEDB, or CLI program. Here is an example of the statement using parameter markers:

```
SELECT DESCRIPTION FROM PARTS WHERE  PARTID =  ?
```

The ? symbol informs the optimizer that this is an unknown value at this time. The optimizer will optimize the statement with the idea that, when it is executed, the program will give it a value to bind into the parameter marker. The advantage of parameters is that the AS/400 can now store the statement in a package file. Any time your application or program runs and attempts to execute the statement, the AS/400 will forgo optimization and use the stored execution plan in the package file.

How you use packages depends on the programming environment you are using, and is beyond the scope of this book. If you are using ODBC, JDBC, or OLEDB, see the respective IBM programming guides to those interfaces. Package use for precompiler applications is determined by the options used in creating the program.

Finally, remember this motto: Static Good, Dynamic Bad.

Example of Parameter Markers

One of the reasons that I wrote SQLThing was to test parameterized SQL queries and evaluate their performance without having to write a program. Type the following query into the SQLThing editor window and execute it to produce a screen like the one shown in Figure 6.11:

```
SELECT * FROM SQLBOOK.WEBTEMP2
        WHERE REQTS BETWEEN ? AND ?
        AND GEOID = ?
```

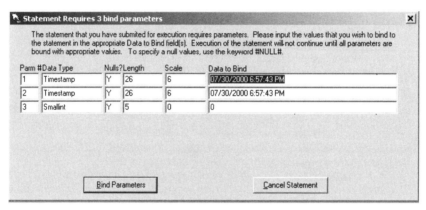

Figure 6.11: SQLThing will allow you to test parameterized statements without having to write a program.

Once you have entered a parameter value in the screen, click Bind Parameters to have SQLThing bind the parameter data into the statement and execute the statement. If you were to look at the job log for this job, you would notice that the statement was prepared. However, if you subsequently executed this statement, you should not notice additional messages about the access path being prepared. This is because the statement will reuse the ODP created by its first use, even though you are executing the statement with many different parameter values. SQLThing will try to type-check the values you are attempting to pass to a parameterized query.

Using Parameter Markers in Client Applications

Figure 6.12 shows a sample Visual Basic program that uses ActiveX Data Objects and an ODBC data source to connect to the AS/400 and execute a parameterized query.

164

```
Dim CON1 as New ADODB.Connection
Dim CMD1 as New ADODB.Command
Dim RS as New ADODB.RecordSet

'open the connection
CON1.Open "DSN=MYAS400;UID=HOWARD;PWD=SECRET"
'Associate ADO command object with statement
CMD1.ActiveConnection = CON1
'Set the statement into the command object
CMD1.CommandText = "SELECT * FROM SQLBOOK.WEBTEMP2 " & _
    "WHERE GEOID=?"
'Get the parameter definitions
CMD1.Parameters.Refresh
'Set the parameter
CMD1.Parameters(0).Value = 3
'Tell the recordset object to cache requests
RS.CacheSize = 200
'Open the recordset
RS.Open CMD1
'read all of the records
While not RS.Eof
    'Print column 1 to the debug window
     Debug.Print Rs.Fields(0).Value
    'Move to the next record
   RS.MoveNext
Wend
'Clean up memory
RS.Close
Set RS=Nothing
Set CMD1=Nothing
CON1.Close
Set CON1=Nothing
```

Figure 6.12: This Visual Basic program will prepare an SQL statement, set its parameters, execute the statement, and then print the returned data.

Performance Tips

The following sections contain information on performance tips and techniques for use in your SQL statements. While not comprehensive, they should serve as a basic do's and don'ts list to SQL programming. Most of these tips will serve the embedded SQL programmer as well as the Web and client/server SQL programmer. If a tip is only for a certain environment, that information is noted.

Nudge the Optimizer with the FOR X ROWS Clause

You can sometimes influence the behavior of the query optimizer by adding the FOR X ROWS clause to the end of your query. This is a "hint" to the optimizer that you expect it to read only X number of rows from the query, even though it might return many more rows. This is most effective on statements that have OR-DER BY or GROUP BY elements. Consider the following two statements:

```
SELECT REQUSER, REQTS FROM SQLBOOK.WEBTEMP2 WHERE
    REQTS BETWEEN '1999-10-01-00.00.00.000000'
    AND '1999-10-30-23.59.59.999999'
    ORDER BY REQUSER, REQTS
    OPTIMIZE FOR 1 ROW;

SELECT REQUSER, REQTS FROM SQLBOOK.WEBTEMP2 WHERE
    REQTS BETWEEN '1999-10-01-00.00.00.000000'
    AND '1999-10-30-23.59.59.999999'
    ORDER BY REQUSER, REQTS
    OPTIMIZE FOR 10000 ROWS
```

The first query lets the optimizer know that you only expect to read one row of the data that is returned by the request. The optimizer still estimates the number of rows that will satisfy your query, but it will bias the search of access paths in favor of finding data quickly. This will tend to make the optimizer favor using an index to retrieve results.

The second query lets the optimizer know that you expect to read many rows from the query. The optimizer will bias the evaluation of access paths in favor of using a sort on the resulting query data and lessen the effect of available indexes.

Join and Select on Data Types That Don't Require Conversion

A bad performance mistake is to join tables that have dissimilar data types. For example, if you have a table of transactions that contains a DECIMAL(6,0) field for the customer number, and join it to the customer table where it is defined as an integer, the join requires that the decimal number be cast to an integer for comparison. This operation takes valuable computing resources. If you are going to join on it, ensure the types are the same.

166

In addition, using selection criteria whose data types do not match can cause a performance hit. For example, suppose you have a transaction table with a SMALLINT (2-byte) column that indicates the branch location the transaction is applied to. There is also an index over this column. When you attempt a query for branch-13 transactions, the number 13 is incorrectly passed to the query as an INTEGER (4-byte) number. Not only will the query optimizer generate a warning because of the data type difference in operator comparisons, it will also be unable to use the index made over the branch location column. This is because the AS/400 has to convert the SMALLINT to an INTEGER before it can compare the values, thus making the index unusable for comparison.

To find these situations, monitor the job log for the message "CPI432E - Selection columns mapped to different attributes." If you get this message a lot, consider altering the table to the data type you need.

Indexes Cannot Be Evaluated with Scalar Functions

Another bad mistake is to expect the optimizer to use an index when performing a query with a scalar function, for example:

```
SELECT * FROM SQLBOOK.WEBTEMP WHERE MONTH(REQTS)=10
```

Even though there is in index with the REQTS column as the key, the optimizer will not be able to use that index. This is because the MONTH operation is being performed against the column REQTS and then compared to the integer 10. This query would be better expressed as follows:

```
SELECT * FROM SQLBOOK.WEBTEMP
         WHERE REQTS BETWEEN '1999-10-01-00.00.00.000000'
         AND '1999-10-01-23.59.59.999999'
```

Even though the timestamp values are being given as a string, the AS/400 will be able to compare them using the index over the REQTS column, thereby saving execution time. If you needed multiple years of data for only October, the query could be expressed like this:

```
SELECT * FROM SQLBOOK.WEBTEMP
        WHERE (REQTS BETWEEN '1999-10-01-00.00.00.000000'
        AND '1999-10-01-23.59.59.999999')
        OR
        (REQTS BETWEEN '1998-10-01-00.00.00.000000'
        AND '1998-10-01-23.59.59.999999')
```

Note that the OR allows for the selection of October records from two distinct years. Multiple OR clauses could be added to include more years. This query will most likely use the REQTS index and optimize well. Also, even though the parentheses operators are not required, they help ensure that the OR logic is processed correctly. I highly recommend that you use parentheses in your queries when using OR conditions.

Create Indexes to Assist Join Operations and Frequent Searches

If you have a query that routinely joins two tables together, you should consider indexes on the child table's join key to assist in this processing. In addition, if you consistently use the same search criteria against the same columns with different queries, consider indexing those columns. Which type of index you create should depend on the data type and selectivity of the data. (See the following section on EVI indexes for when they might be appropriate.)

Traditional indexes lend themselves to ordering and search criteria. Also, traditional indexes are more appropriate for multikey files. Experiment with the order of the keys to see which key ordering gives you best performance.

For example, consider a transaction table that contains a date value and a transaction type value. There are over 1,300 distinct dates, but only five distinct transaction types. Most queries against the data are for a range of dates and a single data type. The most appropriate index would be on the date column first and then the type column. In this manner, the leftmost key of the index is very selective and more likely to be picked by the query optimizer.

Another situation in the transaction table might be joining transactions to the part master table to retrieve part descriptions and other information. These queries are also usually run for a date range. It would not be appropriate to create an index on the date column and then the part ID column. That index would not be used during the join operation because the leftmost key of the index would not match the join criteria. The more appropriate index would be by part ID and then date.

Designing indexes for relational systems is a combination of understanding the optimizer and experimenting. Try several variations to see where you get the best performance. In addition, always keep in mind the ways in which your users and applications will likely query the data, and ensure that you have access paths available.

Finally, monitor the job log for the message "CPI4321 - Access path built for file &1." This indicates that the AS/400 is creating an index on the fly to satisfy your query. Look at the details of the message to get the key fields the AS/400 is using to build the index. Consider making a permanent access path for that table.

When to Use Vector Indexes

EVI indexes can really boost performance, but they need to be used judiciously. Think about how many distinct data values are in a column that you are going to index before indexing the column. Too many distinct values can hurt you. With regular indexes, poor selectivity makes the index less likely to be used by the optimizer; remember that multiple EVI indexes can be combined in memory. Therefore, it might be appropriate to make an EVI on a column with very few distinct values.

Timestamps are terrible candidates for EVI indexes. Remember that the timestamp has precision down to the microsecond. As a result, almost every timestamp column in a table will be unique. There is probably never a case where you should use a timestamp in an EVI.

Dates, however, might be appropriate for EVI indexes. Think about a scenario where a table of part transactions spans five years (with 200 or more transactions per day). Five years of data would yield roughly 1,825 distinct values. That is not too many values for an EVI index.

Most of the time, an individual EVI index should be created over only one column of data, but there are exceptions to this rule. Again, experimentation and evaluation of access plans and query performance should be your guide. EVI indexes lend themselves best to situations and tables where large amounts of ad hoc queries will be performed.

Remember that EVI indexes can be combined. (Even I tend to forget this.) A query that elects to use a traditional index will only open one logical file. If the optimizer elects to use EVI indexes, it can open one or more EVI indexes and combine them dynamically in memory. So, it might be appropriate to have several EVI indexes on the transaction table in the previous example: one on the part ID, one on the date, and one on the transaction type. A query asking for several different parts over a period of time with a certain transaction type might elect to use an EVI to satisfy the query.

I have found EVI indexes invaluable for tables that receive a lot of ad hoc query requests. For example, I have a table with columns for newspaper issue, the operator who entered the issue, and a count of records in the issue. This table is maintained by my production systems and has over 400,000 records in it. I created EVI indexes over the operator, date, and paper number fields (each as a separate EVI index). If I issue a query such as "list the issues worked on by operators whose initials start with the letter *H*, with the paper ID between 100 and 400, and the issue date between 01/01/1999 and 03/01/1999," the AS/400 will elect to merge the EVI indexes as opposed to performing a table scan. A table scan against this table takes approximately 24 seconds. In contrast, merging the EVI indexes and retrieving the data takes less than one second.

Normalizing and Table Design

When designing databases, people sometimes do stupid things that seem smart at the time. If you are a victim of bad design, don't be afraid to redesign the database schema if you can. Also, you can rename a table and then create a view with the same structure as the old tables. In this way, older code doesn't have to be changed. That code will still reference the original table name. However, the table is now a view that is a combination of the tables that you have separated.

170

A good candidate for normalization is a character column that has repeating values. I recently consulted on a database with 20 million rows of data. The database had a CHAR(20) column that contained a shipping status. When examining the data, I found that there were only 20 distinct strings that ever appeared in the column. A CHAR(20) column to hold this type of repeating data is the worst type you can create. It is just plain wasteful of space and affects logical files created on that column. I created a table of the 20 values and added a CHAR(1) column to serve as the primary key. Next, I altered the base table to include a new CHAR(1) column to accept the new relational value. I then updated the table to set the CHAR(1) column to reflect the ID of the character string stored in the record. I was then able to drop the original CHAR(20) column and free a lot of space.

Because the relational table had so few values, the join could be accomplished in memory and was not noticeable in query execution times compared to the original table layout. In addition, the logical files that now contained a reference to the column were significantly smaller. Finally, the overall system performance improved because the individual table rows were smaller in size; more rows could fit on a database page. More rows on a page mean more records retrieved from disk in one I/O step and more records retained in cache.

You're not always in a position to normalize, but be aware that this option exists. Also, always try to make the smallest row size possible when designing a table. Ask yourself, do I really need an integer when a SMALLINT might do? Does this column warrant this many characters? Also, avoid LONG VARCHAR if at all possible. Instead, use CLOB or BLOB types. Finally, stay away from VARCHAR unless you need it. Sometimes a fixed row size can optimize better than rows with VARCHAR columns.

De-normalizing

Okay. So, sometimes you should join and sometimes you just have to de-normalize for performance reasons. This shouldn't be undertaken lightly, however, as application programs and updates must take into account that the database is de-normalized unless you elect to use triggers to maintain data integrity.

Triggers are attached to a physical file and can be launched on the insertion, update, or deletion of a record from the table. Triggers can ensure that a calculation is performed or a value is grabbed from another table to ensure that a record is consistent. In addition, a trigger must complete successfully for the row to be altered, and no application can bypass the effects of a trigger. Because of this, you can be sure that a trigger will maintain the proper state of your data (as long as the trigger is programmed correctly, that is).

Consider this situation, where I de-normalized a database for performance reasons: A database contained records of business financial activity, and included information such as the business identifier, activity location, and the date of the activity. There were over 30 million records in the table. There was also a table of businesses that identified each unique business, offered a description, and had codes for the type of business. This table had well over a million records. The type of business related to a table that classified the business types to a meta-category. A common query was to look at meta-category expenditures by activity for a period of time. Because you could only get to the meta-category by a three-way join, (base table/business table/meta-category table), grouping data by the meta-category was inefficient, and the optimizer typically did table scans when searching for more than one category of data.

In this situation, I employed the use of triggers on both the business and main data tables and added the business type column to the main data type. Then, if the business type of the business was changed, the trigger updated each record in the main table that referred to that business with the new business type. If the main table was changed, its trigger ensured that the business type was retrieved from the business table and placed into the record image. Therefore, queries requiring category or meta-category grouping did not need to join to the intermediate table

To explore programming triggers in more detail, see *DB2 UDB for AS/400 Database Programming*, available online from IBM.

De-normalizing for OLAP

Because the AS/400 does not allow you to create indexes based on the value of scalar functions, and because it will not use an index if the target column is massaged by a scalar function, you might want to de-normalize tables that are targets of OLAP queries.

Assume a hypothetical table of part transactions with several million rows. The table contains a timestamp value to indicate the moment of the transaction. You need to produce a report of product sales by year and month. The following query could be used to do this:

```
SELECT PARTID,
       YEAR(TRANSDATE),
       MONTH(TRANSDATE),
       SUM(QUANTITY*PRICE)
       FROM SQLBOOK.MYTRANS
       WHERE DATE(TRANSDATE)>='1998-01-01'
       AND DATE(TRANSDATE)<'2000-01-01'
       GROUP BY PARTID, YEAR(TRANSDATE), MONTH(TRANSDATE)
```

Even if an index exists on the PARTID and TRANSDATE columns, it might not be used in the query. In addition, you cannot create an index on the year of the TRANSDATE column because AS/400 does not allow indexes on scalar functions. If you were to collapse the table to include SMALLINT columns to hold the year and month part of the date field, you could index by these fields and possibly improve the processing of the query.

Who Is ODP and What Did He Do to My Performance?

No. ODP is not Ron Howard's character from *Mayberry RFD*. ODP stands for *open data path*. When the AS/400 is finished optimizing an SQL statement, it has to open the file in order to implement the SQL statement. This operation results in an ODP.

ODPs are not necessarily discarded after the SQL statement has been run, even if the cursor or handle associated with the statement in the host-programming environment is destroyed. The AS/400 will keep an ODP alive in case the application program needs that access path again. This can be a blessing and a curse.

ODPs are a blessing if your application is well designed and uses static SQL. Because the AS/400 retains the ODP paths, the number of file-open requests is reduced, and performance and overall throughput of the application increases. Keeping ODPs can be a curse in applications that use dynamic SQL. The overhead of so many open data paths reduces memory and resources available to all programs on the AS/400, thereby decreasing performance.

One real-life example that shows the tragedy of dynamic SQL and open ODPs involved converting a client/server application from Centura's SQLBase to the AS/400. The AS/400 was used as an industrial-strength data server because the database had grown beyond the limits of a PC database server. All client applications were in Visual Basic and used ODBC to connect to the AS/400. All data manipulations were done via SQL. Because I needed to complete the conversion quickly, I did not implement any of the SQL statement to use parameters. All statements were put together as strings in RAM and then passed to ODBC for preparation and execution. This worked fabulously on V3R6.

The client then upgraded to V3R7. One of its improvements was that the AS/400 would reuse ODPs from SQL statements. Because my application used dynamic SQL, this resulted in the AS/400 not knowing that an ODP could be reused with the next execution of an almost identical statement. Because the lengths of the statements were different, the AS/400 assumed it needed a new ODP, and opened one. Within 20 minutes of operation, the client program would have over 200 ODPs open on the AS/400. Multiply 200 open ODPs by 40 users, and you have a serious number of ODPs loaded into RAM. It brought the AS/400 to its knees.

The only solution was to recode the application using parameter markers rather than dynamic SQL. This reduced the number of ODPs down to only 10. Because the ODPs were reused constantly during the execution of the application, application performance and throughput increased dramatically.

Here's the point: Use static SQL with parameter markers. Not only will you save optimizer-processing time, you will reuse open data paths, which will reduce file-open and file-close operations. Also, avoid statements that require data conversion because this can make an ODP unable to be reused.

The Ugly DDS Logical Trick

Now for the neatest thing I have ever discovered about the AS/400. Completely by accident, one day I discovered that DDS-based indexes can be used in the FROM portion of an SQL statement. This was a revelation to me because I always considered AS/400 logical files to be indexes and never understood that they are actually a cross between an index and a view. On all other SQL platforms, you cannot name an index in the FROM clause of an SQL statement because, on all other SQL platforms, a view is just an SQL statement that is executed when you attempt to read the virtual table. On the AS/400, a DDS logical is a weird beast that doesn't conform.

Because I always created indexes using the SQL CREATE INDEX statement, I could not name them in the FROM clause. Imagine my surprise when, at a client site, I accidentally typed the name of a logical file in the FROM clause and the SELECT statement worked! I had discovered the nebulous relationship between AS/400 logical files that come into being because of the CREATE INDEX statement, and AS/400 logical files that come into being because of DDS and the CRTLF command. Again, DDS logicals are more like views than indexes. This difference can make a huge impact in SQL performance, as you will see in this scenario:

I have a client who has an order-detail table with over 10 million records in it. Each record has about 138 fields. Part of the reason for the large number of fields is that the system is quite old and separates each date into four fields: MONTH, DAY, YEAR, and CENTURY. The main table has about five different date values, which means that over 20 fields in the system are just for storing information about when the event happened.

Now, the job I was performing for the client was to make an interactive Web-based EIS system to allow employees to drill through sales information. To accomplish this, I wrote queries that would roll up order-detail data into summary tables by customer, year, and month. These queries executed each night in order to rebuild the summary tables.

Only the last two months of data could ever change in the legacy database. Therefore, I didn't need to rebuild the entire summary table (only the data for the last two months). My batch operation would delete the summary records for CURRENT_DATE – 2 MONTHS, and then execute a query to reinsert the summary data from the production files.

Remember that date fields in this system are actually combinations of four different fields. The indexes available to my query were typically of the form "Century, Year, Month, Day, Customer, Invoice Number." This index lends itself to the RPG programs that needed to use the logical for batch processing, but note that it starts with a very nonselective key field. Because the leftmost key field is century, and there are only two values for this field (19 and 20), the query optimizer would constantly deem all of these indexes unsuitable for my query. My query only needed two months' worth of records, about 400,000 out of 10,000,000 records, but the optimizer could not recognize this fact because of the selectivity of the indexes available.

The optimizer repeatedly chose to implement the query with a table scan. The table scan took over 10 minutes to process. No matter how I changed the query, I could not force the optimizer to use any of the access paths that might help it operate more efficiently. I was also not allowed to create additional access paths over the physical file that might be more appropriate to my query. The physical file already had 43 logical files associated with it, and the shop did not want any more. This situation was a real pickle.

I solved the problem by naming the DDS logical file that I wanted the AS/400 to use as an index in the FROM clause of my query instead of naming the physical file in the FROM clause. This trick forced the optimizer to read from the DDS logical rather than directly from the physical. Because the logical forced the records to be in century, year, month, day, and customer order, the AS/400 was able to use key row positioning to find the target record set efficiently. This resulted in taking the query processing time from 10 minutes down to less than 40 seconds.

This brings up two suggestions and a few caveats. First, never create indexes using the SQL CREATE INDEX statement on an AS/400. If you always use DDS to create indexes, you will be able to use them in FROM clauses to help influence optimizer behavior. The only indexes that should be created with SQL syntax are EVI indexes; there is no way to create these indexes via DDS.

Second, never assume that you know more than the optimizer. Always name the physical file in the FROM clause first, and see what the optimizer does to implement your query. If it does not choose the appropriate index, experiment with changing the query syntax. Only after exhausting *all* variations of the statement should you attempt to use a force. The optimizer, most of the time, picks the most efficient way to access your data. Make sure you compare the CPU utilization, I/O requests, etc. of your force to that of the optimizer's original execution plan. You might cause the result to come faster, but at a high resource price.

Finally, using the index rather than the table name in the FROM clause should be thought of as only a suggestion to the query optimizer. It doesn't guarantee that the optimizer will use that access path. It just seems to give it a little more weight during the optimization process.

Only Ask for What You Need

One of the easiest optimizations is the simplest. I was called in on some performance problems with a Web-based system that was reading legacy data via ODBC to an NT box. The performance was terrible. The programmer was reading order-detail records and writing the part number, price, quantity, and total to the browser, but it took almost 20 seconds to retrieve 150 records. Here is the SQL statement the programmer was using:

```
SELECT * FROM ORDERDTL WHERE ORDERID=?
```

It looked good to me. Does it look good to you? The statement is a perfectly fine example of good SQL programming—it even uses parameter markers. The problem did not become apparent until I looked at the structure of the ORDERDTL table. The legacy system had over 200 fields in the ORDERDTL table. There were seven different date values, and five fields were required to represent each date value because the design of the system predated the SQL DATE data type. Each record in the legacy system took over 3KB of space. For 150 records, that's 450KB of data transmission.

But that wasn't the only problem. The programmer was using Microsoft ADO to request the data. Now, ADO is really fast and convenient, but when ADO prepares an SQL statement, it requests the data type, length, and name for each column that will be returned in the result set. Because the programmer was selecting all columns, ADO had to request information on 200 columns. All of this takes time (about 2 seconds), and that time was wasted because the programmer only wanted the part ID, quantity, and price. Here is the new SQL statement:

```
SELECT ITEMID, PRICE, QUANTITY, PRICE*QUANTITY
        FROM ORDERDT WHERE ORDERID=?
```

It executed and returned the 150 records in less than 1second. The moral of the story is to only put on your plate what you plan to eat.

Avoid Type Conversion

Finally, your biggest enemy is type conversion during processing of SQL statements. This can happen for a variety of reasons. For example, you could be doing math operations against a SMALLINT column that cause it to be cast to INTEGER. If you then attempt to compare the result to another SMALLINT column, you are forcing SQL to promote that column to INTEGER to do the comparison. If there was an index available on the SMALLINT column, it could no longer be used in optimization of the query because of the type promotion. These type promotions are usually noted in the job log. Look for the following messages:

```
SQL7919 - Data conversion required on FETCH or embedded SELECT

SQL7939 - Data conversion required on INSERT or UPDATE

CPI432E - Selection columns mapped to different attributes
```

Chapter Summary

This chapter contains a lot of information. In it, you have been exposed to the query optimizer and how it makes decisions about the implementation of your query. You also have been shown how to get information about the decisions the optimizer made in implementing queries. In addition, you now have the concept of static versus dynamic SQL and many useful suggestions for enhancing query performance. You should now be familiar with the following:

- How to retrieve optimizer information.

- How to interpret this information into performance enhancement.

- The difference between static and dynamic SQL.

- Why static SQL is always preferable to dynamic SQL.

- The role of packages on the AS/400.

- Tips and techniques for enhancing your SQL performance.

7

STORED PROCEDURES

The AS/400 has fantastic support for using stored procedures. This chapter introduces you to stored procedures, explains what they are, shows you how to call CL and RPG programs as stored procedures, and shows you how to create your own procedures using the AS/400 stored-procedure language. Stored procedures are an excellent way to reduce your communications overhead, encapsulate business logic on the server, and make your client and server programs more robust.

A Stored Procedure Is Just a Program

At its heart, a stored procedure is just a mechanism for calling a program on the AS/400. That program can be written in any language that executes natively on the AS/400 (like C, CL, RPG, Java, or COBOL). The stored procedure contains the declaration of the variables that need to be passed to and returned from the program you are calling, the definition of the language that the program was written in, and other information about the program you want to run.

When you declare a procedure, the definition of the procedure and its parameters are stored in the system catalog. When a program wants to call the procedure, the

AS/400 uses the procedure definition to correctly marshal arguments back and forth between the caller and the host. The nice thing about this is that the AS/400 and SQL handle all of the messy details, like platform data conversion, for you. Stored procedures are a cool way to open up business logic on your AS/400 to other platforms.

Why Use Stored Procedures?

Every day I consult with client companies that ask the same basic question, "How do we re-architect our legacy application to support multiple presentation layers?" If the logic of your application is sound, why on earth would you want to re-architect? To get the fastest possible path to client/server and Web deployment of your applications, you should reuse every piece of code you possibly can.

A company has a huge investment in legacy code. Like fine Scotch, legacy systems take years to properly mature. Now that they are mature, why invest money in rewriting the applications in CORBA, in ILE, or as Java Servlets? RPG and COBOL code have run your business fine for all of these years; there is no need to abandon code that works.

Once a program is defined as a procedure, it can be called from any platform that supports SQL. By implementing procedures, you gain *client platform independence* while maintaining your business logic next to your data on the AS/400. Client platform independence means that you can make a 5250 interface, a Web interface, or a GUI Visual Basic interface for your business logic. This is the world as it should be.

Rants About Politically Correct Platform Independence

This takes me to my favorite punching bag: platform independence. I think that platform independence is way too big of a buzzword right now. Everyone is talking about writing things in Java so that they can run on any platform. Why? I say you pick the proper platform for the job you want to perform and the best language that lets you use the skill sets and resources you own. There are a lot of RPG and COBOL programmers, but not a lot of Java programmers.

Additionally, I have no desire to move my business logic from my AS/400 system. It is one of the best transaction-processing environments around. I also have a huge investment in the business logic that already exists on my AS/400. Why rewrite that code in Java? Platform independence is no reason to rewrite in Java. Heck, I can write platform-independent code in C using POSIX; all I do is copy it to the target platform and recompile. This search for platform independence reminds me of the search for the Holy Grail, a pointless waste of time and resources.

When you design your systems, pick the appropriate tool for the job. There are times when Java is important and there are times when RPG is important. There also are cases where Visual Basic, Excel, and other PC technologies are necessary. The point is not to rewrite, but to reuse. Because you have all of this logic available, stored procedures are a wonderful way to reuse years' worth of systems development.

Your First Procedure

The best way to learn is by doing. Setting up a small CL program on the AS/400 and then calling it as a stored procedure will expose you to all of the elements of the procedure definition and the mechanisms available for calling the procedure from a client application. In this manner, you will come to understand the concept and some of the conventions of stored procedures. Later in this chapter, you will see more complex examples that show how you can really benefit from this technology.

The stored procedure you are about to create is a useful little program if you do client/server programming. It returns the job number under which your SQL connection is currently running. This can be used to get job-log information or to issue a START DEBUG request for the target program quickly and easily. Start by creating a source physical file on your AS/400 called QCLSRC in the library SQLBOOK:

```
CRTSRCPF  FILE(SQLBOOK/QCLSRC)
```

This file will hold the CL source for the retrieve job-log program. Next, issue the following command to create a new member in the file called RTVJOBN:

```
ADDPFM FILE(SQLBOOK/QCLSRC) MBR(RETJOBN)
```

This member will be used to hold the source of the stored procedure command. Finally, issue the following command so that you can edit the new member:

```
STRSEU SRCFILE(SQLBOOK/QCLSRC) SRCMBR(RETJOBN) TYPE(CLP)
```

Enter the source code shown in Figure 7.1 into the member. Press F3 to get the SEU exit options. Make sure that you put a *Y* in the Change/Create Member option and then press the Enter key to get back to the AS/400 command prompt.

```
PGM          PARM(&JOBN)
DCL          VAR(&JOBN) TYPE(*CHAR) LEN(6)
RTVJOBA      NBR(&JOBN)
```

Figure 7.1: This CL source will be used in the procedure to retrieve your current job number.

This program is very simple. You call it with a single argument and it returns your job number by calling the Retrieve Job Attributes (RTVJOBA) command. Now let's create the CL program with the following command:

```
CRTCLPGM PGM(SQLBOOK/RETJOBN) SRCFILE(SQLBOOK/QCLSRC)
```

At this point, you have a program called RETJOBN that exists in the SQLBOOK library. Now, you need to call the program as a stored procedure. To do this, first start SQLThing, log into your AS/400, and select File New to get a new SQLEditor Window. In the window, type and execute the following statement:

```
CREATE PROCEDURE SQLBOOK.MYPROCTEST
        (OUT JOBN CHAR (6))
        LANGUAGE CL
        NOT DETERMINISTIC
        NO SQL
        CALLED ON NULL INPUT
        EXTERNAL NAME SQLBOOK.RETJOBN
        PARAMETER STYLE GENERAL
```

This statement declares that there is a procedure available on this AS/400. The first line indicates the procedure is called MYPROCTEST and exists in the library SQLBOOK. Even though the program to be called is RETJOBN, the procedure declaration can name the procedure anything it wants. In addition, the procedure does not have to be declared in the same library as the program to be called. In fact, when I want to declare procedures that will be called by lots of programs that have different library lists, I usually declare them in the QGPL library. All users have access to these procedures. A side benefit is that QGPL is usually in a user's library list.

The second line tells SQL about the parameters to the procedure. This procedure takes one parameter called JOBN that is of data type CHAR(6). Notice that OUT precedes the declaration of the parameter. This informs SQL that the variable is an output-type parameter. A parameter can be declared as IN, OUT, or INOUT. IN tells SQL that the parameter will be passed, but the caller is not interested in a return value. OUT informs SQL that the caller is interested in reading the return value from the called procedure. INOUT indicates that the variable will travel into and be read from the procedure. Even if a parameter is declared OUT, SQL will still pass any data that you choose to put in it to the called program. I typically declare my parameters as to their input output function mainly so that the declarations serve as documentation.

The next line indicates the language of the procedure. In this case, the procedure is a CL program. You do not have to specify this unless the language of the program is REXX, but it helps SQL ensure that any variables are correctly massaged when they are passed to the program being called. If it is not specified, SQL will look at the program attributes of the procedure to determine the language in which it was written.

NOT DETERMINISTIC is a very important instruction to SQL. This indicates that if you call the procedure over and over with the same parameters, it will return different results. If a procedure is declared as DETERMINISTIC, SQL might elect not to execute the procedure in subsequent calls, and instead return results from the previous call to the procedure if the parameters are exactly the same. It is important that you define a procedure as deterministic or nondeterministic because this can effect whether the procedure program is executed or not.

NO SQL informs SQL that the procedure does not contain any SQL statements. It is not really that important to specify this argument, but if a procedure does not contain SQL statements, it is a good idea to tell SQL so. This helps SQL determine how to best execute the procedure call. In addition, you could specify that the procedure CONTAINS SQL, READS SQL DATA, or MODIFIES SQL DATA. These arguments, which are discussed in detail later in this chapter, place restrictions on the type of SQL statements that can be used in the program being called. Omitting them informs the SQL interpreter that no SQL statements will be issued within the context of this procedure.

CALLED ON NULL INPUT indicates that the procedure should be called even if null values are passed as input parameters to the procedure. Because this procedure has no input variables, this is actually a no-op. However, it is always best to give SQL the most information possible about any procedure that you want to declare. Therefore, this statement is included for SQL's reference.

EXTERNAL NAME SQLBOOK.RETJOBN tells SQL the name of the external program that it will call when this procedure is executed. In this case, it informs SQL to call the RETJOBN program in the library SQLBOOK.

Finally, PARAMETER STYLE GENERAL indicates that the procedure will not accept null values as input parameters. Null-parameter passing requires special handling within the procedure code. The procedure code must accept an additional argument that is not passed from the caller of the procedure, but instead is passed via SQL during the invocation of the procedure. This argument is an array of indicator variables that tells whether an argument is a null value or not. Because the CL program does not need a null value, you can declare the call as PARAMETER STYLE GENERAL and save a few processing steps when calling the program.

Calling the Procedure

So far, you have created a CL program and a procedure definition. Now, you need to call the program from an SQL client. Procedures are invoked using the CALL statement. Here is the SQL that calls the MYPROCTEST procedure:

```
CALL SQLBOOK.MYPROCTEST (?)
```

The CALL keyword informs SQL that you are going to invoke a procedure. Next, you specify the name of the procedure you want to invoke. Finally, you pass a parameter marker to indicate that the procedure needs one parameter.

When you execute this statement in SQLThing, the Parameters Window will be shown. This window allows you to specify a value for the parameter marker. Just put a blank character into the value field and then click the Bind Parameters button. This causes SQLThing to execute the procedure and show the Output Parameters Window. A sample of this window is shown in Figure 7.2.

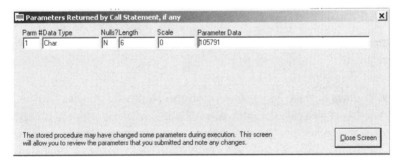

Figure 7.2: This is the SQLThing Parameters window. Note that the Parameter data field contains the job number of the current ODBC connection SQLThing used to execute the procedure.

Calling procedures is one of the main reasons that I created SQLThing in the first place. Note that almost all procedures have parameters that need to be passed or viewed. The interactive SQL on the AS/400 doesn't prompt you for procedure parameters and it doesn't show the output of procedure parameters. The only way to test a procedure is to issue a CALL from a programming environment, pass each required parameter, and then write code to retrieve and evaluate the parameters. SQLThing can help you test procedures as a simple tool that allows you to pass and view parameters, whether they are for parameterized SQL statements or for SQL procedures.

Calling the Procedure from Visual Basic

Figure 7.3 shows a simple Visual Basic program that can call the MYPROCTEST procedure. This program uses ActiveX Data Objects (ADO) and ODBC to connect to the AS/400. Note that it uses an ODBC data source called WORKSQL.

```
Dim Con1 As New ADODB.Connection
Dim Cmd1 As New ADODB.Command
Con1.Open "DSN=WORKSQL;UID=MYUSERID;PWD=SECRET;"
Cmd1.ActiveConnection = Con1
Cmd1.CommandText = "{CALL SQLBOOK.MYPROCTEST (?)}"
Cmd1.Parameters.Refresh
Cmd1.Execute
Jobnum = Cmd1.Parameters(0).Value
MsgBox "Your Job Number is " & Jobnum
Set Cmd1 = Nothing
Con1.Close
Set Con1 = Nothing
```

Figure 7.3: This Visual Basic program sets up the call to the stored procedure, refreshes the parameters, calls the procedure, and then returns your current job number.

The first two lines declare ADO connection and command objects. The connection object is used to communicate with your AS/400, and the command object is used to execute SQL statements. The next line uses the OPEN method of the connection object to open a connection to your AS/400. Next, the command object is associated with the connection object by setting the command object's ActiveConnection property. The VB environment is now ready to execute an SQL statement.

The CommandText property of the command object is set to the SQL statement that you want to run. In this case, it is set to {CALL SQLBOOK.MYPROCTEST(?)} The curvy brackets let ADO know that it should use ODBC calling conventions when executing this procedure call. It is important that you always do this when calling procedure via ADO. Otherwise, ADO will incorrectly retrieve procedure parameter information that can cause your program to malfunction.

The next line of code tells the command object to refresh its parameters collection. The parameters collection is what you use to set and get the parameters of a stored procedure call. The Execute method of the command object is called, which causes the command to be run on the AS/400. The next line of code retrieves the parameter value from the parameters collection of the command object into a variable called JOBNUM. Finally, a message box is displayed that shows the job number, and then the program disconnects and cleans up its data stores.

It is interesting to note that this code will not only execute in the Visual Basic development environment, but also within Word, Excel, PowerPoint, Visio, Windows Scripting Host, and Active Server Pages. This is because Microsoft has standardized on ADO as the technology for building database applications, using Visual Basic as the macro language in all of its products. If you want to write client/server programs that talk to your AS/400, Visual Basic is definitely a language you want to learn. Visual Basic is portable among all Microsoft products and technologies. In addition, many other vendors have licensed the VB language as the macro language for their products.

Calling Any Program on the AS/400

Officially, a stored procedure needs to be declared in order to pass parameters and record sets back and forth from the client to the server. However, *any* AS/400 command or program can be called using the stored procedure mechanism, even if it is not declared as a stored procedure. This is accomplished through the QCMDEXC API that resides in the QSYS library.

QCMDEXC takes two arguments: the command you want the AS/400 to execute, and a DECIMAL(15,5) number indicating the length of the string you are passing in the command. Here is an example of calling the Start Debug (STRDBG) command using this facility:

```
CALL QSYS.QCMDEXC('STRDBG UPDPROD(*YES)',0000000020.00000)
```

The AS/400 looks for a procedure definition. Not finding one, it immediately looks to see if there is a program called QCMDEXC in the library QSYS. Because there is, the AS/400 calls that program and passes the two arguments to it. QCMDEXC, in turn, invokes the command string specified in its first argument. Because QCMDEXC is quite stupid, you must pass it that ugly number as its second argument so that it knows how big the command string is. As soon as you do, your job is in debug mode and all messages are being written to the AS/400 job log. Cool.

For another example of calling an AS/400 command, suppose you want to read the database relations for a file within a client program. The easy way to do this is using the Display Database Relations (DSPDBR) command to display the files related to the target file. One option of the command is that its output can be redirected into a physical file. You could then use SQL to read the results back to your client program.

Let's try this using SQLThing to look at the relationships of the WEBTEMP2 table. First, execute the following command:

```
CALL QSYS.QCMDEXC('DSPDBR FILE(SQLBOOK/WEBTEMP2) OUTPUT(*OUTFILE)
            OUTFILE(QTEMP/PEST)',0000000066.00000)
```

Now, you should have a file in the QTEMP library called PEST, which has the results of the DSPDBR command in it. Next, execute this SQL statement to view the relationships:

```
SELECT WHREFI AS FILE, WHRELI AS LIBRARY FROM QTEMP.PEST
```

This statement reads the columns WHREFI (containing the name of the related file) and WHRELI (containing the name of the library where the file is located) from the PEST table that the previous command created. The output of the command should look something like Figure 7.4.

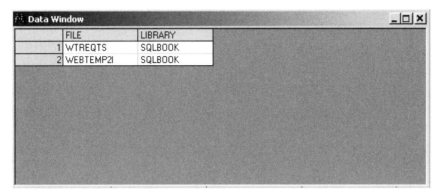

Figure 7.4: This is the output from the DSPDBR command. The cool thing about calling AS/400 commands is that your client programs can get this type of information without API calls.

Finally, for another neat use of calling QCMDEXC, let's say you have a source physical file with a lot of members, but you want to read the contents of a single member using an SQL statement. Instead of issuing a CREATE ALIAS command to point to the member, you can issue an Override Database File (OVRDBF) command to cause the SQL statement to read from the selected member. This might be more appropriate than an alias because an alias stays in the system until it is dropped. On the other hand, an override only stays in effect for the calling program until the termination of the caller.

First, execute the following command to cause the QCSRC file in SQLBOOK to be overridden to the RETJOBN member:

```
CALL QSYS.QCMDEXC('OVRDBF FILE(QCLSRC) TOFILE(SQLBOOK/QCLSRC)
        MBR(RETJOBN) OVRSCOPE(*JOB)',0000000070.00000);
```

This statement causes any SELECT statement made by this job to be pointed at the RETJOBN member of the QCLSRC file. The OVRSCOPE(*JOB) means that this override will remain in effect until the job ends. Now, execute the following statement:

```
SELECT * FROM SQLBOOK.QCLSRC
```

You should see results like those that are shown in Figure 7.5.

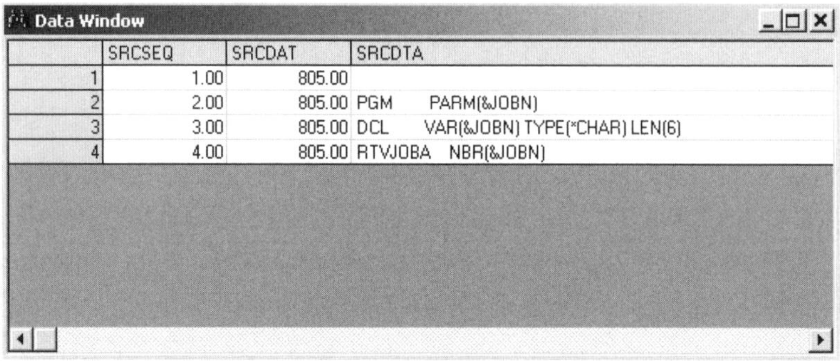

	SRCSEQ	SRCDAT	SRCDTA
1	1.00	805.00	
2	2.00	805.00	PGM PARM(&JOBN)
3	3.00	805.00	DCL VAR(&JOBN) TYPE(*CHAR) LEN(6)
4	4.00	805.00	RTVJOBA NBR(&JOBN)

Figure 7.5: Here are the results of selecting after the override has been issued. Overrides can guarantee you are selecting from the proper member of a multimember file.

Commitment Control in Stored Procedures

Before delving further into stored procedures, it is important to know how to use commitment control within a procedure and how certain program options can affect stored procedures. First, always compile a stored procedure by setting the ACTGRP(*CALLER) option, so that it runs in the same activation group as the calling program. This ensures that the calling program and the procedure share the same commitment boundaries. If the activation group is not set to CALLER, the stored procedure will run in a different commitment scope from the calling application. This can be very bad for transactional integrity, as COMMIT and ROLLBACK will not affect the changes made by the procedure.

Let's consider a simple client/server scenario to see how the activation group can affect the program. Suppose you have a client program that inserts a payment record into a table and then calls a stored procedure that updates the customer master record to indicate a new balance. (Yes, it's a stupid program, but I want to keep it simple!)

Now, let's pretend that the stored procedure was compiled to run in the caller's activation group. The payment record is inserted, and the procedure is called to update the customer balance. Control returns to the client application, and the client issues a ROLLBACK. Both the update of the customer master record (caused by the procedure) and the inserted payment record are removed from the database by the ROLLBACK. Now, if the procedure were recompiled and the activation group were not set to the caller, ROLLBACK will only undo the insertion, as the stored procedure program ran under a different activation group. This can definitely be a problem because your database is now inconsistent.

In addition, if the stored procedure is running under a different activation group and issues a COMMIT, it will only apply to changes that the stored procedure made to the database. It will not commit the changes made by the caller. While this behavior might be desirable on some planets, I have yet to find a use for it on this one.

One other reason to make sure the activation group is set to *CALLER is for performance. The AS/400 will have to create the new activation group, and this takes time. For example, I had a procedure, running under a different activation group, which could be called only two times per second. Changing the procedure to be in the same activation group as the calling program allowed me to execute the procedure over 25 times per second.

AS/400 Stored Procedure Language

Starting in V4, the nice folks at IBM put an integrated stored procedure language on the AS/400. This is a welcome addition to the platform because it gives you a simple language to use in the creation of your stored procedures. However, to use the language, you must have the ILE C compiler and the AS/400 Query and SQL Development Kit licensed on your machine. At the time of this writing, these programs cost money. However, I hope that a future release will include these programs as part of the base operating system. If you are one of the lucky few who has these two products, you can write stored procedures in this nifty language. If you don't, you can still write them in RPG, C, or COBOL.

The stored procedure language is quite simple. You can define a procedure by either typing it into the interactive SQL interpreter or by placing the procedure source in a physical file and using the RUNSQLSTM command to run the source code. In addition, you'll find a cute little procedure-editor program on the CD that accompanies this book.

Once the AS/400 begins to create your procedure, it creates a source physical file called QSQLSRC in the QTEMP library. It adds a member to the file and names the member with the name of your procedure. The AS/400 then interprets the SQL procedure language and writes an ILE C program with embedded SQL in it. The ILE C program is compiled using the CRTSQLCI command. If the compilation is successful, you have a stored procedure.

One advantage of using the procedure language is its simplicity. It is very easy to read, and you will pick it up quickly. Also, try the utility on the CD for editing procedures. It has a neat option that sucks the generated ILE C code out of the QSQLSRC file during the creation of the stored procedure. This can be really useful for learning how to use embedded SQL. Also, I use the stored procedure language as a C program generator. I let the AS/400 interpret my SQL procedure into C code, and then I edit the code and make refinements to it.

Getting a Sequence Number with a Procedure

There is no better way to learn than by doing. So, let's do a procedure! This example is a useful program that generates unique sequence numbers. Because I believe that all tables should have a primary key, most of the tables I create have an integer column that acts as the unique identifier for the record.

The problem is generating those unique numbers. Many SQL databases have a facility for auto-numbering records, but the AS/400 does not support this type of field. My solution is to make a table with two columns: SEQID and VLU. SEQID contains the name of the sequence number, and VLU is an integer representing the current sequence value. When I need a sequence number, I read the current contents of the VLU field for the SEQID that I am interested in, add one to it, and then issue an update to the record to reflect the new number. Making a stored procedure that does this is really simple.

Issue the following SQL statement to create the table that the procedure needs:

194

```
CREATE TABLE SQLBOOK.SEQCTRL
         (SEQID CHAR(10) NOT NULL PRIMARY KEY,
          VLU INTEGER NOT NULL WITH DEFAULT)
```

Next, issue the following two SQL statements to put seed records into the database. Because the VLU column was created as NOT NULL WITH DEFAULT, it will be set to zero by the AS/400:

```
INSERT INTO SQLBOOK.SEQCTRL (SEQID) VALUES ('WORK ORDER');
INSERT INTO SQLBOOK.SEQCTRL (SEQID) VALUES ('PONUM')
```

Now, use STRSQL, Operations Navigator, or the procedure-editing program from the CD to enter the SQL procedure shown in Figure 7.6.

```
CREATE PROCEDURE SQLBOOK.GETSEQ
(REQKEY IN CHAR(10),
 RETVAL INOUT INTEGER)
LANGUAGE SQL NOT DETERMINISTIC

BEGIN
DECLARE C1 CURSOR FOR
  SELECT VLU+1 FROM SQLBOOK.SEQCTRL
  WHERE SEQID = REQKEY FOR UPDATE OF VLU;
OPEN C1;
FETCH C1 INTO RETVAL;
UPDATE SQLBOOK.SEQCTRL SET VLU=RETVAL
  WHERE CURRENT OF C1;
END
```

Figure 7.6: This is the SQL procedure code for the stored procedure to generate sequence numbers.

Now, you can use SQLThing to call the procedure with the following SQL statement:

```
CALL SQLBOOK.GETSEQ(?,?)
```

When SQLThing prompts you for the values, enter WORK ORDER for the first parameter and the number zero for the second parameter. Clicking Bind Parameter will cause SQLThing to pass the parameters. The procedure will execute and you should see a screen like the one shown in Figure 7.7.

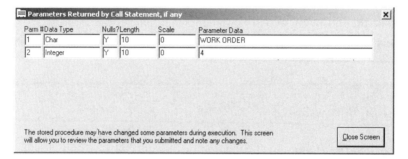

Figure 7.7: If your procedure created successfully, you should be able to execute it from SQLThing and see the results.

Congratulations, you just made a useful stored procedure! But, what is it doing? Let's look at each line of code so that you understand exactly what is happening. The top of the procedure declaration names the procedure GETSEQ and tells the AS/400 that it will have two arguments. The first argument is a 10-character input value called REQKEY. The second argument is an integer output variable called RETVLU. The rest of the header tells SQL that the procedure is in the SQL procedure language (LANGUAGE SQL), and that the procedure is not deterministic (does not always return the same output with the same input variables).

The action really starts at the BEGIN keyword. This tells SQL that the procedure code is starting. After the BEGIN keyword, each SQL statement or procedure action must be terminated by a semicolon. This is how SQL parses each line of the procedure and tells one action from another.

The next line of code declares a cursor named C1 for the SQL statement that follows. Remember, a cursor is like a pointer. It can be moved forward or backward through a file and can be used for positioned UPDATE and DELETE statements. Now, look closely at the SQL statement's WHERE clause. It says to look for the record where the SEQID column is equal to the REQKEY value. This is an example of using a host variable in a procedure. REQKEY is the variable that is passed into the procedure when it is called. In addition, notice that the SQL statement is not

196

selecting the VLU column directly; it is selecting VLU+1. This is a cheap way to get SQL to increment the counter for you.

The statement has the FOR UPDATE OF VLU clause appended to it to ensure that SQL will lock the record when it is read. Also, if another program has a shared lock on the record, the procedure will not read the record until the shared lock is released. In addition, the WITH CS added to the end of the SQL statement ensures that the statement will execute with Cursor Stability isolation level. This combination ensures that the procedure always creates a unique serial number.

The next line tells SQL to open the cursor C1. This causes the SQL statement associated with C1 to be executed and the cursor to be positioned to the first row of data that meets the selection criteria. The line FETCH C1 INTO RETVAL causes SQL to read the record at the current position of C1 and place the single column returned by the SELECT statement into the variable RETVAL. At this point, the procedure now has RETVAL instantiated with the value of the VLU column plus one.

Next, the procedure issues the UPDATE statement to set the VLU column equal to the contents of the RETVAL variable.Because RETVAL is VLU+1, this is equivalent to incrementing the VLU variable. Note the WHERE clause of the UPDATE statement. This is a perfect example of when a positioned update is appropriate. You positioned the cursor to the record you wanted with the SELECT statement; now you are updating the record at that position.

The END keyword lets SQL know that it is at the end of the procedure logic. Figure 7.8 shows the C source code generated by the AS/400. Study this code because it uses embedded SQL to accomplish the goals of the stored procedure. Even if you do not know C, the code demonstrates how SQL can be embedded into other host languages such as C, RPG, or COBOL.

```
#include <stdlib.h>
#include <stdio.h>
#include <string.h>
#include <decimal.h>
#include <wcstr.h>
#include <stddef.h>
#include <sqlproc.h>
EXEC SQL SET OPTION SQLMODE = *SQLPROC;
EXEC SQL BEGIN DECLARE SECTION;
struct SQLDLINK * SQLDLPTR;
typedef _Packed struct SQLDLINK
{
short SQL_DL_LEN;
char SQL_DL_VERS[5];
char SQL_DL_TYPE[4];
char SQL_DL_URLLEN[5];
char pad8[8];
char SQL_DL_URLCMMT[32718];
 };
long SQLP_INT_VAR;
long SQLCODE;
char SQLSTATE[5];
SQLCA* sqlcap;
short SQLP_IND0 = 0;
short* SQLP_IND_PTR = &SQLP_IND0;
struct {
char REQKEY[10];
short SQLP_I1;
long RETVAL;
short SQLP_I2;
} GETSEQ;
short *SQLP_IND;
int SQLPROCH(void);
short SQLP_DATE_FMT=SQL_ISO;
char SQLP_DATE_SEP = 0;
short SQLP_TIME_FMT=SQL_HMS;
char SQLP_TIME_SEP = ':';
int SQLPROC1(void);
EXEC SQL END DECLARE SECTION;
void main(int argc, char* argv[]) {
SQLP_IND = (short int*) argv[3];
sqlcap = (SQLCA*) argv[4];
SQLInitSQLCA((SQLCA*)&sqlca);
GETSEQ.SQLP_I1 = *(SQLP_IND+0);
if (GETSEQ.SQLP_I1 != SQLP_NULLIND)
    {
memcpy(GETSEQ.REQKEY, argv[1],10);
```

Figure 7.8: This is the source code that the AS/400 generated to perform the steps in the GETSEQ procedure. (Part 1 of 3)

198

```
    }
else {
}
GETSEQ.SQLP_I2 = *(SQLP_IND+1);
if (GETSEQ.SQLP_I2 != SQLP_NULLIND)
    {
GETSEQ.RETVAL = * (long *) argv[2];
    }
else {
GETSEQ.RETVAL = 0;
}
for ( ; ; ) {
SQLP_L2:
sqlca.sqlcaid[6] = 0x00;
EXEC SQL
DECLARE C1
CURSOR FOR SELECT VLU + 1 FROM SQLBOOK . SEQCTRL WHERE SEQID =
:GETSEQ.REQKEY :
GETSEQ.SQLP_I1 FOR UPDATE OF VLU ;
EXEC SQL
OPEN C1 ;
if (SQLPROCH() == 1)
    goto SQLP_END_GETSEQ;
EXEC SQL
FETCH C1 INTO  :GETSEQ.RETVAL :GETSEQ.SQLP_I2 ;
if (SQLPROCH() == 1)
    goto SQLP_END_GETSEQ;
EXEC SQL
UPDATE SQLBOOK . SEQCTRL SET VLU =  :GETSEQ.RETVAL :GETSEQ.SQLP_I2 WHERE
CURRENT
 OF C1 ;
if (SQLPROCH() == 1)
    goto SQLP_END_GETSEQ;
SQLP_END_SQLP_L2:
if (sqlca.sqlcade == 0) {
    EXEC SQL CLOSE C1;
    SQLInitSQLCA((SQLCA*)&sqlca);
    }
break;
}
SQLP_END_GETSEQ:
*(SQLP_IND+1) = GETSEQ.SQLP_I2;
if ( GETSEQ.SQLP_I2 != SQLP_NULLIND)
* (long *) argv[2] = GETSEQ.RETVAL;
sqlcap->sqlcode = sqlca.sqlcade;
memcpy(sqlcap->sqlstate, sqlca.sqlstote, 5);
if (sqlca.sqlerrml > 0) {
```

*Figure 7.8: This is the source code that the AS/400 generated to perform the steps in the
GETSEQ procedure. (Part 2 of 3)*

```
    sqlcap->sqlerrml = sqlca.sqlerrml;
    memcpy(sqlcap->sqlerrmc, sqlca.sqlerrmc,sqlca.sqlerrml); }
return; }
int SQLPROCH(void) {
  int mc0, mc1, mc2;
  mc0 = memcmp(sqlca.sqlstote, "00", 2);
  mc1 = memcmp(sqlca.sqlstote, "01", 2);
  mc2 = memcmp(sqlca.sqlstote, "02", 2);
  if (mc0 != 0 && mc1 != 0 && mc2 != 0)
    return(1);
  return(0); }
```

Figure 7.8: This is the source code that the AS/400 generated to perform the steps in the GETSEQ procedure. (Part 3 of 3)

Writing a Stored Procedure in RPG

Now that you've seen a stored procedure created using the SQL procedure language, let's create it using RPG and call it from SQL. Because this is what you will be doing with a lot of your OPM programs to make their logic available to Web applications, it's a good exercise. Also, it will help you understand some of the problems in passing parameters from the PC environment to an RPG stored procedure.

The program is the same as in the previous section: It takes a sequence ID as an argument and returns the next available sequence number for that ID. To begin, create a source physical file called QRPGSRC in the SQLBOOK library and add a new member in the file called RPGETSEQ. Enter the source shown in Figure 7.9.

Next, issue the following command to add the SQLBOOK library to your library list:

```
ADDLIBLE LIB(SQLBOOK)
```

Then, execute the following command to compile the program:

```
CRTRPGPGM PGM(SQLBOOK/RPGETSEQ) SRCFILE(SQLBOOK/QRPGSRC)
```

```
FSEQCTRL UF  E           K         DISK
F              SEQCTRL                        KRENAMERSEQCT
 *
C            *ENTRY    PLIST
C                      PARM              REQKEY 10
C                      PARM              VLU    0090
C                      PARM              IND    0090
 *
C            REQKEY    CHAINRSEQCT                  98
C            *IN98     IFEQ '0'
C                      ADD  1           VLU
C                      UPDATRSEQCT
C                      ELSE
C                      MOVE -1          IND
C                      ENDIF
 *
C                      RETRN
```

Figure 7.9: This is the RPG record-level access source code that performs the equivalent operation to the GETSEQ stored procedure.

Creating the Procedure Definition

At this point, you should have a program called RPGETSEQ that exists in the SQLBOOK library. Now you need to call the program as a stored procedure. Before you can call it, you need to add a procedure definition to your AS/400 system catalog. To add the procedure definition, use SQLThing to issue the following SQL statement:

```
CREATE PROCEDURE SQLBOOK.MYPROCTEST
        (SID IN CHAR (10),
        VLU OUT DECIMAL(9,0),
        RC OUT DECIMAL(9,0))
        LANGUAGE RPG
        NOT DETERMINISTIC
        NO SQL
        EXTERNAL NAME SQLBOOK.RPGETSEQ
        PARAMETER STYLE GENERAL
```

The SQL statement declares that there is a procedure available on your AS/400. The second line of the procedure tells SQL about the parameters of the procedure. This particular procedure takes three parameters. The first is an IN parameter of data type CHAR(10), with the parameter name SID.

201

Notice the DECIMAL(9,0) data type of the second parameter. If you look at the SQL that creates the SEQCTRL table, you will see that the VLU column is an integer. However, because you are dealing with RPG, you need to declare the data type as DECIMAL(9,0) for RPG to return the correct value to the calling program. Try declaring the data type as an integer, and it will not get passed back to the caller. This is a weird RPG quirk that you should watch out for.

The clause EXTERNAL NAME SQLBOOK.RPGETSEQ tells SQL the name of the external program that it will be calling when this procedure is executed. In this case, you are telling SQL to call the RPGETSEQ program in the library SQLBOOK.

Finally, the clause PARAMETER STYLE GENERAL indicates that the procedure will not accept null values as input parameters. Null-parameter passing requires special handling within the procedure code. The procedure code must accept an additional argument that is not passed from the caller of the procedure, but passed via SQL during the invocation of the procedure. This argument is an array of indicator variables that tell SQL whether or not an argument is a null value. Because this RPG program does not need a null value, you can declare the call as PARAMETER STYLE GENERAL and save a few processing steps in calling the program.

Calling the Procedure from VB

So far, you have created an RPG program, compiled it, and created a procedure definition. The code in Figure 7.10 shows a simple VB program that can call the MYPROCTEST procedure. This program uses ActiveX Data Objects and ODBC to connect to the AS/400. Note that it uses an ODBC data source name (DSN) called WORKSQL, just like the one you created during the installation of SQLThing, as well as an ID and password. (You will need to use your own user ID and password for this example to work on your machine.) You must also ensure that the SQLBOOK library is in the library list in the ODBC data source, or the procedure will not run. (This was also done during the installation and setup of SQLThing). The procedure will not be able to find the SEQCTRL file if the SQLBOOK library is not in the library list.

The first two lines declare ADO connection and command objects. The connection object is used to communicate with your AS/400, and the command object is used to execute SQL statements. The next line uses the OPEN method of the connection object to open a connection to your AS/400. Next, the command object is associated with the connection object by setting the command object's ActiveConnection property. Now, the VB environment is ready to execute an SQL statement.

```
Dim Con1 As New ADODB.Connection
Dim Cmd1 As New ADODB.Command
Con1.Open "DSN=WORKSQL;UID=ARNER;PWD=KAB742C;"
Cmd1.ActiveConnection = Con1
Cmd1.CommandText = "{CALL SQLBOOK.MYPROCTEST (?,?,?)}"
Cmd1.Parameters.Append Cmd1.CreateParameter("P1", adChar, adParamInput, 10)
Cmd1.Parameters.Append Cmd1.CreateParameter("P2", adDouble, adParamOutput)
Cmd1.Parameters.Append Cmd1.CreateParameter("P3", adDouble, adParamOutput)
Cmd1.Parameters("P1").Value = "PONUM"
Cmd1.Execute
If Cmd1.Parameters("P3").Value = -1 Then
  MsgBox "There was an error!"
Else
  X = Cmd1.Parameters("P2").Value
  MsgBox "Your Sequence Number is " & X
End If
Set Cmd1 = Nothing
Con1.Close
Set Con1 = Nothing
```

Figure 7.10: This Visual Basic code calls the RPG program RPGETSEQ, which is declared as the procedure MYPROCTEST.

The CommandText property of the command object is set to the SQL statement that you want to run. In this case, it is set to {CALL MYTEST.MYPROCTEST(?,?,?)}. The curvy brackets tell ADO that it should use the ODBC calling convention when executing this procedure call. It is important that you always do this when calling a procedure via ADO with ODBC. Otherwise, ADO will incorrectly retrieve procedure parameter information if you use the PARAMETERS REFRESH method. Even with the curvy brackets, ADO will incorrectly identify the decimal columns as character columns. That's why I never use the PARAMETERS REFRESH method, and I always declare my parameters by hand.

The next three lines of code describe the procedure parameters to ADO by adding items to the parameters collection. In the parameters collection, you set and get the parameters of a stored procedure call. The Append method places the item in the parameters collection. The CreateParameter method creates a new parameter object and takes the following arguments: parameter name, data type, parameter direction, data type size, and parameter value. The first declaration declares a parameter called P1, which is a 10-character input parameter. The next parameter is called P2, and it is a double-precision numeric-output parameter. It is declared as double, even though the procedure has it declared as DECIMAL(9,0), because ADO will mess up the retrieval of the data if you try to declare the parameters as integers or decimals when marshaling data to RPG programs. When retrieving parameters from RPG stored procedures, I typically use the adDouble data type for any numeric variables.

By creating your parameters manually, without using the PARAMETERS REFRESH method, you save time in program execution by reducing the amount of information retrieved from the server. The next line of code sets the value of the P1 parameter to PONUM. This value could have been passed when the parameter was created, but I wanted you to see how to set it by referencing the parameters collection.

Next, the Execute method of the command object is called. This causes the command to be run on the AS/400.

The next line of code evaluates whether P3 is equal to –1. If it is, the program shows you a message informing you that there was an error during execution of the procedure. Otherwise, the value of parameter P2 is loaded into the variable X and displayed via the MsgBox function.

Remember that this code will execute not only in the VB development environment, but also in Word, Excel, PowerPoint, Visio, Windows Scripting Host, and ASP because Microsoft has standardized on ADO and VB.

Ramifications of Non-ILE Programs and Commitment Control

Because this program was compiled as an OPM program and not an ILE, it does not run in the same commitment definition as the calling program (*CALLER). Therefore, once the procedure returns control to the calling application, all updates are committed. (See this chapter's section on Commitment Control in

Stored Procedures.) A ROLLBACK will not undo the changes that OPM programs have made to AS/400 tables. Exiting the OPM program causes all of its changes to be committed, but this will not commit any pending changes that the calling program has made.

Advanced Sequence-Number Procedure

The sequence-number generator is a neat little program—and now you've seen how to emulate it in RPG—but at present it has no error recovery. Because this program is really simple, it doesn't really need traditional error recovery. Nevertheless, there is a nice related feature you could supply to users. Right now, if a user passes an invalid ID, the program fails and returns an error message to the calling program. The program does not fail because a record is not found for the ID; it fails because the positioned update is not pointing at a current record.

If you add a handler for the NOT FOUND condition, you can add code to cover that condition. A *handler* is a piece of code that gets executed when a certain event is fired. In this case, you want the code to be executed if the target record is not found. Figure 7.11 shows the revised code with a handler installed.

```
CREATE PROCEDURE SQLBOOK.GETSEQ2
(REQKEY IN CHAR(10),
 RETVAL INOUT INTEGER)
LANGUAGE SQL NOT DETERMINISTIC

BEGIN
DECLARE X INTEGER DEFAULT 0;
DECLARE C1 CURSOR FOR
  SELECT VLU+1 FROM SQLBOOK.SEQCTRL
  WHERE SEQID = REQKEY FOR UPDATE OF VLU;
DECLARE CONTINUE HANDLER FOR NOT FOUND
SET X=1;
OPEN C1;
FETCH C1 INTO RETVAL;
IF X=0 THEN
UPDATE SQLBOOK.SEQCTRL SET VLU=RETVAL
  WHERE CURRENT OF C1;
ELSE
```

Figure 7.11: This SQL code creates a procedure that has a handler for the NOT FOUND message (part 1 of 2).

```
SET RETVAL=1;
 INSERT INTO SQLBOOK.SEQCTRL (SEQID,VLU)
 VALUES (REQKEY,1);
 END IF;
END
```

Figure 7.11: This SQL code creates a procedure that has a handler for the NOT FOUND message (part 2 of 2).

The added feature enables the stored procedure to start a new counter record if you pass a sequence identifier that is not on file. This is accomplished by the following changes:

1. Add an integer variable called X and set its value to zero in the procedure line DECLARE X INTEGER DEFAULT 0.

2. Add a handler condition so that if the target record is not found, the program sets X to one. This is done by DECLARE CONTINUE HANDLER FOR NOT FOUND SET X=1. Several types of handlers can be created. In this case, a *continue handler* is used. If the condition occurs (in this case, the record is not found), then execute the code that follows the handler and continue the procedure with the line of code after the line that caused the handler to fire. The code defined within the handler sets the value of the variable X to 1. Any condition or SQL state value can be trapped with a handler. Other handlers are discussed later in this chapter.

3. Add an IF THEN statement to the procedure to test the value of X. If X is zero, then the record was found for the ID that was passed; therefore, you should increment the base record pointed to by cursor C1. If X is not zero, then the handler code was fired (indicating that a record was not found for the ID passed). In this case, insert a new record that has the requested counter ID, and return a counter value of 1.

This version of the procedure is a vast improvement over the previous version in that it can either create or increment a counter. To test the procedure, fire up SQLThing and issue the following SQL statement:

```
CALL SQLBOOK.GETSEQ2 ('NEWCTR',?)
```

You are asking SQLThing to call the procedure, pass NEWCTR as the first parameter, and pass a variable for the second parameter. Choosing Statement Execute causes the procedure to be called. Click the Bind Parameters button on the Parameters windows to cause the statement to complete running. Because NEWCTR is not in the SEQCTRL table, the procedure will insert the record and then return the parameter value as 1. If you execute the following statement, you should see a result (as shown in Figure 7.12) where the new value was added to the SEQCTRL table and set to the current counter number:

```
SELECT * FROM SQLBOOK.SEQCTRL
```

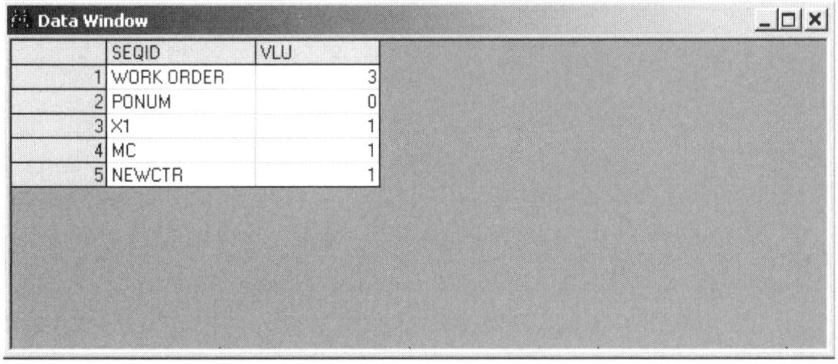

Figure 7.12: Your SEQCTRL table should look like this after the execution of the GETSEQ2 procedure.

The C source code generated by the AS/400 is shown in Figure 7.13.

```
#include <stdlib.h>
#include <stdio.h>
#include <string.h>
#include <decimal.h>
#include <wcstr.h>
#include <stddef.h>
#include <sqlproc.h>
EXEC SQL SET OPTION SQLMODE = *SQLPROC;
EXEC SQL BEGIN DECLARE SECTION;
struct SQLDLINK * SQLDLPTR;
typedef _Packed struct SQLDLINK
{
```

Figure 7.13: On the AS/400, C source code is generated to create the GETSEQ2 procedure (part 1 of 4).

```
short SQL_DL_LEN;
char SQL_DL_VERS[5];
char SQL_DL_TYPE[4];
char SQL_DL_URLLEN[5];
char pad8[8];
char SQL_DL_URLCMMT[32718];
 };
long SQLP_INT_VAR;
long SQLCODE;
char SQLSTATE[5];
SQLCA* sqlcap;
short SQLP_IND0 = 0;
short* SQLP_IND_PTR = &SQLP_IND0;
struct {
char REQKEY[10];
short SQLP_I1;
long RETVAL;
short SQLP_I2;
} GETSEQ2;
short *SQLP_IND;
int SQLPROCH(void);
 struct {
long X;
short SQLP_I3;
 } SQLP_L2;
short SQLP_DATE_FMT=SQL_ISO;
char SQLP_DATE_SEP = 0;
short SQLP_TIME_FMT=SQL_HMS;
char SQLP_TIME_SEP = ':';
long SQLP_RC1 = 0;
int SQLPROC1(void);
int SQLPROC2(void);
EXEC SQL END DECLARE SECTION;
void main(int argc, char* argv[]) {
SQLP_IND = (short int*) argv[3];
sqlcap = (SQLCA*) argv[4];
SQLInitSQLCA((SQLCA*)&sqlca);
GETSEQ2.SQLP_I1 = *(SQLP_IND+0);
if (GETSEQ2.SQLP_I1 != SQLP_NULLIND)
    {
memcpy(GETSEQ2.REQKEY, argv[1],10);
    }
else {
}
GETSEQ2.SQLP_I2 = *(SQLP_IND+1);
if (GETSEQ2.SQLP_I2 != SQLP_NULLIND)
    {
GETSEQ2.RETVAL = * (long *) argv[2];
    }
else {
GETSEQ2.RETVAL = 0;
}
for ( ; ; ) {
```

Figure 7.13: On the AS/400, C source code is generated to create the GETSEQ2 procedure (part 2 of 4).

```
SQLP_L2:
sqlca.sqlcaid[6] = 0x00;
SQLP_L2.X = 0;
SQLP_L2.SQLP_I3 = 0;
EXEC SQL
DECLARE C1
CURSOR FOR SELECT VLU + 1 FROM SQLBOOK . SEQCTRL WHERE SEQID =
:GETSEQ2.REQKEY
 :GETSEQ2.SQLP_I1 FOR UPDATE OF VLU ;
EXEC SQL
OPEN C1 ;
if (SQLPROC1() == 1)
    goto SQLP_END_SQLP_L2;
if (SQLPROCH() == 1)
    goto SQLP_END_GETSEQ2;
EXEC SQL
FETCH C1 INTO  :GETSEQ2.RETVAL :GETSEQ2.SQLP_I2 ;
if (SQLPROC1() == 1)
    goto SQLP_END_SQLP_L2;
if (SQLPROCH() == 1)
    goto SQLP_END_GETSEQ2;
SQLP_RC1 = 0;
if (SQLP_RC1 != -1 &&
(SQLP_L2.SQLP_I3 != SQLP_NULLIND &&
SQLP_L2.X==0)
 ) {
EXEC SQL
UPDATE SQLBOOK . SEQCTRL SET VLU =  :GETSEQ2.RETVAL :GETSEQ2.SQLP_I2 WHERE
CURRENT OF C1 ;
if (SQLPROC1() == 1)
    goto SQLP_END_SQLP_L2;
if (SQLPROCH() == 1)
    goto SQLP_END_GETSEQ2;
}
 else if (SQLP_RC1 != -1)
 {
GETSEQ2.RETVAL = 1;
GETSEQ2.SQLP_I2 = 0;
if (SQLPROC1() == 1)
    goto SQLP_END_SQLP_L2;
if (SQLPROCH() == 1)
    goto SQLP_END_GETSEQ2;
EXEC SQL
INSERT INTO SQLBOOK . SEQCTRL ( SEQID , VLU ) VALUES (  :GETSEQ2.REQKEY
:GETSEQ2
.SQLP_I1 , 1 ) ;
if (SQLPROC1() == 1)
    goto SQLP_END_SQLP_L2;
if (SQLPROCH() == 1)
    goto SQLP_END_GETSEQ2;
}
if (SQLPROC1() == 1)
    goto SQLP_END_SQLP_L2;
```

*Figure 7.13: On the AS/400, C source code is generated to create the GETSEQ2 procedure
(part 3 of 4).*

```
if (SQLPROCH() == 1)
    goto SQLP_END_GETSEQ2;
SQLP_END_SQLP_L2:
if (sqlca.sqlcade == 0) {
    EXEC SQL CLOSE C1;
    SQLInitSQLCA((SQLCA*)&sqlca);
    }
break;
}
SQLP_END_GETSEQ2:
*(SQLP_IND+1) = GETSEQ2.SQLP_I2;
if ( GETSEQ2.SQLP_I2 != SQLP_NULLIND)
* (long *) argv[2] = GETSEQ2.RETVAL;
sqlcap->sqlcode = sqlca.sqlcade;
memcpy(sqlcap->sqlstate, sqlca.sqlstote, 5);
if (sqlca.sqlerrml > 0) {
    sqlcap->sqlerrml = sqlca.sqlerrml;
    memcpy(sqlcap->sqlerrmc, sqlca.sqlerrmc,sqlca.sqlerrml); }
return; }
int SQLPROCH(void) {
  int mc0, mc1, mc2;
  mc0 = memcmp(sqlca.sqlstote, "00", 2);
  mc1 = memcmp(sqlca.sqlstote, "01", 2);
  mc2 = memcmp(sqlca.sqlstote, "02", 2);
  if (mc0 != 0 && mc1 != 0 && mc2 != 0)
    return(1);
  return(0); }
 int SQLPROC1( void ) {
if( (memcmp(sqlca.sqlstote,"02",2)==0)
 ){
SQLP_L2.X = 1;
SQLP_L2.SQLP_I3 = 0;
SQLInitSQLCA((SQLCA*)&sqlca);
return(0); }
return(0); }
```

Figure 7.13: On the AS/400, C source code is generated to create the GETSEQ2 procedure (part 4 of 4).

More Information About Handlers

The previous section mentions that you can declare several types of handlers:

- Continue
- Exit
- Undo

When you code stored procedures, it is important to understand how these handlers operate. They also can affect the way your procedures operate and how you code the client application that calls the procedure.

As mentioned earlier, a continue handler fires on the condition defined in the handler, and then the code continues with the next line of code after the condition is fired. An exit handler does not continue with any code after the condition is fired; it ends the procedure. An undo handler is like an exit handler, but it also forces a ROLLBACK to the last checkpoint. Remember, if your procedure is called in a different activation group from the calling program, it will only undo changes made within the procedure itself. Procedures created using the AS/400 procedure language are, by default, called in the calling program's activation group. Therefore, a ROLLBACK will apply to changes made in the calling application as well.

A handler can be called for any condition that might be thrown by an SQL statement. There are certain built-in conditions you can call without knowing the associated SQLSTATE. These are NOT FOUND, SQLEXCEPTION, and SQLWARNING. Let's look at SQLSTATE a little further before really getting into the definition of these constants.

SQLSTATE is the return code that the AS/400 sets for any SQL statement that it runs for you. If a statement runs correctly, the CLASS portion of the SQLSTATE is set to 00, 01, or 02. A class of 00 means that the statement ran correctly, and the program received no errors or warnings. You do not have a keyword for catching a 00; you don't need one because the statement ran correctly.

An SQLSTATE class of 01 means that the SQL statement ran successfully, but a warning was issued during its processing. A handler can catch a warning by being defined against the keyword SQLWARNING. A warning can be issued because data is truncated or for other reasons. The SQLSTATE and warning messages are detailed in the book *SQL Programming Concepts*, available online in the technical documents section at *www.AS400.IBM.com*. Here is an example of a statement that will cause a warning:

```
DELETE FROM <TABLE>
```

SQL will perform this statement, but it will issue a warning that all records will be deleted from the target table because no WHERE clause was specified. Review the SQL warnings, as there might be conditions that you want to catch based on the warning codes.

A state of 02 means that a statement was run, but no records were found during the execution of the statement. This can be caught by the keyword NOT FOUND. Typically, this will be the handler condition that you declare most often because it is the most common condition that you will find.

Using a Handler to Exit from a Loop

The code in Figure 7.14 is an example snippet that declares a handler for the not-found condition. That handler is used to exit from a WHILE loop in an SQL procedure.

```
DECLARE X INTEGER DEFAULT 0;
DECLARE CONTINIUE HANDLER FOR NOT FOUND SET X=1;
DECLARE C1 CURSOR FOR
SELECT <SOME-COLUMN> FROM <SOME-TABLE>;
WHILE X=0 DO
        FETCH C1 INTO Z;
        ...More Code
END WHILE;
```

Figure 7.14: This procedure snippet uses a handler to exit from a WHILE loop.

The handler will fire when all records have been read from the cursor C1, causing X to be set to 1. Since X is no longer zero, the WHILE loop will exit.

Returning Result Sets

From an embedded SQL statement within an RPG, COBOL, or C program, or within an SQL stored procedure, you can return a result set to the calling program. This is accomplished by using the SET RESULT SETS keywords and leaving the cursor open at the end of your program execution. Here is an example procedure that returns a result set to the calling program:

```
CREATE PROCEDURE SQLBOOK.TRESULT
        LANGUAGE SQL NOT DETERMINISTIC
        RESULT SETS 1
        BEGIN
         DECLARE C1 CURSOR FOR
         SELECT * FROM SQLBOOK.WEBTEMP2 WHERE GEOID=1;
        OPEN C1;
        SET RESULT SETS C1;
        END
```

Pay particular attention to the procedure declaration, as it now identifies that the procedure is expected to return one result set to the calling program. An SQL procedure call returns any number of result sets, but at any given time, it can have only 100 pending result sets for return. This effectively limits the number of result sets to 100 for most situations.

Try the procedure call from SQLThing using the following syntax:

```
CALL SQLBOOK.TRESULT
```

If you have the option Send Select Data to Data Window checked, you should see a screen like the one shown in Figure 7.14. Note that in order to retrieve result sets from procedures, you must use ODBC, ADO, or the CLI interface. At this time, embedded SQL on the AS/400 cannot process result sets returned from stored procedure calls. However, you can create procedures using RPG, COBOL, or C that return result sets to client programs.

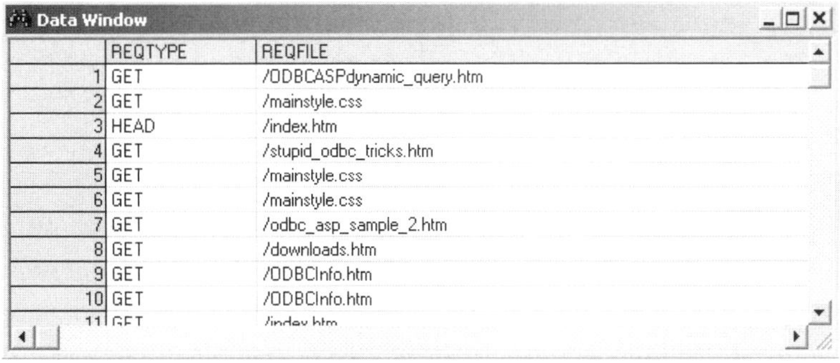

	REQTYPE	REQFILE
1	GET	/ODBCASPdynamic_query.htm
2	GET	/mainstyle.css
3	HEAD	/index.htm
4	GET	/stupid_odbc_tricks.htm
5	GET	/mainstyle.css
6	GET	/mainstyle.css
7	GET	/odbc_asp_sample_2.htm
8	GET	/downloads.htm
9	GET	/ODBCInfo.htm
10	GET	/ODBCInfo.htm
11	GET	/index.htm

Figure 7.14: The TRESULT procedure should return output like this.

Error Reporting and Recovery

The last important thing to know about procedures is how to return errors to the client application. I have a preferred method, which includes always passing two additional parameters back to the calling application besides any parameters the procedure might require. Figure 7.15 contains a revised version of the GETSEQ procedure that passes back an error message to the calling program.

```
CREATE PROCEDURE SQLBOOK.GETSEQ3
(REQKEY IN CHAR(10),
 RETVAL INOUT INTEGER, |
ERRIND INOUT INTEGER,
ERRMSG INOUT CHAR(80))
LANGUAGE SQL NOT DETERMINISTIC

BEGIN
DECLARE C1 CURSOR FOR
 SELECT VLU+1 FROM SQLBOOK.SEQCTRL
 WHERE SEQID = REQKEY FOR UPDATE OF VLU;
DECLARE CONTINUE HANDLER FOR NOT FOUND SET ERRIND=1;
SET ERRIND=0;
SET ERRMSG=' ';
OPEN C1;
FETCH C1 INTO RETVAL;
IF ERRIND=0 THEN
UPDATE SQLBOOK.SEQCTRL SET VLU=RETVAL
 WHERE CURRENT OF C1;
ELSE
SET RETVAL=-1;
 SET ERRMSG='Requested ID Key Not In Database';
  END IF;
END
```

Figure 7.15: This procedure returns execution-status information to the calling program by setting the value of a procedure variable.

Notice the two new variables in the procedure: ERRIND and ERRMSG. When the calling program calls the procedure, if the record associated with the passed ID is not found, the procedure will set ERRIND to a nonzero number and pass back the reason for the error in the ERRMSG field. In the client application, you need only check that ERRIND is zero. If it is not, simply display the contents of the ERRMSG field to the user.

Try issuing the call to the stored procedure from SQLThing with the following command:

```
CALL SQLBOOK.GETSEQ3 ('INVALID',?,?,?)
```

When the Parameters window appears, click Bind Parameters to cause the procedure to execute. A screen like the one shown in Figure 7.16 should appear. Note that the screen has the error message in parameter 3, showing that the ID passed was invalid.

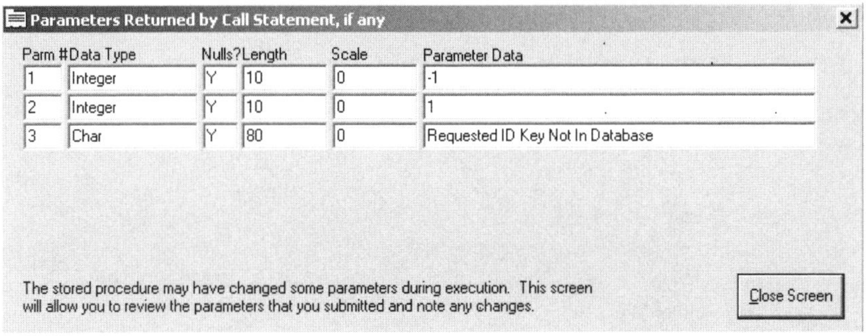

Figure 7.16: Here are the results of calling GETSEQ3 with an invalid ID.

Of course, this is a really simple procedure that has few points of failure. However, I have written procedures that have over 30 SQL statements and complex business logic. In these procedures, there are a lot of points of failure. Therefore, this technique enables my client application to be much simpler. I just ensure that the procedure call worked or I display the contents of the ERRMSG field and issue a ROLLBACK in my client code.

Chapter Summary

In this chapter, you have been exposed to the power of stored procedures. I hope that you see how powerful they are and how they can help you encapsulate operations on your AS/400. They allow you to reuse your legacy code and simplify your client code by having single points of call.

215

You should now have a good working knowledge of the following concepts:

- Procedures can return result sets.

- Any program can be called as a procedure, whether declared or not.

- Procedures allow for encapsulating business logic and making it available to other platforms.

- Procedures can be called from almost any platform.

- Commitment control depends on the activation group of the procedure job.

- You can call OPM RPG programs as stored procedures.

8

EMBEDDED SQL in RPG

One of the really neat and powerful features of the AS/400 is the capability to use embedded SQL in languages like RPG, COBOL, and C. Actually, the built-in stored procedure language relies on the fact that the AS/400 supports embedded SQL because it generates C programs that contain embedded SQL to run your procedures. However, as an RPG or COBOL programmer, you might be asking yourself why you would ever want to use embedded SQL when you have record-level access (RLA) available. The short answer is that SQL can help you do your job faster than RLA in certain situations. The key here is the phrase "in certain situations."

What Is Embedded SQL
and Why Should You Use It?

Embedded SQL allows you to place an SQL statement directly into the logic of your program. When coding a traditional AS/400 program, you concern yourself with opening physical files or logical files and positioning your file pointer with the CHAIN or READ commands to access the records that interest your application.

When using embedded SQL, instead of concerning yourself with opening logicals and physicals, you craft an SQL statement that will return the records you want. You then move through the returned record set using a construct called a cursor. Moving the cursor is like using a CHAIN or READ; it moves the file pointer from one record to another. Instead of opening an actual file, with embedded SQL you are opening a virtual file (a table) that can act like a physical file, but doesn't really exist at all.

The big difference, then, between embedded SQL and RLA, is that with RLA you worry about the physical layout of the database. It becomes very important to know what logical and physical files you have. Using embedded SQL, you are more concerned with what records you want and what order you read them in, not how they are retrieved from the physical database.

Another big difference is that you can access fields that do not really exist at all. Remember some of the statements from chapter 4 that pulled totals by day of the week? Day of the week as a column does not exist in the real universe; it is a virtual column created by a function. Also, the totals do not exist in a physical file; they exist only in the virtual table that the SQL statement creates. SQL gives you access to "files" that exist only in the imagination of your AS/400. Now, I realize you can accomplish some of this kind of stuff using logical files and open query files (although not the day of the week function). However, it's a bit more cumbersome with open query files and more permanent with logical files and, in both cases, a lot less flexible.

With that said, don't even think about using SQL for writing everyday data entry and manipulation programs. SQL should be your helper when it is the appropriate solution: for reporting, ad hoc queries, and dynamic selection and sorting.

For example, suppose you have a physical file of retail transactions and you want to allow people to view transaction summaries in any of three ways: by store with a date range, by state with a date range, or by vendor and a date range. If you have logical files by vendor and date, by store and date, and by state and date, you are sitting pretty because you can easily write the programs using RLA. However, what if you don't? What if you want to allow your user to pick any field out of the data set and run the summary? This type of thing is not suited to RLA, but it is suited to SQL.

Another reason for using SQL is for ease of reporting. Remember the query in chapter 4 that totaled parts and showed them as a percentage of the total in the warehouse? What if you wanted to design an RPG program that would compute that? That's not an easy task, but it's really easy if you use embedded SQL because all data access, sorting, and totaling is taken care of by one statement. You might be surprised that the SQL-based program will out-perform the RLA program in these situations. This is due to the set-based approach that SQL takes to data access. It allows for easier scanning of tables and manipulation of data in blocks rather than individual records.

Also, what about that procedure you only run once in a blue moon? You know the one—it requires that special logical file that sorts your data by X, Y, and Z; it's the one that no other program ever uses. Here is another possibility for using embedded SQL: Write the data access and manipulation in SQL so that you can get rid of that rarely used logical file. Fewer logical files equal less maintenance of the file system, which translates directly into more processor available for other tasks.

Finally, embedded SQL is a good tool for data export. I once took a job to help automate data extraction from an AS/400 to an SQL server database. The programmers wrote an RLA RPG program that read the database and placed records into a file that needed to be exported. The SQL server program then read the file and transported the records to itself. The RLA program took over 8 hours to read the physical files in the database and write the records to the target file that needed to be exported. After looking at the logic of the program, I replaced it with a single SQL statement that did the entire run in less than 20 minutes. This is due to the block fetch and copy optimization of SQL. I did not write any special code to use these techniques; I left it up to the optimizer to find the best way to extract the data. It found better ways than the human programmers were able to write. This is an example of using the right tool for the job at hand.

SQL has its place in the RPG programmer's arsenal. In certain situations, it makes the most sense. And in other situations, it makes no sense. The rest of the chapter is devoted to showing you when it makes sense and giving you ideas on how to incorporate embedded SQL into your RPG applications.

Dynamic Sorting

SQL embedded into your RPG program allows you to sort and select the data as you want, but it also provides the user with some added power. Let's say multiple users from different departments are going to use your subfile program, but, as is often the case with users, each one wants to see the data in a different order. You can certainly accomplish this by including enough logical files in your program to cover every possible sorting criterion, but that might amount to many logical files (especially if the users want secondary and tertiary sorts). Besides, you might create unnecessary access-path administration by the system if all the logical files are created for this one application. It also makes for an ugly subfile-build routine in your RPG program.

An alternative way to allow dynamically sorted subfiles is to use the Open Query File (OPNQRYF) command. You could create one OPNQRYF for each possible sort or dynamically create the OPNQRYF command based on what the user wants to do. Either way, you would be passing parameters back and forth between the RPG and CL programs to either build the OPNQRYF command or select which specific OPNQRYF command to use.

I've messed around with the latter method and the CL can get a bit cumbersome if you try to give the user complete flexibility by allowing them to sort on more than one field at a time. I love users, but that's a lot of work just to provide them a different view of the same data. In addition, as of V4R5, IBM is not going to support new SQL functions and capabilities with the OPNQRYF command. Therefore, if you build an SQL view that uses these new functions, a program that uses OPNQRYF will never be able to open and read that view.

The answer is SQL. By embedding SQL, you can dynamically build your SELECT statement—based on how a user wants to sort the data—all in one neat little subroutine. You also can use techniques that allow you to provide this capability very efficiently and, with a couple of minor changes, for data on other AS/400s. Let's see how it's done.

DDS

The first example is a simple subfile program that lists the Web-hit database (WEBTEMP2). It uses a standard self-extending subfile, where the program will handle each time a new page of records is added and OS/400 will page back and forth through existing subfile pages. A window record format allows the user to select fields on which to sort. I could have made this window a subfile window, but there are only three fields from which to choose. Therefore, I decided to make the selection window a regular format and not a subfile. Figure 8.1 shows the window for the display file (SQL001DF). The entire DDS code for the display file can be found on the CD-ROM included with the book. (For more information on subfile programming, see *Subfiles in RPG IV: Rules, Examples, Techniques, and Other Cool Stuff* by Kevin Vandever, published in 2000 by Midrange Computing.)

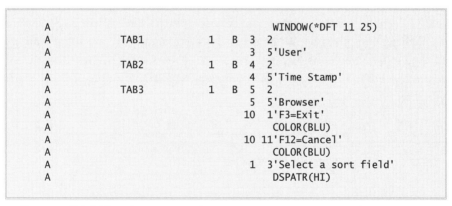

```
     A                                     WINDOW(*DFT 11 25)
     A            TAB1         1   B  3  2
     A                                  3  5'User'
     A            TAB2         1   B  4  2
     A                                  4  5'Time Stamp'
     A            TAB3         1   B  5  2
     A                                  5  5'Browser'
     A                                 10  1'F3=Exit'
     A                                     COLOR(BLU)
     A                                 10 11'F12=Cancel'
     A                                     COLOR(BLU)
     A                                  1  3'Select a sort field'
     A                                     DSPATR(HI)
```

Figure 8.1: This DDS code creates the window where a user can select the field for sorting.

F-specs

Now let's take a look at the RPG program SQL001RG. There is only one F-spec (Figure 8.2), but that is used for the display file. There are no F-specs for the data files. They will be accessed using embedded SQL. This F-spec defines a basic self-extending subfile program to list the Web hits from the file. This program allows the user to display a window using the F4 key and select a field on which to sort. When the user presses the Enter key after selecting a field, the data will be sorted by that field and redisplayed on the screen. Cool, huh?

```
Fsql001df  cf   e              workstn
F                                       sfile(sfl1:rrn1)
F                                       infds(info)
```

Figure 8.2: The only F-specification in the program defines the display file with the subfile.

Compiling the RPG/SQL

Before digging into the RPG code itself, you'll need to know about the compile options necessary to make this work. First, this source member is type SQLRPGLE, not RPGLE. This tells the compiler that there are going to be embedded SQL statements in this RPG code. The command used to create a program using a SQLRPGLE source member is Create SQL RPG ILE (CRTSQLRPGI). This command will verify, validate, and, if you choose, prepare the embedded SQL statements during compile time. When using this command, there are some options you need to take into consideration. Figure 8.3 shows some of the parameters that you might want to tinker with when compiling SQLRPGLE source code.

```
* COMPILING. In order to compile this program you will need
*            to use options that allow it to work correctly
*            between machines. These options are
*               COMMIT = *NONE
*               RDB    = Machine name that you will connect to.
*               DLYPRP = *YES
*               SQLPKG = The name & library that you want to
*                        use for the package. This will put the
*                        package on the RDB machine that you
*                        specify.
```

Figure 8.3: Compiling with embedded SQL is a little different from compiling with just RPG.

The Relational Database parameter (RDB) indicates which database you are using. This can be the name of your local DB2 database or, if you are networked using Distributed Relational Database Architecture (DRDA), it can contain the name of a remote AS/400 database. If you use a remote database in the RDB parameter, you will need to tell the compiler where to create the SQL package. You do this by entering a library and package name in the SQLPKG parameter. For example, if you wanted to run a program on AS/400a to look at data on AS/400b, you would put the name of the DRDA entry for AS/400b in the RDB parameter. You can find this name by asking someone or by typing the WRKRDBDIRE command to list the remote DB2 locations.

The Delay Preparation (DLYPRP) parameter asks you if you want to delay dynamic statement preparation for a PREPARE statement until the OPEN, EXECUTE, or DESCRIBE statement is run. Answer *YES to this parameter because you do not want to perform redundant access path validation. If you entered *NO, access path validation would be performed when the PREPARE statement was run and again when either the OPEN, EXECUTE, or DESCRIBE statement was run. By entering *YES, the access path validation is done only once, during the PREPARE statement.

The Commitment Control (COMMIT) parameter specifies whether to run the SQL statements in the program under commitment control and, if so, how. This affects only the embedded SQL statements. It doesn't affect any files defined in the RPG with F-specs. Entering anything other than *NONE requires that the journal function be on for the tables and views used in the embedded SQL statements. Refer to chapter 5 for a more detailed explanation on commitment control and how it affects updates, inserts, and record locking.

These are the common parameters related specifically to embedded SQL. They provide you some flexibility on how to run your application. Now let's take a look at some actual code. That's what you're really here to see, isn't it?

The D-specs

Now that you know how to compile an RPG program containing embedded SQL, you probably would like to know how to code one. Start by creating the basis for your dynamic selection capability, with the help of D-specs.

Define a stand-alone field, SelectOne, that's 500 bytes long to hold your initial SQL statement. The number 500 was selected at random. You need a variable large enough to hold your SQL statement. Initialize this field with the SQL statement shown in Figure 8.4.

```
D SelectOne       S              500A   INZ('SELECT requser,reqts,  -
D                                       browser  -
D                                       FROM webtemp2  -
D                                       ORDER BY')

D SelectTwo       S              500A   INZ(' ')
D OrderBy         S               20A   INZ('requser')
```

Figure 8.4: These D-specs are used to build the initial SELECT statement.

Next, define a second stand-alone field, SelectTwo, also 500 bytes long, to hold the user-defined SQL statement. This SQL statement will be made up of the initial SQL statement from SelectOne, plus the selection criteria assigned by the user. Also define a stand-alone field called OrderBy and initialize it to "requser," which is the name of the user field in the database file. The OrderBy variable will be used to append the field selected by the user to the ORDER BY clause in the SelectOne variable.

Rules and Regulations

You've set up the D-specs, but you've still not embedded any SQL. Before you do, you need to understand the rules involved. All blocks of SQL code must begin with a slash (/) in position 7, followed by the EXEC SQL statement. They must also end with a slash in position 7, followed by the END-EXEC statement. Between EXEC and END-EXEC you place all your SQL code. Each line will be signified by a plus sign in position 7. The RPG compiler uses these slashes and pluses to help it interrogate your SQL code.

If you look at a compiled listing, you will see where the compiler has removed your SQL statements and replaced them with data structures, calls to SQL APIs, and other RPG syntax. There is no need for you the check this code out other than to see what happens at compile time and to impress your friends and neighbors.

Figure 8.5 marks the first section of embedded SQL. The CONNECT RESET statement will connect to the local DB2 database. If you were going to connect to a database on another machine, you would connect to that remote database here by replacing the RESET parameter with the name of the remote database.

```
C/EXEC SQL
C+ CONNECT RESET
C/END-EXEC
```

Figure 8.5: Embedded SQL connects your program to your local database.

Prepare, Declare, and Open

Now let's look at the rest of the main routine. Start with Figure 8.6, which is the PREP subroutine. This is where the dynamic SQL statement will be built.

```
C       prep          BegSr
 *
 * Clear the subfile
 *
C                     Eval      *in31 = *on
C                     Write     sf1ctl
C                     Eval      *in31 = *off
C                     Eval      rrn1 = 0
C                     Eval      Lastrrn = 0
 *
 * Prepare the SQL statement for validation, since the program was
 * compiled with DLYPRP (*YES), it will wait until it is used before
 * it prepares th cursor.
 *
C                     Eval      SelectTwo = %TRIMR(SelectOne) + ' '
C                                         + OrderBy
 *
C/EXEC SQL
C+    PREPARE sel FROM :SelectTwo
C/END-EXEC
 *
 * Declare the SQL cursor to hold the data retrieved from the SELECT
 *
C/EXEC SQL
C+ DECLARE MYCSR SCROLL CURSOR FOR SEL
```

Figure 8.6: The PREP subroutine prepares the SQL statement for validation (part 1 of 2).

225

```
C/END-EXEC
 *
 * Open the SQL cursor.
 *
C
C/EXEC SQL
C+ OPEN MYCSR
C/END-EXEC
 *
C                    EndSr
 *
```

Figure 8.6: The PREP subroutine prepares the SQL statement for validation (part 2 of 2).

The first thing to do after clearing the subfile and initializing subfile fields and indicators is to create the dynamic SQL statement from what the user selected. Because this is the first time through, the default value is used for the OrderBy variable. This is set in the D-specs. Subsequent times through this subroutine, the user will have selected a field to sort on, and that data will be placed in the OrderBy variable. Once you have appended the data in OrderBy to the original SELECT statement defined in the D-specs, you have a completed SELECT statement that will retrieve your data and order it appropriately.

Now you'll use that SELECT statement to retrieve data. Start with the PREPARE statement to prepare a statement called SEL using the SelectTwo variable that was just created. The PREPARE statement will validate the SQL statement contained in the SelectTwo variable. Next, declare a cursor called MYCSR using the DECLARE statement. This cursor, which will be able to scroll, is created from the SEL statement prepared in the previous statement. Finally, open the cursor using the OPEN command.

Clear as spaghetti code, right? Okay, before going on, let's review cursors. When SQL runs a SELECT statement, the resulting rows create a result table. A cursor provides a way to access that table. It's like a subfile in its own right. The cursor is used within an SQL program to maintain a position in the result table. SQL uses the cursor to work with the data in the result table and make it available to your program. Your program may contain several cursors (although each must have a unique name).

There are two types of cursors: *serial* and *scrollable*. A serial cursor is defined without using the SCROLL keyword. This type of cursor allows you to fetch each row once—and only once. If you want to retrieve a row more than one time, you must close the cursor and reopen it. This kind of cursor is perfect for a LOAD ALL subfile; you want to see the data only once before loading into your subfile. In this case, the subfile will allow scrolling of the data.

The scrollable cursor is being used in this example, though. The advantage of a scrollable cursor is that you can move back and forth through the rows of data. Using different parameters in a FETCH statement, you can read the next or prior row, navigate to the first or last row, read the same row over again, or position any number of rows forward or backward from the current row. This type of cursor can be used if you are building your subfile one page at a time, or self-extending, as in this example. The data remains in the cursor and is loaded into your subfile only one page at a time.

You have successfully validated the SELECT statement contained in your variable using the PREPARE command, created a scrollable cursor that will contain the result table from your SELECT statement using the DECLARE command, and opened the cursor using the OPEN command. You are now ready to load the subfile from the cursor.

Fetch

Take a look at Figure 8.7. Instead of loading the subfile directly from the database file, it is loaded from the cursor using SQL's FETCH command.

```
     *
     * Process the 1 page of records in the SQL cursor or
     *     until the return code not = 0
     *
C                       Do          SubfilePage
     *
     * Get the next row from the SQL cursor.
     *
```

Figure 8.7: You can retrieve records from the cursor using FETCH instead of reading from a data file (part 1 of 2).

```
C/EXEC SQL
C+    FETCH NEXT FROM mycsr
C+        INTO :requser, :reqts, :browser
C/END-EXEC
   *
C                    If        sqlcod = 0
C                    Eval      rrn1   = rrn1  + 1
C                    Write     sfl1
C                    Else
C                    Leave
C                    EndIf
   *
C                    EndDo
```

Figure 8.7: You can retrieve records from the cursor using FETCH instead of reading from a data file (part 2 of 2).

Notice that the FETCH command is inside the DO loop, with the results placed into the display file's field names. Because this is a scrollable cursor, the NEXT parameter is used with FETCH. If this were a serial cursor, you would simply use FETCH because you could access each record in the cursor only once. SQLCOD is used to determine whether to write to the subfile record format. If you are astute (and I know you are), you might have noticed that SQLCOD is not defined anywhere in the program or the display file. So where did it come from? Well, when you embed SQL in your program and use the CRTSQLRPGI command to create the program, a data structure not unlike the file information data structure is included in your program. It is filled with all sorts of information about the SQL statements embedded in your program.

One example of that information is the error code returned when an SQL statement is run. It is contained in the SQLCOD variable and is set to zero upon successful execution of an SQL statement. For more information on the SQL Data Area (SQLDA), refer to IBM's *SQL AS/400 Programming* manual. For this program, the only data needed from the SQLDA is contained in the SQLCOD variable. Once the subfile is loaded, you are ready to display it. Now let's go back to the main routine.

Prompt for Sort Criteria

When displaying the subfile the first time, you will see the data sorted by user because the OrderBy variable was initialized to the user field. Now that the person running this program has control of the data, he or she can press F4 to sort the data another way.

When F4 is pressed, a number of subroutines will be executed. First, the SORT subroutine will determine what to place in the OrderBy variable. Then, the CLEAN subroutine closes the cursor, MYCSR, using the CLOSE command. Once the sort criterion is determined and the cursor is closed, the PREP and SFLBLD routines are executed again. You've already seen what they do. Figure 8.8 shows what happens when F4 is pressed.

```
     *
     * prompt to selection sorting criteria
     *
     C                    When       cfkey = prompt
     C                    ExSr       sort
     C                    ExSr       clean
     C                    ExSr       prep
     C                    ExSr       sflbld
```

Figure 8.8: When F4 is pressed, this block of code sorts, cleans, and prepares the SQL statement before loading the subfile.

Let's take a closer look at the SORT subroutine (shown in Figure 8.9). There is no new, exciting embedded SQL code in this routine, but there is some code that might interest you.

```
     C     sort           BegSr
     *
     C                    ExFmt      window1
     *
     C                    Select
     *
     C                    When       tab1 <> *blank
```

Figure 8.9: This routine determines which field to sort by (part 1 of 2).

```
C                    MoveL(p)  'requser'    OrderBy
C                    Clear                  tab1
 *
C                    When      tab2 <> *blank
C                    MoveL(p)  'reqts'      OrderBy
C                    Clear                  tab2
 *
C                    When      tab3 <> *blank
C                    MoveL(p)  'browser'    OrderBy
C                    Clear                  tab3
 *
C                    EndSl
 *
C                    EndSr
 *
```

Figure 8.9: This routine determines which field to sort by (part 2 of 2).

This subroutine determines what field to append to the ORDER BY clause in the dynamic SQL statement. A window is displayed that lists the fields contained in the subfile. The user can select one of these fields and press Enter. The program then determines which field was selected and places that field in the OrderBy variable. Figures 8.10 through 8.12 show what this all looks like.

```
SQL001RG              Dynamic Sort with Embedded SQL              10/09/00
                                                                 15:04:47

User           Time Stamp                        Browser
000000001      2000-09-19-18.35.10.000000        X
000000001      1999-11-04-19.33.13.000000        IE 5.0
000000001      1999-11-04-19.33.13.000000        IE 5.0
000000001      1999-11-04-19.33.22.000000        IE 5.0
000000001      1999-11-07-02.09.45.000000        IE 4.01
000000001      1999-11-07-02.09.45.000000        IE 4.01
000000001      1999-11-07-02.10.05.000000        IE 4.01
000000001      1999-11-07-02.10.08.000000        IE 4.01
000000001      1999-11-07-02.10.08.000000        IE 4.01
000000001      1999-11-15-08.23.32.000000        IE 5.0
000000001      1999-11-15-08.23.32.000000        IE 5.0
000000001      1999-11-15-08.55.55.000000        IE 5.0
000000001      1999-11-15-08.56.12.000000        IE 5.0
000000001      1999-10-07-02.09.45.000000        IE 4.01
000000001      1999-10-07-02.09.45.000000        IE 4.01
000000001      1999-10-07-02.10.05.000000        IE 4.01
000000001      1999-10-07-02.10.08.000000        IE 4.01
                                                            More...
F3=Exit    F4=Sort   F12=Cancel
```

Figure 8.10: Here is the initial display, sorted by user.

When the user presses F4 to request a change in sort order, the screen (shown in Figure 8.11) is displayed. After the user makes a choice and presses Enter, the file is re-sorted and redisplayed, as shown in Figure 8.12.

```
 SQL001RG              Dynamic Sort with Embedded SQL      10/09/00
 ...........................                               15:04:47
 :   Select a sort field    :
 :                          :                      Browser
 :     User                 : 35.10.000000        X
 :     Time Stamp           : 33.13.000000        IE 5.0
 : 1   Browser              : 33.13.000000        IE 5.0
 :                          : 33.22.000000        IE 5.0
 :                          : 09.45.000000        IE 4.01
 :                          : 09.45.000000        IE 4.01
 :                          : 10.05.000000        IE 4.01
 : F3=Exit   F12=Cancel     : 10.08.000000        IE 4.01
 :                          : 10.08.000000        IE 4.01
 :..........................: 23.32.000000        IE 5.0
   000000001       1999-11-15-08.23.32.000000     IE 5.0
   000000001       1999-11-15-08.55.55.000000     IE 5.0
   000000001       1999-11-15-08.56.12.000000     IE 5.0
   000000001       1999-10-07-02.09.45.000000     IE 4.01
   000000001       1999-10-07-02.09.45.000000     IE 4.01
   000000001       1999-10-07-02.10.05.000000     IE 4.01
   000000001       1999-10-07-02.10.08.000000     IE 4.01
                                                          More...

   F3=Exit   F4=Sort   F12=Cancel
```

Figure 8.11: The user has pressed F4 and chosen to sort by browser.

Pretty simple, huh? Well, if you really want to separate this technique from what's easily implemented using logical files and OPNQRYF, you can allow the user to select more than one field. The user could, for example, sort by user ID, browser, and timestamp by entering a 1 next to User, a 2 next to Browser, and a 3 next to Timestamp after pressing F4. Place the logic in your SORT routine to interrogate all the fields selected, put them in the correct order, and put that information in the OrderBy variable. Instead of the OrderBy variable containing one field to append to the ORDER BY clause, it would now contain three.

Go ahead, give it a try.

231

```
SQL001RG              Dynamic Sort with Embedded SQL        10/09/00
                                                            15:10:40

User            Time Stamp                    Browser
000000106       1999-11-08-04.02.34.000000    IE 3.0
000000142       1999-11-08-16.35.59.000000    IE 3.0
000000142       1999-11-08-23.43.54.000000    IE 3.0
000000129       1999-11-09-00.50.34.000000    IE 3.0
000000117       1999-11-09-01.16.48.000000    IE 3.0
000000117       1999-11-09-01.38.22.000000    IE 3.0
000000117       1999-11-09-01.59.14.000000    IE 3.0
000000122       1999-11-09-02.17.33.000000    IE 3.0
000000122       1999-11-09-02.35.02.000000    IE 3.0
000000122       1999-11-09-02.51.43.000000    IE 3.0
000000114       1999-11-09-03.07.50.000000    IE 3.0
000000114       1999-11-09-03.23.17.000000    IE 3.0
000000114       1999-11-09-03.38.09.000000    IE 3.0
000000114       1999-11-09-03.52.42.000000    IE 3.0
000000121       1999-11-09-04.07.19.000000    IE 3.0
000000121       1999-11-09-04.24.33.000000    IE 3.0
000000121       1999-11-09-04.38.16.000000    IE 3.0
                                                             More...
F3=Exit   F4=Sort   F12=Cancel
```

Figure 8.12: The list is now sorted by browser.

Parameter Markers

How about kicking this application up a notch by allowing the user to key a date range to shorten the Web hit list? Adding this to the dynamic sort doesn't seem like a big deal at first. You can use a logical view, sorted by timestamp, to set a lower limit at the FROM timestamp and read through the file until you reach the TO timestamp.

Well, that's great if you always want the data sorted by timestamp, but what if you still want it sorted by user or browser? You're back to using multiple logical files and negotiating through them to get the desired data. With fixed-list SELECT statements (that is, SELECTs that contain a fixed number of parameters of the same data type), you can use one or more placeholders inside the SELECT statement and substitute them with data at a later time (like when a user enters a date range). To do this, simply use a question mark inside your SELECT where your data would normally go. Figure 8.13 shows a modified version of the SelectOne D-spec from the previous example.

Notice that the WHERE clause states that the timestamp, REQTS, inside WEBTEMP2, should be greater than or equal to some data to be determined later, and less than or equal to some other data to be determined earlier. Let's take a look at the data to be determined later. Figure 8.14 shows the entry screen that allows the user to key in a date range. Defaults have been set in the timestamps so that, even if the user presses Enter without entering anything, the SQL will still contain valid FROM and TO timestamps.

```
D SelectOne      S             500A   INZ('SELECT requser, reqts,  -
D                                      browser, UCASE(reqfile)  -
D                                      FROM webtemp2 -
D                                      WHERE reqts >= ?  And  -
D                                      reqts <= ? ')
```

Figure 8.13: Using parameter markers allows user-entered data to be easily inserted into SELECT statements.

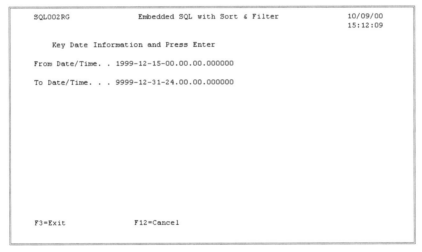

```
SQL002RG              Embedded SQL with Sort & Filter          10/09/00
                                                               15:12:09

    Key Date Information and Press Enter

From Date/Time. . 1999-12-15-00.00.00.000000

To Date/Time. . . 9999-12-31-24.00.00.000000









F3=Exit              F12=Cancel
```

Figure 8.14: The user has selected everything greater than December 15, 1999.

Now that the user has entered timestamps, or taken the defaults, these entries can be inserted into the SELECT statement from Figure 8.13. This is done during the opening of the cursor. Remember the PREP subroutine? It will contain a minor modification in the OPEN statement. Instead of simply opening MYCSR, you now provide two host variables (you got it, one for each) that will be used to insert data into the SELECT statement. Figure 8.15 shows the modified OPEN statement employing the USING parameter with the FROM and TO timestamps (date1 and date2).

233

```
* Open the SQL cursor.
*
C
C/EXEC SQL
C+ OPEN MYCSR USING :date1, :date2
C/END-EXEC
*
```

Figure 8.15: Open the cursor using date1 and date2 that the user entered from the display screen.

Figure 8.16 shows that the data entered on the first screen is reflected in the subfile list because you only see dates greater than December 15, 1999. To make sure, you can press F4 and choose to sort by timestamp. As you can see, this minor modification to the original dynamic sorting subfile can provide users with added flexibility without adding complicated logic to your program.

```
SQL002RG              Embedded SQL with Sort & Filter            10/09/00
                                                                 15:14:08

User           File Downloaded      Time Stamp                 Browser
000000001      X
                                    2000-09-19-18.35.10.000000  X




                                                                   Bottom

 F3=Exit    F4=Sort    F12=Cancel
```

Figure 8.16: This list contains Web hits since December 15, 1999.

Optional WHERE Clause

You won't always be able to use placeholders with fixed-list SELECT statements. There might be times when you allow optional data to be keyed. Adding to the previous example at little, you might provide capabilities to filter by user and downloaded files, but make them optional; that is, a blank entry in the user field would include all users, just as a blank entry for downloaded files would include all downloaded files. Depending on what was entered, your SELECT statement would change. Figure 8.17 shows the new entry screen.

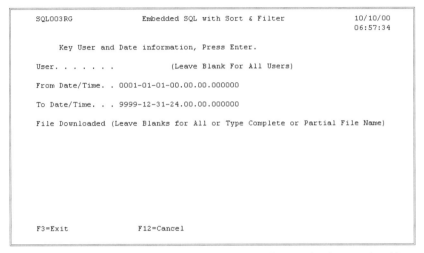

```
SQL003RG              Embedded SQL with Sort & Filter           10/10/00
                                                                06:57:34

        Key User and Date information, Press Enter.

    User. . . . . . .            (Leave Blank For All Users)

    From Date/Time. . 0001-01-01-00.00.00.000000

    To Date/Time. . . 9999-12-31-24.00.00.000000

    File Downloaded (Leave Blanks for All or Type Complete or Partial File Name)




    F3=Exit             F12=Cancel
```

Figure 8.17: Your SELECT statement will change depending on what is entered on this screen.

The D-spec that defines the SELECT statement, SelectOne, becomes much simpler and is built only to the lowest common denominator. The rest of the statement is built based on what is entered on the display screen. This technique was used in the very first example to add the ORDER BY clause but, in this case, it is a little more complex. Figure 8.18 shows the basic SELECT statement.

```
D SelectOne      S          500A    INZ('SELECT requser, reqts,  -
D                                   browser, UCASE(reqfile)  -
D                                   FROM webtemp2')
```

Figure 8.18: The basic SELECT statement is placed in a host variable.

The WHERE and ORDER BY clauses are added to the SELECT statement as the user enters data on the screen. The WHERE clause may take many forms. If no data is entered for the user or downloaded file, then neither would be included in the WHERE clause. However, either or both might be entered and would then be included. Figure 8.19 shows the FILTER subroutine that is called whenever the Enter key is pressed on the first screen.

```
C       filter      BegSr
 *
C                   Clear               WhereClause
 *
C                   Eval      WhereClause = 'WHERE' + ' '
C                                 + DateFilter + ' >= ' + Quo
C                                 + %Char(Date1) + Quote
C                                 + ' And ' + DateFilter + '
C                                 + Quote + %Char(Date2) + Qu
 *
C                   If        User > *zero
C                   Eval      WhereClause = %TrimR(WhereClause) + ' '
C                                 + ' And ' + UserFilter
C                                 + ' = ' + %Char(user)
C                   EndIf
 *
C                   If        file > *blanks
C                   Eval      WhereClause = %TrimR(WhereClause) + ' '
C                                 + ' And ' +  FileFilter
C                                 + ' LIKE ' + quote + '%'
C                                 + %TrimR(file) + '%' + quot
C                   EndIf
 *
C                   EndSr
```

Figure 8.19: This routine interrogates the data and builds the WHERE clause.

The first thing the routine does is clear the WhereClause variable. Then, it performs the timestamp filter evaluation. (I always set FROM and TO timestamp defaults. It's too much work to leave those fields blank and try to figure out if none, one, or both were entered; I default the FROM timestamp to *LOVAL and the TO to *HIVAL.)

Next, the routine checks to see if something was entered in the user field. If so, then that entry is added to the WHERE clause, and the list will only include user IDs matching that entry. The last thing the routine does is check to see if something was entered in the downloaded file field. If so, downloaded files that contain the wildcard entered in the field should be retrieved. For example, if *AS400* was keyed into this field, you would only want to see downloaded files containing *AS400* somewhere in the name. Figures 8.20 and 8.21 show the results.

```
SQL003RG              Embedded SQL with Sort & Filter        10/10/00
                                                             06:57:34

     Key User and Date information, Press Enter.

User. . . . . . . 000000001  (Leave Blank For All Users)

From Date/Time. . 0001-01-01-00.00.00.000000

To Date/Time. . . 9999-12-31-24.00.00.000000

File Downloaded (Leave Blanks for Type or Key Complete or Partial File Name)
AS400




F3=Exit              F12=Cancel
```

Figure 8.20: These entries will significantly shorten the list.

```
SQL003RG              Embedded SQL with Sort & Filter        10/10/00
                                                             07:02:26

User            File Downloaded      Time Stamp              Browser
000000001       /AS400_REPORTS.HTM
                                     1999-10-15-08.23.32.000000   IE 5.0
000000001       /AS400_REPORTS.HTM
                                     1999-11-15-08.23.32.000000   IE 5.0







                                                             Botto
F3=Exit    F4=Sort    F12=Cancel
```

Figure 8.21: The list reflects what was entered on the previous screen.

237

Notice that you have to be very specific when building a SELECT statement this way. Everything must be exact. That is why you see the %TRIMR function used to trim leading and trailing blanks, as well as the quote constant, which is declared in the D-specs, used to surround the data keyed on the screen. For flexibility, it's also a good idea to define constants to hold file field names instead of hardcoding them into the WHERE clause. If you are accustomed to building complicated OPNQRYFS, you should have no problems with this stuff.

Virtual Reality

As the beginning of this chapter mentions, one of the advantages of using embedded SQL is that you can construct very complicated queries containing virtual fields and files, and use built-in functions to very easily display data on a screen or report. Now you'll see how to embed one of those queries into your RPG programs. Using SQL this way can save lots of work in your RPG coding. To be consistent, and because I despise producing reports that never get looked at instead of displaying data to the screen, let's stick to the subfile example. Just understand that any of the examples in this chapter can be sent to the printer instead of the screen. (However, try dynamically sorting a report and let me know how that one works out, will ya?)

Suppose you wanted to take the data from the Web hit file, WEBTEMP2, and calculate the percentage of hits per hour against the total hits, as well as the percentage of how much was downloaded per hour against the total downloaded.

Because there is a query similar to this in chapter 5, I won't spend too much time explaining how the query works. The point here is to see how embedded SQL can save you from overdosing on painkillers as you try to accomplish a similar task using RPG and logical files. Basically, the query will read the WEBTEMP2 file, create virtual tables A and B, and calculate the virtual fields to be housed in those virtual tables. It also will group this data by hour of the day and produce the three columns in which you are interested. Figure 8.22 shows the query.

The only fields that actually exist are those beginning with *REQ*. The only table that exists is WEBTEMP2. All other tables and columns used in this query are virtual, created only for the purpose of this query. Once the cursor is closed, these imaginary entities disappear until the next time it is run.

```
D SelectOne       S            500A  INZ('SELECT A.HR, -
D                                     A.HKB/B.TKB*100 AS PCTKB,  -
D                                     A.HHITS/B.THITS*100 AS PCTHITS -
D                                     FROM (SELECT HOUR(REQTS) AS HR, -
D                                     CAST(SUM(REQSIZE) AS DECIMAL  -
D                                     (10,2)) AS HKB,  -
D                                     CAST(COUNT(*) AS DECIMAL  -
D                                     (10,2)) AS HHITS  -
D                                     FROM WEBTEMP2  -
D                                     GROUP BY HOUR(REQTS)) AS A,  -
D                                     (SELECT CAST(COUNT(*)  -
D                                     AS DECIMAL(10,2)) AS THITS,  -
D                                     CAST(SUM(REQSIZE)  -
D                                     AS DECIMAL(10,2)) AS TKB  -
D                                     FROM WEBTEMP2) AS B  -
D                                     ORDER BY ')
```

Figure 8.22: This query creates virtual tables and columns to generate summary data.

This is not unlike using arrays and work fields in an RPG program. Your arrays and work fields exist only while the program is running. The difference is that built-in functions are used to create the virtual entities in your SQL, saving you from doing it yourself, as in RPG. For instance, the virtual column HR is a result of running the HOUR built-in function against the REQTS column, which is a timestamp. The SUM and CAST functions are also used to produce virtual fields.

RPG has built-in functions, too, and they can do some awesome things, but they can't be used in OPNQRYF or in logical files. This one query saves you from having to read each WEBTEMP2 record, interrogate the timestamp to see which hour of the day it is, store the size and count information in corresponding arrays, as well as keep running totals of the data so that the percent-to-total calculations can be performed later.

Another hassle of performing this stuff in RPG is the dynamic sorting capability. Because you would have to use arrays and work fields to accomplish the summary, alternative sorting would cause some problems. Of course, you could create a temporary physical file to hold your summary data and create logical views or OPNQRYFs over that file to sort your data. Or you could employ the technique you learned earlier in this chapter and use SQL to dynamically sort the data. In this example, the latter option is used. SQL004RG is a copy of SQL001RG, except that the query is a little more complicated. In the F4 sort logic, a choice is added to allow two of the columns to be sorted by ascending or descending order. Figures 8.23, 8.24, and 8.25 show the results of running SQL004RG.

```
SQL004RG               Dynamic Sort with Embedded SQL              10/18/00
                                                                   11:03:17

Hour            Percent of KB to Total          Percent of Hits to Total
 18             1.42418439643686517860000        5.15565804645033767080000
 03             2.24317291489596524700000        3.29435018942513589190000
 22             2.38664950864102292780000        4.44737275572393345410000
 17             2.47369121697961858660000        3.88733322352166035240000
 02             2.64515769340610702830000        1.77894910228957338160000
 06             2.66256603507382616000000        1.91072310986657881730000
 05             2.80763554897148559140000        4.28265524625267665950000
 00             2.83562543165291635230000        3.88733322352166035240000
 12             3.12212349909943121370000        3.09668917805962773840000
 04             3.15432324218416660120000        2.04249711744358425300000
 14             3.16194650291447497920000        4.11793773678141986490000
 23             3.18822968543240386440000        3.12963267995387909730000
 19             3.47063167248651422420000        5.46862131444572558060000
 11             3.56541042156631838600000        2.40487563828034920110000
 15             3.73949383824350970370000        8.49942348871685060120000
 21             3.99265436249628792710000        3.68967221215615219890000
 20             4.69490458977185970010000        9.22418053039038049740000
                                                                     More...

F3=Exit    F4=Sort    F12=Cancel
```

Figure 8.23: The results of the query in 8.22 produce a nice summarized display.

```
SQL004RG               Dynamic Sort with Embedded SQL              10/18/00
..........................                                        11:03:17
:  Select a sort field   :
:                        : o Total          Percent of Hits to Total
:    Hour                : 5178600          5.15565804645033767080000
:    % KB                : 5247000          3.29435018942513589190000
:    % Hits              : 2927800          4.44737275572393345410000
: 1  % KB Descending     : 8586600          3.88733322352166035240000
:    % Hits Descending   : 7028300          1.77894910228957338160000
:                        : 6160000          1.91072310986657881730000
:                        : 5591400          4.28265524625267665950000
: F3=Exit    F12=Cancel  : 6352300          3.88733322352166035240000
:                        : 1213700          3.09668917805962773840000
:........................: 6601200          2.04249711744358425300000
 14             3.16194650291447497920000        4.11793773678141986490000
 23             3.18822968543240386440000        3.12963267995387909730000
 19             3.47063167248651422420000        5.46862131444572558060000
 11             3.56541042156631838600000        2.40487563828034920110000
 15             3.73949383824350970370000        8.49942348871685060120000
 21             3.99265436249628792710000        3.68967221215615219890000
 20             4.69490458977185970010000        9.22418053039038049740000
                                                                     More...

F3=Exit    F4=Sort    F12=Cancel
```

Figure 8.24: Press F4 and select to see the hour with the highest percentage of hits.

```
SQL004RG              Dynamic Sort with Embedded SQL            10/18/00
                                                                11:07:13

Hour          Percent of KB to Total        Percent of Hits to Total
 16         11.813437191727282967400        6.720474386427277219500
 09          8.876206210340554950600        4.612090265195190248700
 01          6.205903134525520287500        3.821446219733157634600
 08          5.719607367938385848400        2.635480151540108713500
 13          5.426054939816063234300        5.929830340965244605500
 10          5.285991746398009304900        4.019107231098665788100
 07          5.104398849001409734300        1.943666611760830176200
 20          4.694904589771859700100        9.224180530390380497400
 21          3.992654362496287927100        3.689672212156152198900
 15          3.739493838243509703700        8.499423488716850601200
 11          3.565410421566318386000        2.404875638280349201100
 19          3.470631672486514224200        5.468621314445725580600
 23          3.188229685432403864400        3.129632679953879097300
 14          3.161946502914474979200        4.117937736781419864900
 04          3.154323242184166601200        2.042497117443584253000
 12          3.122123499099431213700        3.096689178059627738400
 00          2.835625431652916352300        3.887333223521660352400
                                                              More...

F3=Exit   F4=Sort   F12=Cancel
```

Figure 8:25: The results show that hour 16, which is 4 P.M., had the most hits.

Voila!

What slick techniques! No OPNQRYF commands and, possibly, no access paths to maintain. Now that you've seen how to use embedded SQL to do some things that might be cumbersome in RPG, remember that it doesn't all come for free. Even though you don't have to manage all the necessary access paths yourself, the system will have to do so for you. When you create sort or a selection criteria on the fly—and the AS/400 isn't already maintaining a similar access path—OS/400 will create a temporary file on the fly, just as it would with OPNQRYF. This might send your users to the coffee machine to grab a cup of coffee and complain about this new application that takes so long to run.

So, be careful. You might want to perform some database analysis before you start, and create a few of the access paths that you know will be used most often. Maybe the majority of the users will sort by timestamp, and you might have provided a timestamp filter. In that case, it might make sense to build a permanent access path by timestamp. However, if only a handful of users cares about sorting by browser, you might let that one get created temporarily, on the fly.

You also can perform multiple row fetches and let SQL handle record-blocking for you. That can certainly speed up your database performance significantly. Just know that there are performance issues to take into consideration before you unleash this powerful mechanism into your RPG applications. Do some research. All in all, though, combining embedded SQL and RPG can take your applications to new heights. Enjoy!

Chapter Summary

This chapter exposes the power that embedded SQL can add to your RPG programs. It also discusses when SQL is appropriate for the RPG developer, and when sticking with record-level access is prudent. I hope that you see the power of embedded SQL and how it can make your everyday programming life easier and more productive. You should now have more through knowledge of the following concepts:

- SQL statements can be placed in RPG variables.

- RPG programs can connect to local or remote databases.

- PREPARE causes SQL statements to be validated and made ready for execution.

- If DLYPRP (*YES) is specified in the CRTSQLRPGI command, the preparation is delayed until the first time the statement is used.

- Cursors can be used to position record pointers in SQL results.

- Cursors can be opened and closed.

- SQL has return codes to indicate the state of cursors or requested operations.

- Parameters are placeholders for data that will be bound before statement execution.

Appendix A

AS/400 SYSTEM CATALOG

This appendix details each AS/400 system catalog view and shows example queries that allow you to get information from the catalog. Some catalog views are available in the QSYS2 library. The following catalog views are automatically created in any SQL collection (which are created with the CREATE DATABASE or CREATE SCHEMA commands):

> SYSCHKCST
> SYSCOLUMNS
> SYSCST
> SYSCSTCOL
> SYSCSTDEP
> SYSINDEXES
> SYSKEYCST
> SYSKEYS
> SYSPACKAGE
> SYSREFCST
> SYSTABLES
> SYSVIEWDEP
> SYSVIEWS

Note that if you are selecting information from a catalog view that was created in an SQL collection, the view will contain information only about the items in the collection. The views in QSYS2, however, contain information about all items on your AS/400.

The following catalogs are available only in the QSYS2 library:

SYSLANGAUGES
SYSFUNCS
SYSPARMS
SYSPROCS
SYSROUTINES
SYSTYPES

SYSTABLES

SYSTABLES is probably the most important catalog table, as it defines the tables and views on the AS/400. It is implemented as a view and actually pulls information from the QADBXREF physical file. It is described in Table A.1.

Table A.1: SYSTABLES

Column Name	Data Type	Description
TABLE_NAME	VARCHAR(128)	The name of the table.
TABLE_OWNER	VARCHAR(128)	The person or account that created the table.
TABLE_TYPE	CHAR(1)	A =Alias L = DDS logical file P = Physical file T = Table V =View
COLUMN_COUNT	INTEGER	The number of columns in the table. If TABLE_TYPE is A, then this is a zero.
ROW_LENGTH	INTEGER	The maximum record length.
TABLE_TEXT	VARCHAR(50)	If you used the LABEL ON statement to add a label to the table, this is the label.
LONG_COMMENT	VARCHAR(2000)	If you used COMMENT ON to supply a comment to the table, this is the comment. It can be null.

Table A.1: SYSTABLES *(continued)*		
Column Name	Data Type	Description
TABLE_SCHEMA	VARCHAR(128)	The SQL library name where the table is found.
LAST_ALTERED_TIMESTAMP	TIMESTAMP	The last time the table was altered.
SYSTEM_TABLE_NAME	CHAR(10)	The AS/400 system table name, if the SQL table name is longer than 10 characters.
SYSTEM_TABLE_SCHEMA	CHAR(10)	The library where the table is found. If the SQL library name is longer than 10 characters, this represents the name of the library on the AS/400.
FILE_TYPE	CHAR(1)	D = Data file or alias S = Source file
BASE_TABLE_SCHEMA	VARCHAR(128)	If this is an alias, this column contains the name of the schema (library) where the base table is found. If this is not an alias, this field is null.
BASE_TABLE_NAME	VARCHAR(128)	If this is an alias, this is the SQL name of the table that the alias refers to. Otherwise, it is null.
BASE_TABLE_MEMBER	VARCHAR(10)	If this is an alias, this column contains the member name if the alias refers to a member. If the alias does not refer to a member, this field contains *first. If this is not an alias record, this column contains null.

SYSTABLES *Queries*

Here are a few interesting queries that you can do against the SYSTABLES catalog:

- Return all tables in the SQLBOOK library:

```
SELECT TABLE_NAME, TABLE_OWNER, TABLE_TYPE, COLUMN_COUNT
FROM QSYS2.SYSTABLES
WHERE TABLE_SCHEMA='SQLBOOK';
```

- Return only views in the SQLBOOK library:

```
SELECT TABLE_NAME, TABLE_OWNER, TABLE_TYPE, COLUMN_COUNT
FROM QSYS2.SYSTABLES
WHERE TABLE_SCHEMA='SQLBOOK' AND
TABLE_TYPE='V';
```

- Find the source tables for aliases in the SQLBOOK library:

```
SELECT BASE_TABLE_NAME, BASE_TABLE_MEMBER
FROM QSYS2.SYSTABLES
WHERE TABLE_TYPE = 'A' AND
TABLE_SCHEMA='SQLBOOK'
```

- Find tables whose row length is greater than 300 bytes:

```
SELECT TABLE_NAME, TABLE_OWNER, TABLE_TYPE, COLUMN_COUNT
FROM QSYS2.SYSTABLES
WHERE ROW_LENGTH>300;
```

- Find all the source files in your system:

```
SELECT TABLE_NAME, TABLE_OWNER, TABLE_TYPE, COLUMN_COUNT
FROM QSYS2.SYSTABLES
WHERE FILE_TYPE='S';
```

- Find logical files that are viewed as tables (DDS-created logicals):

```
SELECT TABLE_NAME, TABLE_OWNER, TABLE_TYPE, COLUMN_COUNT
FROM QSYS2.SYSTABLES
WHERE TABLE_TYPE='L';
```

SYSCOLUMNS

Second most important, the SYSCOLUMNS view lists the columns available in the database, the table they belong to, and information about their data type. SYSCOLUMNS is described in Table A.2.

Table A.2: SYSCOLUMNS

Column Name	Data Type	Description
COLUMN_NAME	VARCHAR(128)	The SQL name of the column.
TABLE_NAME	VARCHAR(128)	The table or view that owns the column.
TABLE_OWNER	VARCHAR(128)	The owner of the table or view.
ORDINAL_POSITION	INTEGER	The offset of the column within the table; one-based.
DATA_TYPE	CHAR(8)	The SQL data type of the column. It can be any of the following: BIGINT, INTEGER, SMALLINT, DECIMAL, NUMERIC, FLOAT, REAL, DOUBLE PRECISION, BLOB, CHAR, VARCHAR, CLOB, GRAPHIC, VARG, DBCLOB, DATE, TIME, TIMESTAMP, DATALINK, or DISTINCT (a user-defined type).
LENGTH	INTEGER	The maximum length of the column in bytes.
NUMERIC_SCALE	INTEGER	The scale of a numeric, binary, or decimal column. Null if not applicable.
IS_NULLABLE	CHAR(1)	Y if the column can contain a null value, else N.
IS_UPDATABLE	CHAR(1)	Y if the column can be updated, else N.
LONG_COMMENT	VARCHAR(2000)	Contains the content of a COMMENT ON statement, else null.
HAS_DEFAULT	CHAR(1)	Y if the column has a default value.
COLUMN_HEADING	VARCHAR(60)	The results of a LABEL ON statement, else null.

247

	Table A.2: SYSCOLUMNS (*continued*)	
Column Name	Data Type	Description
STORAGE	INTEGER	The storage requirements in bytes for the column data.
NUMERIC_PRECISION	INTEGER	Numeric precision if the column is numeric, else null.
CCSID	INTEGER	The CCSID of string columns, or null if not a string.
TABLE_SCHEMA	VARCHAR(128)	The SQL name of the schema where the column is found.
COLUMN_DEFAULT	VARCHAR(2000)	The default value of the column, if it has one, else null.
CHARACTER_MAXIMUM_LENGTH	INTEGER	The maximum length of a string data type, else null.
CHARACTER_OCTET_LENGTH	INTEGER	The number of bytes for CHAR columns.
NUMERIC_PRECISION_RADIX	INTEGER	Null if not numeric, else precision radix.
DATETIME_PRECISION	INTEGER	Indicates microseconds: zero for date and time, six for timestamp, null for all other types.
COLUMN_TEXT	VARCHAR(50)	Contains the results of a LABEL ON statement, else null.
SYSTEM_COLUMN_NAME	CHAR(10)	The system name of the column, which is the same as the SQL name for names 10 characters or less.

Table A.2: SYSCOLUMNS (*continued*)

Column Name	Data Type	Description
SYSTEM_TABLE_NAME	CHAR(10)	The system name of the table, which is the same as the SQL name for names 10 characters or less.
SYSTEM_TABLE_SCHEMA	CHAR(10)	Identifies the library where the table is found. The same as SCHEMA if SCHEMA is 10 characters or less.
USER_DEFINED_TYPE_SCHEMA	VARCHAR(128)	Names the SQL collection where a user-defined type is defined, else null.
USER_DEFINED_TYPE_NAME	VARCHAR(128)	The name of the user-defined type, else null.

SYSCOLUMNS *Query*

The following query is useful to list all of the columns in a SYSCOLUMNS table:

```
SELECT COLUMN_NAME, ORDINAL_POSITION, DATA_TYPE, LENGTH
FROM QSYS2.SYSCOLUMNS
WHERE TABLE_NAME = 'WEBTEMP' AND
TABLE_SCHEMA = 'SQLBOOK'
ORDER BY 2;
```

Note the ORDER BY 2 clause in this query. It ensures that the SELECT statement delivers the columns in the order in which they are defined in the table.

SYSVIEWS

The SYSVIEWS table, shown in Table A.3, contains all the views that have been created against physical files on your AS/400. You can also get a list of views from the SYSTABLES view, but this table has more information about the views.

Table A.3: SYSVIEWS		
Column Name	Data Type	Description
TABLE_NAME	VARCHAR(128)	The name of the view.
VIEW_OWNER	VARCHAR(128)	The creator/owner of the view.
SEQNO	INTEGER	Always one.
CHECK_OPTION	CHAR(1)	N = No check option, Y= Check option, C = Cascade.
VIEW_DEFINITION	VARCHAR(10000)	The SQL statement that built the view, or null if it cannot be shown.
IS_UPDATABLE	CHAR(1)	Y if the view can be updated, N if it is read-only.
TABLE_SCHEMA	VARCHAR(128)	The SQL name of the view schema.
SYSTEM_VIEW_NAME	CHAR(10)	The AS/400 view name if TABLE_NAME is greater than 10 characters, else TABLE_NAME.
SYSTEM_VIEW_SCHEMA	CHAR(10)	The library AS/400 if TABLE_NAME is greater than 10 characters, else TABLE_NAME.

SYSVIEWS Queries

The following queries are useful against the SYSVIEWS view:

- Query to retrieve the SQL statement that created a view:

```
SELECT VIEW_DEFINITION
FROM QSYS2.SYSVIEWS
WHERE TABLE_NAME = 'VTEST' AND
TABLE_SCHEMA = 'SQLBOOK';
```

- Query to list all views on system that can be updated:

```
SELECT TABLE_NAME, TABLE_SCHEMA
FROM QSYS2.SYSVIEWS
WHERE IS_UPDATABLE='Y';
```

SYSVIEWDEP

The SYSVIEWDEP view, shown in Table A.4, allows you to find on which tables a view is dependent. You need this because the DSPDBR will not tell you about view dependencies.

Table A.4: SYSVIEWDEP

Column Name	Data Type	Description
VIEW_NAME	VARCHAR(128)	The view's SQL name.
VIEW_OWNER	VARCHAR(128)	The owner/creator of the view.
TABLE_NAME	VARCHAR(128)	The SQL table name of the dependent table.
TABLE_OWNER	VARCHAR(128)	The owner/creator of the dependent table.
TABLE_SCHEMA	VARCHAR(128)	The SQL collection where the dependent table is found.
TABLE_TYPE	CHAR(1)	T=Table, P=Physical file, V=View, L=DDS logical.
VIEW_SCHEMA	VARCHAR(128)	The name of the view's collection.

Column Name	Data Type	Description
SYSTEM_VIEW_NAME	CHAR(10)	The AS/400 file name of the view, which is VIEW_NAME if VIEW_NAME is 10 characters or less.
SYSTEM_VIEW_SCHEMA	CHAR(10)	The library name where the view is found, which is VIEW_SCHEMA if VIEW_SCHEMA is 10 characters or less.
SYSTEM_TABLE_NAME	CHAR(10)	The system table name of the dependent table, which is TABLE_NAME if TABLE_NAME is 10 characters or less.
SYSTEM_TABLE_SCHEMA	CHAR(10)	The library name where the dependent table is found, which is TABLE_SCHEMA if TABLE_SCHEMA is 10 characters or less.

Table A.4: SYSVIEWDEP *(continued)*

SYSVIEWDEP Query

The following query is useful against the SYSVIEWDEP view to find all tables dependent on the SYSINDEXES view:

```
SELECT TABLE_NAME, TABLE_SCHEMA
FROM QSYS2.SYSVIEWDEP
WHERE VIEW_NAME='SYSINDEXES'
AND VIEW_SCHEMA='QSYS2';
```

SYSINDEXES

SYSINDEXES (Table A.5) lists all of the indexes created against SQL tables. This table details the index name, the physical file referenced by the index, whether the index is unique, and the library and logical file name where the index data is stored. Unfortunately, DDS logical files are not listed as indexes (only indexes created by the CREATE INDEX command). To fix this, an Excel spreadsheet is included on the CD, which finds all of the dependent logical files for a physical file and lists the columns of the physical file. Details on the spreadsheet are given at the end of this appendix.

Table A.5: SYSINDEXES

Column Name	Data Type	Description
INDEX_NAME	VARCHAR(128)	The SQL index name.
INDEX_OWNER	VARCHAR(128)	The owner/creator of the index.
TABLE_NAME	VARCHAR(128)	The name of the table on which the index is defined. This is the SQL table name if one exists; otherwise, it is the system table name.
TABLE_OWNER	VARCHAR(128)	The owner of the table.
TABLE_SCHEMA	VARCHAR(128)	The name of the SQL collection that contains the table on which the index is defined.
IS_UNIQUE	CHAR(1)	D = Duplicates are allowed, V = No duplicates except duplicate nulls, U = No duplicates, including nulls.
COLUMN_COUNT	INTEGER	The number of columns that comprise the key.
INDEX_SCHEMA	VARCHAR(128)	The SQL collection that contains the index.
SYSTEM_INDEX_NAME	CHAR(10)	The AS/400 name of the index, which is INDEX_NAME if INDEX_NAME is 10 characters or less.
SYSTEM_INDEX_SCHEMA	CHAR(10)	The AS/400 library name, which is INDEX_SCHEMA if INDEX_SCHEMA is 10 characters or less.
SYSTEM_TABLE_NAME	CHAR(10)	The AS/400 name of the table the index is based on; TABLE_NAME if TABLE_NAME is 10 characters or less.
SYSTEM_TABLE_SCHEMA	CHAR(10)	The library of the AS/400 table the index is based on; TABLE_SCHEMA if TABLE_SCHEMA is 10 characters or less.
LONG_COMMENT	VARCHAR(2000)	The value of COMMENT ON if you used it to make a comment about the index.

SYSINDEXES *Query*

Because this view only contains the indexes made by CREATE INDEX, it is somewhat limited. The Excel macro defined at the end of this appendix shows a technique using ADO for listing all available indexes (even DDS logicals) that can be used by the query optimizer. Not only that, it does a good job of formatting the information into a nice report.

The following query is useful for finding the indexes related to a table:

```
SELECT INDEX_NAME, INDEX_SCHEMA
FROM QSYS2.SYSINDEXES
WHERE TABLE_NAME='WEBTEMP2';
```

SYSKEYS

This view, shown in Table A.6, lists all of the columns used in making up indexes, similar to the SYSCOLUMNS view for indexes. It lists the index name, column name, column sequence, and sort direction for each column used in an SQL index.

Table A.6: SYSKEYS

Column name	Data Type	Description
INDEX_NAME	VARCHAR(128)	The index's SQL name.
INDEX_OWNER	VARCHAR(128)	The owner/creator.
COLUMN_NAME	VARCHAR(128)	The column name of the key.
COLUMN_POSITION	INTEGER	The offset of the column in the base table.
ORDINAL_POSITION	INTEGER	The position of the column in the key.
ORDERING	CHAR(1)	A=Ascending, D=Descending.

Table A.6: SYSKEYS *(continued)*

Column name	Data Type	Description
INDEX_SCHEMA	VARCHAR(128)	The SQL collection where the index exists.
SYSTEM_COLUMN_NAME	CHAR(10)	The AS/400 name of the column, which is COLUMN_NAME if COLUMN_NAME is 10 characters or less.
SYSTEM_INDEX_NAME	CHAR(10)	The AS/400 name of the index, which is INDEX_NAME if INDEX_NAME is 10 characters or less.
SYSTEM_INDEX_SCHEMA	CHAR(10)	The library name where the index exists, which is INDEX_SCHEMA if INDEX_SCHEMA is 10 characters or less.

SYSKEYS *Query*

The following query lists all of the key fields defined in an index:

```
SELECT COLUMN_NAME, ORDINAL_POSITION, ORDERING
FROM QSYS2.SYSKEYS
WHERE INDEX_NAME = 'WTREQTS'
ORDER BY 2;
```

The ORDER BY 2 clause is included to ensure that the columns are listed in the sequence of the index key.

255

SYSCST

SYSCST provides information about all primary, unique, and foreign key constraints defined against all tables in the SQL database. It is shown in Table A.7.

Table A.7: SYSCST

Column Name	Data Type	Description
CONSTRAINT_SCHEMA	VARCHAR(128)	The SQL collection where the constraint exists.
CONSTRAINT_NAME	VARCHAR(128)	The constraint name.
CONSTRAINT_TYPE	VARCHAR(11)	The type of constraint: UNIQUE, PRIMARY KEY, or FOREIGN KEY.
TABLE_SCHEMA	VARCHAR(128)	The name of the collection containing the table that is constrained.
TABLE_NAME	VARCHAR(128)	The SQL table name the constraint is placed on.
IS_DEFERRABLE	VARCHAR(3)	Always NO.
INITIALLY_DEFERRED	VARCHAR(3)	Always NO.
SYSTEM_TABLE_NAME	CHAR(10)	The AS/400 name of the constrained table, which is TABLE_NAME if TABLE_NAME is 10 characters or less.
SYSTEM_TABLE_SCHEMA	CHAR(10)	The AS/400 library name where the table is found, which is TABLE_SCHEMA if TABLE_SCHEMA is 10 characters or less.

SYSCST *Queries*

The following queries are useful against the SYSCST:

- Find all tables that have a primary key:

```
SELECT TABLE_NAME, TABLE_SCHEMA
FROM QSYS2.SYSCST
WHERE CONSTRAINT_TYPE='PRIMARY KEY';
```

- Find all tables that have a foreign key defined:

```
SELECT TABLE_NAME, TABLE_SCHEMA
FROM QSYS2.SYSCST
WHERE CONSTRAINT_TYPE='FOREIGN KEY';
```

SYSKEYCST

The SYSKEYCST view, shown in Table A.8, contains a listing of the key columns that make up each primary, foreign, or unique key defined on your AS/400. It is useful for finding constraints that have been placed on columns in a table, especially when joined to SYSCST.

Table A.8: SYSKEYCST

Column Name	Data Type	Description
CONSTRAINT_SCHEMA	VARCHAR(128)	The name of the SQL collection containing the constraint.
CONSTRAINT_NAME	VARCHAR(128)	The name of the constraint.
TABLE_SCHEMA	VARCHAR(128)	The name of the SQL schema where the table is found.
TABLE_NAME	VARCHAR(128)	The name of the table where the constraint is placed.
COLUMN_NAME	VARCHAR(128)	The name of the constrained column.
ORDINAL_POSITION	INTEGER	The position of the column within the constraint key.
COLUMN_POSITION	INTEGER	The offset of the column in the table itself.
TABLE_OWNER	VARCHAR(128)	The owner/creator of the table.
SYSTEM_COLUMN_NAME	CHAR(10)	The system name of the column, which is COLUMN_NAME if COLUMN_ NAME is 10 characters or less.

Table A.8: SYSKEYCST (continued)		
Column Name	Data Type	Description
SYSTEM_TABLE_NAME	CHAR(10)	The system name of the table, which is TABLE_NAME if TABLE_NAME is 10 characters or less.
SYSTEM_TABLE_SCHEMA	CHAR(10)	The AS/400 library name where the table is found, which is TABLE_SCHEMA if TABLE_SCHEMA is 10 characters or less.

SYSKEYCST *Queries*

The following query lists all of the constrained columns in the PARTS table:

```
SELECT COLUMN_NAME
FROM   QSYS2.SYSKEYCST
WHERE  TABLE_NAME='PARTS'
```

To find all tables that have a foreign key defined and list their columns, join SYSCST and SYSKEYCST:

```
SELECT  A.TABLE_NAME, A.TABLE_SCHEMA,
COLUMN_NAME, ORDINAL_POSITION
FROM QSYS2.SYSCST A, QSYS2.SYSKEYCST B
WHERE CONSTRAINT_TYPE='FOREIGN KEY' AND
A.CONSTRAINT_NAME=B.CONSTRAINT_NAME AND
A.CONSTRAINT_SCHEMA=B.CONSTRAINT_SCHEMA;
```

SYSCSTDEP

The SYSCSTDEP view, shown in Table A.9, lists all tables that have any type of constraint over any column. This includes primary-key, foreign-key, unique, and check constraints. This is useful only if you want to get a master list of constraints against the table.

Table A.9: SYSCSTDEP		
Column Name	Data Type	Description
TABLE_SCHEMA	VARCHAR(128)	The SQL collection where the table is found.
TABLE_NAME	VARCHAR(128)	The SQL table name.
CONSTRAINT_SCHEMA	VARCHAR(128)	The SQL collection where the constraint is found.
CONSTRAINT_NAME	VARCHAR(128)	The constraint name.
SYSTEM_TABLE_NAME	CHAR(10)	The AS/400 table name, which is TABLE_NAME if TABLE_NAME is 10 characters or less.
SYSTEM_TABLE_SCHEMA	CHAR(10)	The AS/400 library name where the table is found, which is SCHEMA_NAME if SCHEMA_NAME is 10 characters or less.

SYSCSTDEP Query

The following query is useful for finding any table in the SQLBOOK library that has any type of constraint:

```
SELECT TABLE_NAME, TABLE_SCHEMA
FROM QSYS2.SYSCSTDEP
WHERE SYSTEM_TABLE_SCHEMA='SQLBOOK';
```

SYSCHKCST

SYSCHKCST, shown in Table A.10, lists only check constraints defined against tables in the SQL database. Note that the CONSTRAINT_CATALOG field is new to V4R5.

Table A.10: SYSCHKCST		
Column Name	Data Type	Description
CONSTRAINT_CATALOG	VARCHAR(128)	The SQL catalog where the constraint exists.
CONSTRAINT_SCHEMA	VARCHAR(128)	The SQL schema where the constraint exists.
CONSTRAINT_NAME	VARCHAR(128)	The name of the constraint.
CHECK_CLAUSE	VARCHAR(2000)	The SQL name of the check constraint.

SYSCHKCST Queries

The following queries are useful against the SYSCHKCST:

- Retrieve the SQL text of a check constraint:

```
SELECT *
FROM QSYS2.SYSCHKCST
WHERE CONSTRAINT_NAME = 'QSYS_PRIKEYCHKCST_000002';
```

- Retrieve tables that have check constraints in the SQLBOOK library:

```
SELECT  A.TABLE_NAME
FROM QSYS2.SYSCST A, QSYS2.SYSCHKCST B
WHERE A.CONSTRAINT_NAME=B.CONSTRAINT_NAME
AND A.CONSTRAINT_SCHEMA=B.CONSTRAINT_SCHEMA
AND A.TABLE_SCHEMA='SQLBOOK';
```

- Retrieve the constraint text of the constraints on the tables in the SQLBOOK library:

```
SELECT  A.TABLE_NAME, CHECK_CLAUSE
FROM QSYS2.SYSCST A, QSYS2.SYSCHKCST B
WHERE A.CONSTRAINT_NAME=B.CONSTRAINT_NAME
AND A.CONSTRAINT_SCHEMA=B.CONSTRAINT_SCHEMA
AND A.TABLE_SCHEMA='SQLBOOK';
```

SYSREFCST

Table A.11 lists all of the foreign-key constraints defined against your tables.

Table A.11: SYSREFCST		
Column Name	Data Type	Description
CONSTRAINT_SCHEMA	VARCHAR(128)	The name of the SQL collection containing the constraint.
CONSTRAINT_NAME	VARCHAR(128)	The name of the constraint.
UNIQUE_CONSTRAINT_SCHEMA	VARCHAR(128)	The schema that contains the unique key constraint that this constraint references.
UNIQUE_CONSTRAINT_NAME	VARCHAR(128)	The name of the unique constraint referenced by the referential constraint.
MATCH_OPTION	VARCHAR(7)	Always NONE.
UPDATE_RULE	VARCHAR(11)	Can be NO ACTION or RESTRICT.
DELETE_RULE	VARCHAR(11)	Can be NO ACTION, CASCADE, SET NULL, SET DEFAULT, or RESTRICT.
COLUMN_COUNT	INTEGER	The number of columns in the foreign key.

SYSREFCST *Queries*

The following SYSREFCST queries can be useful:

- List all foreign key constraints that cause de-referenced records to be deleted:

```
SELECT *
FROM QSYS2.SYSREFCST
WHERE DELETE_RULE='CASCADE'
```

- Find the table names for constraints that restrict deletion of records by joining the SYSREFCST view to the SYSCST view:

```
SELECT A.TABLE_NAME
FROM QSYS2.SYSREFCST B, QSYS2.SYSCST A
WHERE DELETE_RULE='CASCADE'
AND A.CONSTRAINT_NAME=B.CONSTRAINT_NAME
```

SYSCSTCOL

SYSCSTCOL, shown in Table A.12, details each column referenced in a constraint. There are only records for columns in the primary-key, unique-key, and referencing columns of referential constraints.

Table A.12: SYSCSTCOL

Column Name	Data Type	Description
TABLE_SCHEMA	VARCHAR(128)	The name of the SQL schema where the table that the constraint is dependent on is found.
TABLE_NAME	VARCHAR(128)	The SQL name of the table the constraint is dependent on.
COLUMN_NAME	VARCHAR(128)	The SQL column name the constraint is placed on.

Table A.12: SYSCSTCOL (continued)

Column Name	Data Type	Description
CONSTRAINT_SCHEMA	VARCHAR(128)	The schema where the constraint is found.
CONSTRAINT_NAME	VARCHAR(128)	The name of the constraint.
SYSTEM_COLUMN_NAME	CHAR(10)	The system name of the column, which is COLUMN_NAME if COLUMN_NAME is 10 characters or less.
SYSTEM_TABLE_NAME	CHAR(10)	The system name of the table, which is TABLE_NAME if TABLE_NAME is 10 characters or less.
SYSTEM_TABLE_SCHEMA	CHAR(10)	The AS/400 library name, which is TABLE_SCHEMA if TABLE_SCHEMA is 10 characters or less.

SYSCSTCOL *Query*

The following query lists all of the columns that are constrained in the SQLBOOK library:

```
SELECT DISTINCT COLUMN_NAME
FROM QSYS2.SYSCSTCOL
WHERE SYSTEM_TABLE_SCHEMA='SQLBOOK';
```

SYSPROCS

The SYSPROCS view, shown in Table A.13, is found in QSYS2. It contains a record for each stored procedure or user-defined function on your AS/400. User-defined functions are created with the CREATE FUNCTION command and are referenced as routines in the SYSPROCS and SYSPARMS catalogs.

Table A.13: SYSPROCS

Column Name	Data Type	Description
SPECIFIC_SCHEMA	VARCHAR(128)	The SQL schema where the procedure is found.
SPECIFIC_NAME	VARCHAR(128)	The specific name of the procedure. This may be different from the name you created the procedure under.
ROUTINE_SCHEMA	VARCHAR(128)	This should be the same as SPECIFIC_SCHEMA.
ROUTINE_NAME	VARCHAR(128)	The original name the procedure was created under.
ROUTINE_CREATED	TIMESTAMP	The date and time when the procedure was created.
ROUTINE_DEFINER	VARCHAR(128)	The creator's AS/300 user profile.
ROUTINE_BODY	VARCHAR(8)	This defines the type of procedure. It can be EXTERNAL (the procedure is an external program call) or SQL (the procedure is an AS/400 SQL language procedure).
EXTERNAL_NAME	VARCHAR(279)	The name of the external program; null if this is an SQL procedure.
EXTERNAL_LANGUAGE	VARCHAR(8)	The language of the external program. If SQL, the column is null. Possible values are C, C++, COBOL, COBOLLE, FORTRAN, RPG, RPGLE, REXX, PL1, or JAVA.
PARAMETER_STYLE	VARCHAR(7)	The parameter passing style: DB2GNRL, DB2SQL, GENERAL, JAVA, SQL, or NULLS.
IS_DETERMINISTIC	VARCHAR(3)	YES or NO.
SQL_DATA_ACCESS	VARCHAR(8)	This lets you know if the procedure contains SQL, and the extent to which SQL is used. It can be NONE, CONTAINS, READS, or MODIFIES.
SQL_PATH	VARCHAR(558)	The routine path; null if not a routine.

Table A.13: SYSPROCS (continued)

Column Name	Data Type	Description
PARM_SIGNATURE	VARCHAR(510)	The routine signature.
RESULT_SETS	SMALLINT	Identifies the number of result sets the procedure returns, where 0 = none.
IN_PARMS	SMALLINT	The number of IN parms, where 0 = none.
OUT_PARMS	SMALLINT	The number of OUT parms, where 0 = none.
INOUT_PARMS	SMALLINT	The number of INOUT parms, where 0 = none.
PARSE_TREE	VARCHAR(350)	Not applicable; for internal use only.
PARM_ARRAY	VARCHAR(6600)	Not applicable; for internal use only.
LONG_COMMENT	VARCHAR(2000)	The COMMENT ON you might have applied to the procedure, else null.
ROUTINE_DEFINITION	VARCHAR(18432)	The SQL procedure language that created this procedure, if it is an SQL procedure, else null.

SYSPROCS Queries

The following queries can be used to find out useful things about your procedures:

- Find the specific name of a procedure so that you can drop that particular instance:

```
SELECT SPECIFIC_SCHEMA, SPECIFIC_NAME,
ROUTINE_NAME, ROUTINE_SCHEMA
FROM QSYS2.SYSPROCS
WHERE ROUTINE_NAME = 'GETSEQ';
```

- Find all procedures that were written in RPG:

```
SELECT ROUTINE_NAME, ROUTINE_SCHEMA
FROM QSYS2.SYSPROCS
WHERE EXTERNAL_LANGUAGE='RPG';
```

- Find procedures with more than 10 parameters:

```
SELECT ROUTINE_NAME, ROUTINE_SCHEMA,
IN_PARMS, OUT_PARMS, INOUT_PARMS
FROM QSYS2.SYSPROCS
WHERE IN_PARMS+OUT_PARMS+INOUT_PARMS>10;
```

SYSPARMS

The SYSPARMS view, shown in Table A.14, is found in QSYS2. It contains a record for each parameter defined against a stored procedure or user-defined SQL function.

Table A.14: SYSPARMS

Column Name	Data Type	Description
SPECIFIC_SCHEMA	VARCHAR(128)	The schema where the procedure is found.
SPECIFIC_NAME	VARCHAR(128)	The specific name of the procedure.
ORDINAL_POSITION	INTEGER	The numeric position of the parameter in the call statement.
PARAMETER_MODE	VARCHAR(5)	The direction of the parameter: IN, OUT, or INOUT.
PARAMETER_NAME	VARCHAR(128)	The name of the parameter, or null if the parameter was not given a name.

Table A.14: SYSPARMS (continued)

Column Name	Data Type	Description
DATA_TYPE	VARCHAR(128)	The data type of the parameter, any legal SQL data type, including user-defined. Returns BIGINT, INTEGER, SMALLINT, DECIMAL, NUMERIC, FLOAT, REAL, DOUBLE PRECISION, BLOB, CHAR, VARCHAR, CLOB, GRAPHIC, VARG, DBCLOB, DATE, TIME, TIMESTAMP, DATALINK, or DISTINCT (a user-defined type).
NUMERIC_SCALE	INTEGER	The scale of the data if it is numeric, else null.
NUMERIC_PRECISION	INTEGER	The numeric precision of numeric data, else null.
CCSID	INTEGER	The CCSID of non-numeric data.
CHARACTER_MAXIMUM_LENGTH	INTEGER	The maximum length if character data, else null.
CHARACTER_OCTET_LENGTH	INTEGER	The maximum bytes for character data.
NUMERIC_PRECISION_RADIX	INTEGER	The number of binary digits of precision for numeric columns, else null.
DATETIME_PRECISION	INTEGER	If DATE or TIME is zero, TIMESTAMP is six, else null.
IS_NULLABLE	VARCHAR(3)	YES means the parameter can be null, NO means it cannot.
LONG_COMMENT	VARCHAR(2000)	The value of an SQL comment placed with the COMMENT ON statement. It can be null.
ROW_TYPE	CHAR(1)	The type of row: P (parameter), R (result before casting), or C (result after casting). Only applies to a routine; null if the parameter is for a procedure.

Table A.14: SYSPARMS *(continued)*		
Column Name	**Data Type**	**Description**
DATA_TYPE_SCHEMA	VARCHAR(128)	If the parameter is UDT, the schema where the UDT is defined, else null.
DATA_TYPE_NAME	VARCHAR(128)	If the parameter is UDT, the name of UDT, else null.
AS_LOCATOR	VARCHAR(3)	YES if the parameter is a locator, else NO.

SYSPARMS *Query*

The following query is useful against the SYSPARMS table to find all parameters for a given procedure name:

```
SELECT PARAMETER_NAME, PARAMETER_MODE,
DATA_TYPE, ORDINAL_POSITION
FROM QSYS2.SYSPARMS
WHERE SPECIFIC_NAME = 'RETJOBINFO'
ORDER BY ORDINAL_POSITION;
```

Note that the query specifies the order by ORDINAL_POSITION. This is to ensure that the parameters are returned in the sequence in which they must be passed to a call statement.

SYSTYPES

The SYSTYPES view is found in QSYS2. It contains a record for each user-defined type available on your AS/400. The definition of SYSTYPES is not relevant to the material in this book. To see its column definitions, look in the *DB2 SQL Reference*.

SYSTYPES Query

The following query against the SYSTYPES view finds all user-defined types, who created the type, the schema where the type is stored, and the type that the UDT is based on:

```
SELECT USER_DEFINED_TYPE_NAME,
USER_DEFINED_TYPE_SCHEMA,
USER_DEFINED_TYPE_DEFINER,
SOURCE_TYPE
FROM QSYS2.SYSTYPES;
```

SYSFUNCS

SYSFUNCS is found in QSYS2 and contains an entry for each user-defined function available on your AS/400. The fields defined in the SYSFUNCS view are not relevant to the material in this book. To see its column definitions, see the *DB2 SQL Reference*.

SYSFUNCS Queries

The following are useful SYSFUNCS queries:

- Find all of the user-defined functions available on your AS/400:

```
SELECT SPECIFIC_NAME, SPECIFIC_SCHEMA,
ROUTINE_SCHEMA, ROUTINE_NAME,
ROUTINE_DEFINER
FROM QSYS2.SYSFUNCS;
```

- Find the external name of a specific user-defined routine:

```
SELECT EXTERNAL_NAME, EXTERNAL_LANGUAGE
FROM QSYS2.SYSFUNCS
WHERE SPECIFIC_NAME='SEX0001'
```

SYSROUTINES

SYSROUTINES contains one row for every procedure and function on your AS/400. It is very similar to SYSPROCS and is included for compatibility with other DB2 products. To see a complete definition of SYSROUTINES, see the *DB2 SQL Reference*.

SYSROUTINES Query

The following query returns only a list of procedures from the SYSROUTINES view:

```
SELECT SPECIFIC_NAME, SPECIFIC_SCHEMA, ROUTINE_NAME
FROM QSYS2.SYSROUTINES
WHERE ROUTINE_TYPE='PROCEDURE';
```

SQL_LANGUAGES

SQL_LANGUAGES is found in QSYS2 and contains a record for each language supported on your AS/400. The SQL_LANGUAGES view is documented in the *DB2 SQL Reference*.

SQLLANGUAGES Query

The following query lists all development languages supported on your AS/400:

```
SELECT SQL_LANGUAGE_BINDING_STYLE,
SQL_LANGUAGE_PROGRAMMING_LANG
FROM QSYS2.SQL_LANGUAGES;
```

Spreadsheet to List Indexes and Columns Related to a Table

When I took a job with a new client in January, 2000, I was exposed to the most obtuse field names I have ever seen in my life. They had absolutely nothing to do with the underlying type of data, and there was no rhyme or reason to the naming conventions. Normally, this is not too much of a problem, but the system I was designing had to access over 70 out of 1,000 files in a single library, each file having about 100 fields and at least 4 logical files (indexes). Most of the physical files had a minimum of 1,000,000 records to contend with. All of this points to spending a lot of time trying to optimize the data access of my queries, and I did not relish using my handy decoder ring each time I wanted to search for an index that might be appropriate for the query I was optimizing.

The Display File Field Definitions utility, DSPFFD, is wonderful if you like browsing through "green" data, but I needed a friendly listing of indexes that decoded the obfuscated field names into their column headers. This would be a handy reference to have during the query optimization process. I developed a spreadsheet to aid in query optimization and illuminate the dark world of the target data.

The Components

The spreadsheet uses ADO (ActiveX Data Objects) to retrieve a list of indexes for a target physical file on the AS/400. It then uses another ADO method to retrieve the column headers for the fields, in the target physical file, so that it can print a report of the available indexes. The macro that produces the report uses a technique called *disconnected record sets* to manipulate the collection of column headers as it iterates through each index entry retrieved from the AS/400. This technique is a valuable addition to your toolbox because it allows you to massage and manipulate sets of records that you obtain from a database. The resulting spreadsheets also are useful; let's walk through the macro and see how it works.

First, the user enters the library, table name, data source name, user ID, and password in an Excel form, as shown in Figure A.1. Clicking the List Indexes button causes the macro GetIndexInfo to be executed. GetIndexInfo starts by declaring an ADO connection object and connecting to the specified data source. (Note that this spreadsheet is not 400 specific. It will connect to any ODBC data source and produce an index report on any defined database table.)

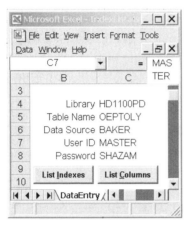

Figure A.1: The user enters physical-file information in the Excel spreadsheet.

ADO connection objects have a method available called OpenSchema that can be used to retrieve information about a database to which ADO is connected. The OpenSchema method takes arguments that allow you to specify the type of information you want to retrieve about the database and limit the scope of the query to only certain tables, views, or indexes. The first argument of OpenSchema is an enumerator (integer constant) indicating the schema that you want to open. There are enumerators for column information, indexes, tables, and other listings that you can ask for. The second argument is an array of arguments that affect the records returned by the OpenSchema method. Each schema enumeration takes different arguments. These can be found in the *Microsoft Platform SDK* documentation for database access, in the ADO and OLEDB sections.

Let's look at the adSchemaColumns enumerator. Note that adSchemaColumns returns a record set containing a list of database columns. If it is called with all arguments empty, it will return all columns in all tables in the entire database, which could take quite a lot of time (so don't try this at home!). Here are two examples of arguments passed to the OpenSchema method requesting the adSchemaColumns collection:

```
Set ColRs = Con1.OpenSchema(adSchemaColumns,array(Empty,"FOO","BAR",Empty))
Set ColRs = Con1.OpenSchema(adSchemaColumns,array(Empty,"FOO",Empty,Empty))
```

The keyword EMPTY specifies that we do not care about that particular argument to the query. The first example would create COLRs as a record set containing all columns for the BAR table in library FOO on your AS/400. The second example would return a record set of all columns for all tables in library FOO on your AS/400. Once you had the record set, you could easily navigate it to find information about the columns in your physical files.

The Excel Macro

The macro shown in Figure A.2 is available as an Excel spreadsheet on the CD accompanying this book. The only requirements to run the macro are that you have some sort of ODBC connection available to your AS/400 (like the Client Access ODBC driver) and that you have a good version of ADO installed and referenced. ADO can be obtained from *www.microsoft.com/data*. To reference ADO in the spreadsheet, select Tools References in the Visual Basic editor and make sure ADO is selected.

```
Public Sub GetIndexInfo()
Dim con1 As New ADODB.Connection
'make it fast
Application.ScreenUpdating = False
Worksheets("DataEntry").Activate
Range("A1").Activate
Library = UCase(Range("C4").Value)
Table = UCase(Range("C5").Value)
DSN = Range("C6").Value
UID = Range("C7").Value
PWD = Range("C8").Value
DSNSTR = "DSN=" & DSN & ";UID=" & UID & ";PWD=" & PWD
con1.Open DSNSTR
ArgArray = Array(Empty, Library, Table, Empty)
Set cs = con1.OpenSchema(adSchemaColumns, ArgArray)
cs.MoveLast
cs.ActiveConnection = Nothing
cs.MoveFirst
ArgArray = Array(Empty, Library, Empty, Empty, Table)
Set rs = con1.OpenSchema(adSchemaIndexes, ArgArray)
Worksheets("TableIndexes").Activate
Cells.ClearContents
Range("A1").Activate
Range("A1").Value = "Available Indexes"
Range("A1").Font.Size = 12
Range("A1").Font.Bold = True
Range("A1", "E1").MergeCells = True
Range("A2").Value = Library & "/" & Table
Range("A2").Font.Size = 12
Range("A2").Font.Bold = True
Range("A2", "E2").MergeCells = True
Range("A4").Activate
```

Figure A.2: This macro generates a list of indexes and then decodes their values (part 1 of 3).

```
R = 0
ActiveCell.Offset(R, 0).Font.Size = 10
ActiveCell.Offset(R, 0).Font.Bold = True
ActiveCell.Offset(R, 0).Font.Underline = True
ActiveCell.Offset(R, 0).Value = "Index Name"
ActiveCell.Offset(R, 1).Font.Size = 10
ActiveCell.Offset(R, 1).Font.Bold = True
ActiveCell.Offset(R, 1).Font.Underline = True
ActiveCell.Offset(R, 1).Value = "Unique?"
ActiveCell.Offset(R, 2).Font.Size = 10
ActiveCell.Offset(R, 2).Font.Bold = True
ActiveCell.Offset(R, 2).Font.Underline = True
ActiveCell.Offset(R, 2).Value = "SortSeq"
ActiveCell.Offset(R, 3).Font.Size = 10
ActiveCell.Offset(R, 3).Font.Bold = True
ActiveCell.Offset(R, 3).Font.Underline = True
ActiveCell.Offset(R, 3).Value = "ColName"
ActiveCell.Offset(R, 4).Font.Size = 10
ActiveCell.Offset(R, 4).Font.Bold = True
ActiveCell.Offset(R, 4).Font.Underline = True
ActiveCell.Offset(R, 4).Value = "Description"
R = R + 1
c = 0
ixname = ""
While Not rs.EOF
  If rs.Fields(5).Value <> ixname Then
    If c > 0 Then
        'if not the first index then add a blank line
        R = R + 1
    End If
    ActiveCell.Offset(R, 0).Font.Size = 10
    ActiveCell.Offset(R, 0).Font.Bold = True
    ActiveCell.Offset(R, 0).Value = rs.Fields(5).Value
    ActiveCell.Offset(R, 1).Value = rs.Fields(7).Value
    ixname = rs.Fields(5).Value
    c = c + 1
  End If
  If rs.Fields(20).Value = 1 Then
    SS = "Asc"
  Else
    SS = "Desc"
  End If
  ActiveCell.Offset(R, 2).Value = SS
  FldName = rs.Fields(17).Value
  ActiveCell.Offset(R, 3).Value = FldName
```

Figure A.2: This macro generates a list of indexes and then decodes their values (part 2 of 3).

```
    cs.Filter = "COLUMN_NAME = '" & FldName & "'"
    If Not cs.EOF Then
      ActiveCell.Offset(R, 4).Value = cs.Fields(27).Value
    End If
    R = R + 1
    rs.MoveNext
  Wend
  Worksheets("TableIndexes").PageSetup.PrintArea = "A1:E" & R + 4
  Application.ScreenUpdating = True
  Range("A1").Activate
  End Sub
```

Figure A.2: This macro generates a list of indexes and then decodes their values (part 3 of 3).

The macro first generates a record set containing all of the column definitions for the specified physical file. This is accomplished using the OpenSchema method with the adSchemaColumns enumerator, and by passing the target library and table name that the spreadsheet user specified. Next, the spreadsheet uses the MoveLast method of the created record set to move to the last record. This ensures that all column information has been returned to the client record set. It then sets the connection property of the record set to Nothing, which causes the record set to disconnect from the AS/400. At this point, the record set is still active and can be searched, but all search and logic will be local to the client and will not involve positioning of the cursor on the AS/400. This significantly improves the performance when navigating the record set's columns.

The macro then opens a record set of indexes that are available on the target physical file. This is accomplished using the OpenSchema method with the enumerator adSchemaIndexes, and again passing an array of arguments indicating the physical file and library you want. The macro goes into a WHILE loop so that it can process each record and begins printing index information into the spreadsheet.

Inside the WHILE loop, things get interesting. The first IF-THEN condition checks to see if the index name has changed. If so, it moves down the spreadsheet one line and prints the name of the index (offset 5 in the record set), and whether the index is unique (offset 7). It then sets the variable IXNAME equal to the current index name it is processing so that the index name will not be printed unless it

275

changes. (The fields returned by OpenSchema are documented in the *Microsoft Platform SDK* data access documentation.)

Next, the macro examines offset 20 of the record set, which indicates whether the column being indexed is returned in ascending or descending order. It uses the value to print the appropriate response on the spreadsheet. The macro then prints the name of the indexed column (offset 17) and uses the column name to set a filter on the column's record set. The filter is just like an SQL WHERE clause. It restricts the disconnected record set to only the records that match the filter condition. The column's record set has a field called COLUMN_NAME.

The macro is saying, "Only show records in the column's record set where the COLUMN_NAME equals this column." The other records in the record set do not disappear; they are just masked by ADO so that it appears to the program that only one record is in the record set. A byproduct of setting a filter against a disconnected record set is that the record pointer will be moved to the first record in the set that matches the criteria. The next line, "if not CS.EOF," ensures that a matching column definition was found for the indexed column. If it was, the macro prints offset 27 of the column's record set, which represents the column description of the database field. The macro then moves to the next index record via the MoveNext method, and loops.

When all index records have been processed, the macro drops out of the loop and defines the PrintArea of the spreadsheet. The PrintArea is a property of the PageSetup object associated with the current worksheet. Defining PrintArea ensures that if the spreadsheet user chooses File Print, the spreadsheet will only print the information returned by the last call to the macro, and not any empty or erroneous cells. This is a nice convenience to add to any spreadsheet.

Where Can You Go from Here?

Well, you have a neat little utility in the index report generated by this spreadsheet that might help you during optimization of Query400 and SQL queries. Explore the other schemas that can be returned by the OpenSchema method, and you might find other information you want to retrieve.

AS/400 SCALAR FUNCTIONS

T his appendix details the AS/400 scalar functions. To help you develop queries that use the functions, sample queries are included where appropriate.
The functions are arranged by the data type on which they operate. This is easier
than reading a list of alphabetical functions, as you can go directly to the function
category you want.

Numeric Scalar Functions

ABS(X)—Returns the absolute value of X, where X is a number or an expression that can be evaluated to a number. Assuming a table containing the column N with a value of –1, ABS(N) would return 1. The
return value is equal to the data type of the input value/expression except in the following cases: Small integers are upgraded to integers
and single precision numbers are upgraded to doubles. This function
also can be called as ABSVAL(X) for compatibility purposes.

ACOS(X)—Returns the arc cosine of X in radians. X must be a number or an
expression that can evaluate to a number between –1 and 1. A null argument will return null data. If the argument is not null, a double-preci-

sion number will be returned, with a value between zero and pi. Passing a number or expression out of range will result in a null value.

ANTILOG(X)—Returns the antilogarithm of X. X must be a number or an expression that will evaluate to a number. If X is null, the function returns null; otherwise, the function returns a double-precision number.

ASIN(X)—Returns the arc sine of X in radians. X must be a number or an expression that evaluates to a number between –1 and 1. If a null is passed, a null will be returned. Passing an out-of-range value will result in a null being returned. If a value is returned, it will be a double-precision number.

ATAN(X)—Returns the arc tangent of X in radians. X must be a number or an expression that evaluates to a number. If X is null, the function returns null; otherwise, the function returns a double-precision number.

ATANH(X)—Returns the hyperbolic arc tangent of X. X must be a number or an expression that evaluates to a number between –1 and 1. If a null is passed, a null will be returned. Passing an out-of-range value will result in a null being returned. If a value is returned, it will be a double-precision number.

CEIL(X)—Returns the ceiling of X as an integer value. If X is SMALLINT, it will be cast to an integer. This function also can be expressed as CEILING(X) for compatibility with SQL-92 and other versions of DB2. If X is null, CEIL returns null. If X is out of the range of permissible integer values, CEIL will throw an error. Here is a summary of possible inputs and outputs:

Input	Output
4.1	5
4.5	5
-4.1	4
-4.5	4
'23.1'	ERROR
NULL	NULL

COS(X)—Returns the cosine of a number. X must be a number or an expression that evaluates to a number. Somewhere between $1e15$ and $1e16$, COS will start to return null values because the results begin to be meaningless. If X is null, COS will return a null value.

COSH(X)—Returns the hyperbolic cosine of a number. X must be a number or an expression that evaluates to a number. If X is null, COSH will return null.

COT(X)—Returns the cotangent of X. X must be a number or an expression that evaluates to a number. If X is null, COT will return null.

DEGREES(X)—Returns the number of degrees in an angle. X must be a number. If X is null, the result is null.

EXP(X)—Returns a number that is the base of the natural logarithm (e) raised to the power specified by X. EXP returns a double-precision number, and X must be a number or expression that evaluates to a number.

FLOOR(X)—Returns the floor of the number X. X can be a number or an expression that evaluates to a number. The floor of a number is the next integer equal to or smaller than the number. For example, FLOOR(4.5) returns 4, and FLOOR(-4.5) returns -5. FLOOR is useful when you want to get rid of decimal places without rounding.

LN(X)—Returns the natural logarithm of X. X must be a number. If X is value, the result is null.

LOG(X)—Returns the base-10 logarithm of the number X. Can also be expressed as LOG10(X) for compatibility with other versions of DB2. X must be a number or an expression that evaluates to a number.

MOD(X,Y)—Divides X by Y and returns only the remainder. X and Y must be numbers or expressions that evaluate to numbers.

POWER(X,Y)—Raises X to the power of Y. Both X and Y must be numbers or expressions that evaluate to numbers. If either argument is null, POWER will return null.

ROUND(X,Y)—Returns X rounded to the number of decimal places specified by Y. X and Y must both be numbers or expressions that evaluate to numbers.

SIGN(X)—Returns –1 if X is a negative number, 0 if X is equal to zero, or 1 if X is positive. X must be a number or an expression that evaluates to a number.

SIN(X)—Returns the sine of X as a double-precision number. X must be a number or an expression that evaluates to a number.

SINH(X)—Returns the hyperbolic sine of X as a double-precision number. X must be a number or an expression that evaluates to a number.

SQRT(X)—Returns the square root of X. X must be a number or an expressions that evaluates to a number.

TAN(X)—Returns the tangent of X as a double-precision floating-point number. X must be a number or an expression that evaluates to a number.

TANH(X)—Returns the hyperbolic tangent of X as a double-precision floating-point number. X must be a number or an expression that evaluates to a number.

TRUNCATE(X,Y)—Removes Y decimal places from the number X.

Temporal Functions

CURDATE()—Returns the current date as a date; can also be expressed as CURRENT_DATE and CURRENT DATE. This function is useful for expressions where you want to find an activity within a certain amount of time from the current date. For example, assume a date column called D:

```
SELECT * FROM <table> WHERE D BETWEEN CURRENT_DATE - 100 DAYS AND
CURRENT_DATE - 50 DAYS
```

CURTIME()—Returns the current time as a time; can also be expressed as CURRENT TIME or CURRENT_TIME.

DAY(X)—Returns the day part of a date or timestamp field. If the argument is duration, it returns the day part of the duration. The value is returned as a large integer. (See chapter 4 for information on durations.) When used on a date or timestamp, DAY(X) is equivalent to DAYOFMONTH(X). DAYOFMONTH(X) cannot be used on durations.

DAYOFWEEK(X)— Returns a large integer between 1 and 7, where 1 is Sunday and 7 is Saturday. X must be a date or timestamp. For example, if RS is a timestamp column, the following query will count the activity by the day of the week:

```
SELECT DAYOFWEEK(X), COUNT(*) FROM <table>
GROUP BY DAYOFWEEK(X)
```

DAYOFYEAR(X)—Returns a large integer between 1 and 366 representing the day of the year of X, which must be a date or timestamp.

DAYS(X)—Returns the number of days that have elapsed between 01/01/0001 and the date or timestamp value X. DAYS is useful for calculating the number of days between events. For example, assume a work order table, where A is the request date and B is the completion date. The following query shows the number of days from request to completion:

```
SELECT DAYS(B)-DAYS(A) FROM <table>
```

This query will calculate the average, minimum, and maximum days to completion:

```
SELECT MIN(DAYS(B)-DAYS(A)),
    AVG(DAYS(B)-DAYS(A)),
    MAX(DAYS(B)-DAYS(A))
FROM <table>
```

281

HOUR(X)—If X is a timestamp or time, returns the hour of X. If X is a duration, returns the hour part of the duration. (See chapter 4 for an explanation of durations.) The following query could be used to aggregate sales activity by hour of the day, if TS is a timestamp column:

```
SELECT HOUR(TS),COUNT(*), SUM(PRICE*QUANTITY)
FROM <table>
GROUP BY HOUR(TS)
```

MICROSECOND(X)—Returns the microseconds portion of X as a large integer, where X is a timestamp or duration.

MINUTE(X)—Returns the minutes portion of the timestamp, duration, or time value X.

MONTH(X)—Returns the month portion of the date, timestamp, or duration value X. The month is returned as a large integer. For example, if TS is a timestamp in a table of orders, the following query would group sales by month:

```
SELECT MONTH(TS),SUM(QUAN*PRICE)
FROM <table>
GROUP BY MONTH(TS)
```

NOW()—Returns the current timestamp at the server; equivalent to CURRENT_TIMESTAMP. For example, the following INSERT statement would place the current date and time into the timestamp column Z:

```
INSERT INTO <table> (Z) values (NOW())
```

QUARTER(X)—Returns a large integer between 1 and 4 that represents the quarter of the date or timestamp value X. This is useful for aggregating sales by quarter. For example, assume TS is a timestamp field in a table of orders:

```
SELECT QUARTER(X),SUM(QUAN*PRICE)
FROM <table>
GROUP BY QUARTER(X)
```

SECOND(X)—Returns a large integer that represents the seconds part of the date, timestamp, or duration X. (See chapter 4 for an explanation of durations.)

WEEK(X)—Returns a large integer between 1 and 52, which that represents the week of the date. X must be a date or timestamp.

YEAR(X)—Returns a large integer representing the year part of a duration, date, or timestamp. This function is useful for aggregations by year. For example, if TS is a timestamp field in a table of orders, the following query aggregates sales by year and month:

```
SELECT YEAR(TS), MONTH(TS), SUM(QUAN*PRICE)
FROM <table>
GROUP BY YEAR(TS), MONTH(TS)
```

String Functions

CHARACTER_LENGTH(X)—Returns the length of the string X as an integer. Can also be expressed as CHAR_LENGTH or LENGTH.

CLOB(X)—Returns a Character Large Object representation of X. X can be a string, number, timestamp, time, or date.

CONCAT(X,Y)—Returns a string that is the result of concatenating X and Y. Can be used in place of the concatenation operator ‖.

LEFT(X,Y)—Returns a string that is the left Y characters of the string X. If Y is greater than the length of X, X will be returned padded with blanks.

LENGTH(X)—Similar to CHARACTER_LENGTH(X), except LENGTH can take any value. If X is a number, the following table applies:

Type	Length
SMALLINT	2
INTEGER	4
BIGINT	8
FLOAT	4
DOUBLE	8
P	for zoned decimal of precision p
P/2+1	for packed decimal numbers with precision p
TIME	3
DATE	4
TIMESTAMP	10

LOCATE(SS,STR,START)—Returns the starting position of the string SS within the string STR. START is optional. If specified, it is the starting point within STR to begin looking for SS. If SS is not found, zero is returned.

LOWER(X)—Returns string X as a string of all lowercase characters. Can also be specified as LCASE(X). X can be a string or an expression that evaluates to a string.

LTRIM(X)—Removes any blanks from the left of string X. This function is really useful if you are doing HTML-based forms and providing content from CHAR fields on the AS/400. Remember that CHAR fields automatically include trailing blanks up to the length of the field. If you place a CHAR field into an HTML text box, use LTRIM prior to returning the field to the browser. Here is an example:

```
SELECT LTRIM(<char-field>) FROM <table>
```

POSITION(X IN Y)—Returns the starting position of X within Y. If X is not within Y, POSITION returns zero. It also can be called as POSSTR(X,Y) for compatibility purposes and is similar to LOCATE.

RTRIM(X)—Trims leading blanks from string X.

STRIP(E,(BOTH, LEADING, or TRAILING), CHAR)—Removes CHAR from string or expression E. BOTH indicates that STRIP should remove the character from both the beginning and end of the string (equivalent to TRIM). TRAILING indicates that STRIP should remove the character only from the trailing position of the string (equivalent to LTRIM). LEADING indicates that STRIP should remove the character from the beginning of the string (equivalent to RTRIM).

SUBSTRING(X,Y,Z)—Removes a substring from string X beginning at position Y and of length Z. Y cannot be greater than the length of string X. Z can indicate a length longer than the string. If this is the case, the string will be padded with blanks. SUBSTRING(X FROM Y TO Z) AND SUBSTR(Z,Y,Z) are equivalent calls to this function.

TRANSLATE(X,Y,Z,C)—Can be used to translate occurrences of one character in a string to another character. X is the string to translate, Y holds the character(s) to look for, Z holds the characters(s) to replace, and C is an optional single character to use as a pad if the resultant string needs to be padded. Calling TRANSLATE with only the X value is equivalent to calling UCASE. Here is an example:

```
TRANSLATE('MY SOURCE STRING','S','S') yields MY XOURCE XTRING
```

TRIM(X)—Removes trailing blanks from string X. Can also be called as TRIM((LEADING, TRAILING, or BOTH) SC FROM X) Where X is the string to trim; LEADING, TRAILING, or BOTH indicate the type of trim operation; and SC is the single character to remove. This function is equivalent to STRIP.

UCASE(X)— Uppercases string X; also can be called as UPPER(X).

Conversion Functions

The following functions are expressly used to convert from one data type to another data type.

BIGINT(X)—New to V4R5, BIGINT returns X as a big integer. X can be a number, an expression that evaluates to a number, or a character representation of a number. Be aware that this function will remove any precision from the number by truncation, not rounding. If the number cannot be expressed as a big integer, a null will be returned. If the argument is null, the result is null. If the number is out of range, the function will return a null. The BIGINT function is synonymous with CAST(X AS BIGINT). Here is a table of conversions:

Input Value	Return Value
' 23332.999 '	2332
Null	Null
'12ABC32'	Null

CAST(X AS Y)—Takes value X and returns its data type as Y. Y can be any of the following built-in types: SMALLINT, INTEGER, BIGINT, FLOAT, DECIMAL, NUMERIC, REAL, DOUBLE, CHAR, VARCHAR, CLOB, DBCLOB, GRAPHIC, VARGRAPHIC, DATE, TIME, TIMESTAMP, or BLOB. Check the DB2 documentation for which types can be converted to each other.

CHAR(X) [Numeric Rules]—If X is any numeric data type or an expression that results in a numeric data type, the function will return the string representation of X. If X is a decimal or floating-point data type, you can add an optional argument that represents the decimal separator character to use in the string representation of the number. The length of the returned string is in accordance with the data type of X. If the character representation of the number takes fewer spaces than the size of the return string, the string is right-padded with spaces. See the following table.

Data Type	String Length	Value	Sample
SMALLINT	6	123	'123 '
INTEGER	11	456	'456 '
BIGINT	20	789	'789 '
FLOAT/DOUBLE	Number of digits required	123.45	'123.45'
DECIMAL(6,2)	9	6	6.00

The length of a decimal or zoned column is always the precision of the column plus two, plus a space for the sign of the number. Positive numbers are returned with a trailing blank where the sign would be if the number were negative. Leading zeros are never returned, but trailing zeros are always filled in the conversion.

CHAR(X,Y) [String Rules]—Returns string X as a string of length Y. If Y is greater than the length of string X, X is padded with blanks.

CHAR(X) [Temporal Rules]—If X is a timestamp values, CHAR(X) returns a character string representation of X that is always 26 characters, in the form *mm-dd-yyyy-hh:mm:ss.mmmmmm*.

If X is a date or time value, an optional argument can be supplied to choose the format of the returned string. The possible selections are ISO, USA, EUR, JIS, YMD, MDY, or DMY. If no second argument is specified, then the DATEFMT and DATESEP values are used from when the program was compiled, or in the case of time, the TIMESEP and TIMEFMT values are used. If those are not appropriate, the AS/400 system values are used.

CLOB(X)—Returns X as a Character Large Object. The nice thing about CLOB is that the string returned only contains the digits of the number, without spaces. This makes CLOB preferable to CHAR for returning numbers as strings. If X is a null, CLOB returns null. CLOB is equivalent to CAST(X AS CLOB).

DATE(X)—Returns X as a date. X can be a character string representing a date, a timestamp, or a number. If X is a number, it is expressed as the number of days since 01/01/0001. IF X is a timestamp, the time portion is truncated and a date data type is returned. If X is a string, it is converted to a date (if possible).

Use this when you want to aggregate an activity by date and that activity was originally recorded as a timestamp. For example, assume column TS is a timestamp and you want to count activity by day:

```
SELECT DATE(TS),COUNT(*) FROM <table>
GROUP BY DATE(TS)
```

DECIMAL(X,Y,Z) or DEC(X,Y,Z)—Returns X as a packed decimal representation of X. X can be a character string, a number, an expression that evaluates to a number, or an expression that evaluates to a character. If X is some form of a character, you have an optional argument available for passing the character that is being used as the decimal point. Here is an example that would return a decimal number:

```
DECIMAL('123,45',7,2,',')
```

The fourth argument indicates that the comma character represents the decimal marker in the string.

Decimal also can be used as a casting function to guarantee precision and scale of host variables so that they match the precision and scale of columns for selecting and filtering. Suppose you have a table where column A is a DECIMAL(6,0), and there is an index over the column. Your host variable is :AMATCH, and is declared as an integer. You want to ensure that the index is used in a statement when selecting on the A column. The following would help work around a data-type mismatch between the host program and the SQL statement:

```
SELECT * FROM <table> WHERE A = DECIMAL(:amatch,6,0)
```

DIGITS(X)—Returns a string representation of the number X. DIGITS always left-pads the string with zeros. Here is a conversion table for the string length that DIGITS will return:

Data Type	String Size
SMALLINT	5
INTEGER	10
BIGINT	19
DECIMAL(X,Y)	X

DOUBLE(X)—Returns X as a double-precision number. X must be some form of numeric value, a string representation of a numeric values, an expression that evaluates to a number, or an expression that evaluates to a string that can be converted to a number. If X is null, DOUBLE returns null. It is equivalent to CAST(X AS DOUBLE) and is maintained for backward compatibility. DOUBLE_PRECISION(X) also can be used.

FLOAT(X)—Returns a single-precision floating-point representation of X. X can be a number, an expression that evaluates to a number, a character string representation of a number, or an expression that evaluates to a character string representation of a number. FLOAT is maintained for backward compatibility. It is equivalent to CAST(X AS FLOAT).

INTEGER(X)—Returns the integer representation of X. X can be a number, an expression that evaluates to a number, a character string representation of a number, or an expression that evaluates to a character string that represents a number. INTEGER(X), which also can be expressed as INT(X), is equivalent to CAST(X AS INTEGER).

REAL(X)—Returns X as a single-precision floating-point number. X can be a string, a number, an expression that evaluates to a number, or an expression that evaluates to a string that represents a number. REAL(X) is equivalent to CAST(X AS FLOAT) or FLOAT(X).

SMALLINT(X)—Returns X as a small integer. X can be a number, an expression that evaluates to a number, a string representation of a number, or an expression that evaluates to a string representation of a number. SMALLINT(X) is equivalent to CAST(X AS SMALLINT).

TIME(X)—Returns a time-data representation of X. X can be a string representing a time or a timestamp data type. TIME(X) is equivalent to CAST(X AS TIME).

TIMESTAMP(X)—Returns a timestamp-data representation of X. X can be a string representation of a timestamp. This also can be specified as TIMESTAMP(X,Y) where X is the date string and Y is the time string. If this representation is used, you cannot specify microseconds in the type portion. This operation is equivalent to CAST(X AS TIMESTAMP).

VARCHAR(X)—Returns X as a VARCHAR data type. This is equivalent to CAST(X AS VARCHAR). X can be any data type.

VARGRAPHIC(X)—Returns X as a VARGRAPHIC data type. This is equivalent to CAST(X AS VARGRAPHIC). X can be any data type.

ZONED(X,Y,Z)—Returns X as a zoned decimal representation. X can be a character string, a number, an expression that evaluates to a number, or an expression that evaluates to a character. If X is a character type, you have an optional argument available to pass the character that is being used to represent the decimal point. For example, the following would return a zoned decimal number:

```
ZONED('123,45',7,2,',')
```

The fourth argument indicates that the comma character represents the decimal marker in the string. ZONED also can be used as a casting function to guarantee the precision and scale of host variables so that they match the precision and scale of columns for selection and filtering purposes. For example, suppose that you have a table with a column A that is a DECIMAL(6,0) and has an index over the column. Your host variable, :AMATCH, is declared as an integer. You want to ensure that the index is used in a statement when selecting on the A column. The following would help work around a data-type mismatch between the host program and the SQL statement:

```
SELECT * FROM <table> WHERE A = DECIMAL(:amatch,6,0)
```

Logical Functions

COALESCE(X,Y,....Z)—Returns the first expressions that does not evaluate to null. All expressions must be type-compatible, although strings are compatible with date-time values. For example, if QUANTITY is a field that could contain the null value, the following statement would guarantee that the expression could not return a null value:

```
SELECT COALESCE(QUANTITY, 0) * PRICE
FROM <table>
```

IFNULL(X,Y)—Returns Y if X is null. Equivalent to the COALESCE function.

LAND(X,Y,...Z)—Returns a string that is the logical AND of strings X, Y,...Z.

LNOT(X)—Returns a string that is the logical NOT of string X.

LOR(X,Y,...Z)—Returns a string that is the logical OR of X to Y...Z.

MAX(X,Y,...Z)—Returns the maximum value from a set of values. All arguments must be type-compatible (such as all strings, all numbers, or all temporal). MAX can be used with strings, dates, and numbers.

MIN(X,Y,...Z)—Returns the minimum of a set of values. All arguments must be type-compatible (all strings, all numbers, or all temporal). MIN can be used with strings, dates, and numbers.

NULLIF(X,Y)—Returns null if X and Y are equal. X and Y must be type-compatible. If X and Y are not equal, NULLIF returns the first value.

VALUE(X,Y,...Z)—Returns the first argument that is not null; similar to the COALESCE function.

XOR(X,Y,...Z)—Returns a string that is the XOR of strings X, Y,...Z.

SOFTWARE LOADING INSTRUCTIONS

This appendix details how to install the sample data and outfit your PC and AS/400 for running the SQL samples in this book. In order to load the sample data efficiently, I recommend that you use the SQLThing program. If you do not choose to install the SQLThing program, you will need Microsoft Access to move the sample data to your AS/400. Barring that, I have placed a copy of an AS/400 save file of the sample data on the CD. If you can't use the SQLThing program or if you don't have a copy of Microsoft Access, you can use FTP to move the save file to your AS/400 and then do a restore.

Using SQLThing with This Book

SQLThing is a graphical user interface program that runs on a Windows 95/98/NT/ Millennium or 2000 PC and allows you to execute SQL queries against your AS/400 database. You will find that SQLThing is very easy to use. And because the version that comes with this book is free, the cost is just about right! All of the screen shots in the book were taken from the SQLThing program. If you use SQLThing to do the example queries, you should see the exact results on your monitor as they are printed in this book. In addition, SQLThing allows you to perform parameterized queries and to call stored procedures with parameter markers. Because there is no other way—barring writing a program—for you to test queries using parameter markers, you will soon find that SQLThing will become an indispensable tool in your arsenal

SQLThing Requirements

SQLThing uses an Open Database Connectivity (ODBC) driver to communicate with the AS/400. Before you can use SQLThing, you must ensure that you have a suitable ODBC driver and that your Windows installation is capable of using ODBC. If you are using Client Access Express or Client Access for Windows 95/NT, you might already have the ODBC driver installed. To check on the availability of an ODBC driver, go to your Control Panel (available from Start Settings menu) and find the Data Sources (ODBC) driver manager icon. If you do not see the driver manager icon, you are not enabled for ODBC. Therefore, proceed to the DCOM and MDAC installations. After that, you may use the Selective Setup option of Client Access to add the CA ODBC driver to your machine.

If you don't have Client Access installed, I have included a trial version of the HiT Software ODBC driver for you to use. This version of the HiT ODBC driver will work for 60 days after initial installation and should give you time to run all of the sample queries in the book. See the section of this appendix called "Installing the HiT Driver" for how to install the ODBC driver on your machine.

Installing ODBC Prerequisites

Table C.1 details the prerequisites for installing ODBC on various Windows operating system platforms.

So, if you are running Windows ME or Windows 2000, you can skip the next sections and go directly to installing HiT driver or installing the Client Access driver. If you are running Windows 95 or Windows 98, you should ensure that the respective version of DCOM is installed in your machine, and then run the installation for MDAC 2.5 (which is outlined in the following sections.)

Table C.1: Prerequisites for ODBC	
Windows Version	**Required Prerequisites**
95 (both a and b)	DCOM 95MDAC 2.5
98 (both a and b)	DCOM 95/98MDAC 2.5
NT 3.51 and 4.0	MDAC 2.5
ME	\<none\>
2000 (Pro and Server)	\<none\>

Installing DCOM 95/98

If you are running Windows 9*x*, you should ensure that you are running DCOM. DCOM stands for *Distributed Component Object Model* and is a service that is installed by Office 97, Office 2000, IE 4.0, or other programs. If you don't think you have DCOM installed, simply navigate to the DCOM directory on the CD and double-click the DCOM95.EXE file for Windows 95 or the DCOM98.EXE file for Windows 98. This will cause DCOM to install.

If your computer has a current version of DCOM, the setup program will inform you of this and then stop processing. Rest assured that attempting to install DCOM would in no way invalidate a newer version of DCOM on your system. If you don't have DCOM, the setup program will query if you want to install DCOM. If you click YES, the installation process will continue by prompting you to acknowledge the standard Microsoft End User License Agreement. Click YES to consent to the agreement. After the installation is complete, you will be asked to reboot your machine to allow DCOM to take effect.

Installing MDAC 2.5

MDAC 2.5 stands for Microsoft Data Access Components, version 2.5. This set of programs includes all of the ODBC and ISAM drivers needed for SQLThing to function. To install MDAC, simply navigate to the MDAC directory on the CD and double-click the MDAC_TYP.EXE file. MDAC setup will then start. The MDAC setup program will first examine your machine to ensure that you currently don't have a newer version of MDAC installed. If version 2.5 or newer

MDAC is installed on your machine, MDAC setup will inform you of this and stop executing. If MDAC needs to be installed, MDAC will prompt you for consent to the standard Microsoft End User License agreement. Check the box affirming the agreement and then click NEXT to proceed. MDAC setup will ask you if you want to proceed. Click NEXT and the installation will begin. After MDAC is installed on your machine, the system will restart and you may proceed to installation of an ODBC driver.

Configuring Client Access ODBC

In you have Client Access for Windows 95/NT or Client Access Express, you can use the ODBC provided from IBM for communicating with your AS/400. First, you need to ensure that the ODBC driver has been installed on your system. To do this, run the Selective Setup program that is in your Client Access folder. Once selective setup gets going, you should see a screen like the one shown in Figure C.1. If ODBC is checked, as it is in the example screen, you are ready to proceed. If ODBC is not checked, you should check the ODBC box and continue with selective setup to enable ODBC to be installed.

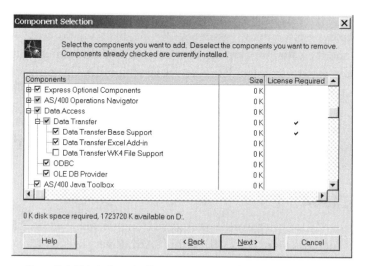

Figure C.1: This is the selective setup screen of Client Access. If ODBC is not checked on your machine, checking it will cause ODBC to be installed.

Once ODBC is installed on your machine, you need to set up an ODBC data source so that the SQLThing program can communicate with your AS/400. To do this, select SETTINGS and then CONTROL PANEL from your Windows START menu. Once the control panel is open, double-click on the ODBC Data Sources (32-bit) icon to start the ODBC Driver Manager. (If you are running Windows 2000, double-click the Administrative Tools icon and then double click the Data Sources [ODBC] icon). Once Driver Manager is started, you should see a screen like the one shown in Figure C.2

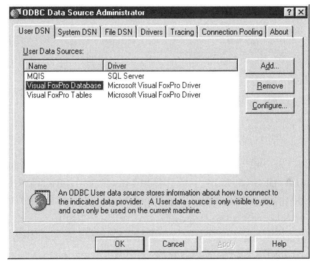

Figure C.2: This is the main interface of the ODBC Driver Manager program.

Click the ADD button and you will be presented with a screen that allows you to choose the driver that you want to configure. Select the Client Access ODBC Driver (32-bit) from the list and then press the FINISH button. You should be presented with a screen like the one shown in Figure C.3.

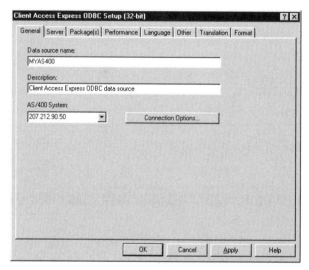

Figure C.3: This screen allows you to configure the properties of the Client Access ODBC connection.

This control panel applet lets you set all of the properties of your new data source. First and most important, you need to name the data source. I recommend you use the name MYAS400 as shown in Figure C.3. Under the AS/400 SYSTEM dropdown list, enter or pick the IP address of the AS/400 to which you will be talking. Next, I recommend that you select the Server tab and then enter a list of libraries that you would like to be your default libraries in the LIBRARY LIST field. In addition to your libraries, I also suggest that you add the library SQLBOOK; that is the library where you will be loading the sample data later in this chapter.

Next, select the Performance tab and make sure that the Extended Dynamic checkbox is not checked. If this box is checked, ODBC will package all of your SQL statements on the AS/400. Right now, you don't want to use packages. Make sure that the check box is unchecked. Finally, press the OK button to apply your settings and save this data source.

Installing the HiT ODBC Driver

If you don't have Client Access, or if you just want to try the HiT ODBC driver, the following instructions detail the installation of the HiT driver and the configuration of a suitable ODBC data source.

First, if you are running Windows 9*x*, ensure that you have DCOM and MDAC 2.5 installed before attempting to continue with the HiT installation. See the previous sections of this appendix for information on installing DCOM and MDAC.

Now, use the Windows Explorer to navigate to the HITODBCDRIVER directory on the CD. In this directory, you will find a program called SETUP.EXE. Double-click on SETUP.EXE to start the HiT installation program. At this point, you will see a welcome screen. Click on the NEXT button to continue the installation and then assent to the HiT Software End User License agreement by pressing the YES button. You will be rewarded for your efforts by a screen like the one shown in Figure C.4. Click on the button next to the text "Standard Client" to begin installation of the ODBC driver. Answer any further prompts with the default information until the driver is installed.

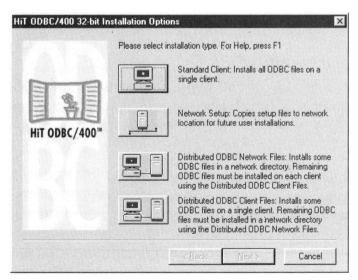

Figure C.4: This screen controls the type of installation you are performing with the Hit driver.

When installation is complete, you will see a screen like the one shown in Figure C.5. Uncheck both boxes on this screen and then click the FINISH button to end the Hit ODBC driver installation. The HiT ODBC driver is now installed on your system and you may proceed to the section on configuring the HiT ODBC Driver.

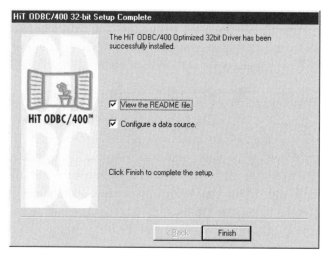

Figure C.5: This screen appears when the driver is finished installing and allows you to proceed to configuration of the ODBC data.

Configuring the HiT ODBC Driver

Once ODBC is installed on your machine, you need to set up an ODBC data source so that the SQLThing program can communicate with your AS/400. To do this, select SETTINGS and then CONTROL PANEL from your Windows START menu. Once the control panel is open, double click on the ODBC Data Sources (32-bit) icon to start the ODBC Driver Manager. (If you are running Windows 2000, double-click the Administrative Tools icon and then double-click the Data Sources [ODBC] icon). Once Driver Manager is started, you should see a screen like the one shown in Figure C.6.

Click the ADD button and you will be presented with a screen that allows you to choose the driver that you want to configure. Choose the HiT ODBC/400 Optimized 32-bit driver from the list of drivers and press FINISH. You will be presented with a screen like the one shown in Figure C.7.

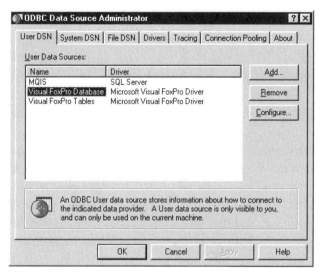

Figure C.6: This is the main interface of the ODBC Driver Manager program.

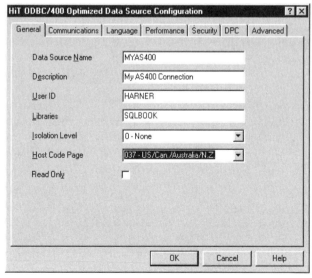

Figure C.7: This control panel applet allows you to configure the HiT ODBC driver to connect to your AS/400.

First, move your cursor to the DATA SOURCE NAME field and enter MYAS400. This will be the name that you use to reference the ODBC connection from programs like Excel, Word, or SQLThing. Next, enter your user ID into the USER ID field and enter the library SQLBOOK into the LIBRARIES fields. You may enter more libraries if you like by separating the libraries with commas. The SQLBOOK library will be created later in the appendix when you load the sample data.

Click on the Communications tab to reveal the panel (as shown in Figure C.8) that allows you to set up communications with your AS/400. The HiT driver supports several communications options—like SNA, AnyNet, APPC, etc.—not available in Client Access. I recommend that you use the TCP/IP Native; this will give the best performance. Enter the IP Address of your AS/400 into the HOST IP ADDRESS field and enter the name of your system into the HOST SYSTEM NAME field. Click the Performance tab and ensure that the Use Packages checkbox is not checked. Finally, press the OK button to cause the ODBC settings to be saved.

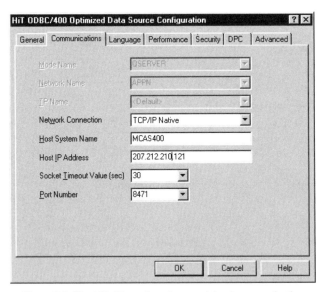

Figure C.8: The HiT driver allows for a variety of communications settings and options.

Installing the SQLThing Program

Once you have installed and configured an ODBC driver, you are ready to use the SQLThing program. To install SQLThing, use Windows Explorer to navigate to the SQLTHING directory on the CD and double-click the SETUP.EXE program. The setup program will prompt you with the screen welcoming you to the SQLThing program. Press the OK button to continue and the program will prompt you for the location where you prefer to install the program (see Figure C.9). Set where you want to install the program and then press the large icon to the left to begin installation of the SQLThing program. Answer any other prompts and allow the installation to complete.

Figure C.9: This is the installation screen presented by SQLThing.

Loading the Sample Data Using SQLThing

Now that ODBC is installed and SQLThing is loaded, you are ready to load the sample data to you AS/400. To begin, select Programs, Client Server Development, and then SQLThing from your START menu to start the SQLThing program. SQLThing will present you with the screen shown in Figure C.10. Use the Data Source dropdown box to select the ODBC data source that you have configured against your AS/400. If you followed my recommendations, this data source is called MYAS400. Next, enter your user ID and password in the respective fields. Press the LOGIN button to attach to your AS/400.

Figure C.10: Select an AS/400 ODBC data source and enter your user ID and password to connect

Once you have successfully logged into your AS/400, you will be presented with the SQLThing main user interface. Choose the FILE menu item and then select NEW to open an editor window (as shown in Figure C.11).

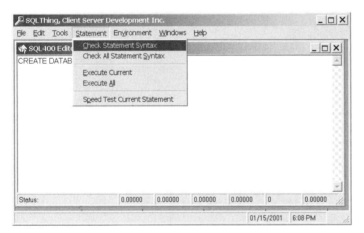

Figure C.11: This is the SQLThing main user interface.

In the editor window, type the following SQL statement:

```
CREATE DATABASE SQLBOOK;
```

Ensure that you end the statement with a semicolon. SQLThing uses the semicolon to tell where one SQL statement ends and the next statement begins. Move your cursor back into the SQL statement. Select the STATEMENT menu and then the EXECUTE CURRENT menu item. This will cause SQLThing to execute the SQL statement where the cursor is currently positioned (thereby creating a library on your AS/400 called SQLBOOK). If the statement executes correctly, you should not receive any messages. However, if you receive an error message, it probably means that you don't have the proper authority to create libraries on your AS/400. Talk to your security officer and get that authority added to your user profile or have the security officer create the database for you by executing the SQL statement.

Once your database library has been created, you are ready to import the sample data. To begin, select the TOOLS menu, then select IMPORT EXTERNAL DATA TO AS/400, and then the ACCESS DATA FORMAT menu item. You should be presented with the screen that allows you to choose a Microsoft Access database. Navigate to the directory SAMPLEDATA on the CD and choose the SAMPLEDATA.MDB file. Then press the OK button. You should now be presented with a screen that allows you to choose a table in the ACCESS database. Choose the WEBHITS2 table and then press the NEXT button to get to a screen like the one shown in Figure C.12.

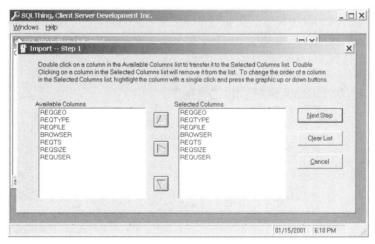

Figure C.12: This screen allows you to identify the fields that you wish to import from an external data source.

Press the middle icon, which represents an arrow that points to the Selected Columns list, to select all columns from the import table. Ensure that your screen looks *exactly* like the one shown in Figure C.12. Then press the NEXT STEP button to reveal a screen like the one shown in Figure C.13.

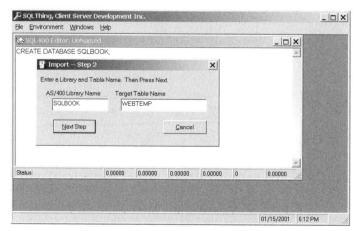

Figure C.13: Enter the library SQLBOOK and table name WEBTEMP on this screen and press NEXT STEP.

Enter the library name SQLBOOK in the library field and the table name WEBTEMP into the TARGET TABLE NAME field, and press NEXT STEP to continue. You will be presented with a screen like the one shown in Figure C.14.

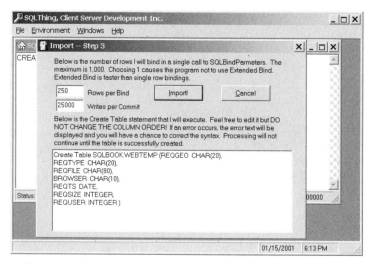

Figure C.14: Ensure that you change the data type of the REQTD field from DATE to TIMESTAMP before continuing.

Figure C.14 shows the final step in using SQLThing to import data. SQLThing has created a CREATE TABLE statement that will create a physical file on your AS/400 in the SQLBOOK library that will hold the sample data. However, because the sample data is stored in an ACCESS database and because ACCESS does not support a TIMESTAMP data type, SQLThing has incorrectly identified the REQTS field as a DATE data type and not a TIMESTAMP data type. Move your cursor to the word DATE in the SQL statement and remove the word DATE. Now, type the word TIMESTAMP. Your modified screen should look like Figure C.15. Once it does, press the IMPORT! button to cause SQLThing to read the sample data and write it to your AS/400.

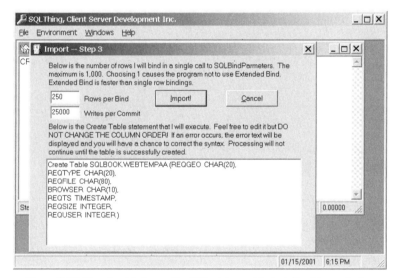

Figure C.15: You should change the SQL statement to look like this one before importing the record to your AS/400.

Once SQLThing is finished importing the data, you may begin running the sample queries in the book.

INDEX

** operator, 55
* operator, 53
% wildcard character, 59-60
; as statement delimiter, xxiii
/ in embedded SQL, as
    delimiter for, 224

A

ABS(X), 277
access path, 142, 158-159, **159**
access plans, in query
    optimizer, 150
ACOS(X), 277-278
Active Server Pages (ASP),
    xvii, 12, 137
ActiveX Data Objects (ADO),
    139, 178, 188, 213, 271-275
    stored procedures and,
        202-204
aggregation, xx, 33, **33**
AIX, xxvi
ALIAS keyword, 40, 41

aliases for members of physical
    files, 7-8
ALL keyword
    in granting/revoking
        privileges, 42-43
    in UNION, 87, **88**
ALLOCATE keyword, 15-17
ALTER keyword, in
    granting/revoking privileges,
    42
ALTER TABLE, 34-35, 38-39
AND, 54, 58
ANTILOG(X), 278
arithmetic operators, 55
AS keyword, 29, 52, 67, 101
AS/400 SQL Reference, 3
AS/400, xvii-xix, xxv-xxvi,
    xxx, 2-3
ASIN(X), 278
ATAN(X), 278
ATANH(X), 278
audio files, 17
Auto Commit option, 133

auxiliary stored pool (ASP), 4
AVG function, 67

B

BETWEEN operator, 58
BIGINT(X), 285
BIGINT, 20*t*, 20-21
binary data, 12
binary long object (see BLOB),
    17
binary radix tree, 146
BLOB, 13, 17-19
block fetch and copy,
    embedded SQL and, 219
business logic, xxi

C

C language, xxix, 39, 163, 181,
    193, 197, 212, 213, 217
Call Level Interface (CLI), xxi

Note: Boldface numbers indicate illustrations, italic t is a table.

Note: Boldface numbers indicate illustrations, italic t is a table.

Note: Boldface numbers indicate illustrations, italic t is a table.

Note: Boldface numbers indicate illustrations, italic t is a table.